THE PUZZLE

Dr Peter Vardy is Vice-Principal and ⟨...⟩
at Heythrop College, University of London and Dr Paul Grosch
lectures in Philosophy and Theology at the College of St Mark and St
John, Plymouth. *The Puzzle of Ethics* has been reprinted many times
since it was first published in 1994 and this new edition is substantially
enlarged, covering significant new areas. The first edition has been
translated into German, Dutch, Polish and Danish, and a separate
edition is published in the United States. In the UK it has become
established as the best-selling title in the field.

Praise for the first edition of *The Puzzle of Ethics*

'A wonderfully clear introduction to moral philosophy and to various
topics of contemporary ethical concern ... This is a book for which
many students and the general reader ... will be grateful.'

David Atkinson

'The great advantage of *The Puzzle of Ethics* over its rivals is that the
authors are so thorough, so balanced and so clear. This is a good book.'

Robin Gill, The Tablet

'The philosopher of religion and gifted communicator Peter Vardy ...
and Paul Grosch ... provide an accessible, balanced and up to date
introduction to moral philosophy.'

The Way

'This book will fill an irritating gap in the current literature available
and provide a valuable resource ... Vardy and Grosch are serious
commentators who have something to say to the general reader; as with
all the *Puzzle* books, accessibility and clarity are the benchmarks of
style.'

Peter Tyler, The Month

The Puzzle of Ethics

PETER VARDY & PAUL GROSCH

Fount
An Imprint of HarperCollinsPublishers

Fount Paperbacks is an Imprint of
HarperCollins*Religious*
Part of HarperCollins*Publishers*
77–85 Fulham Palace Road, London W6 8JB

First published in Great Britain in 1994 by Fount Paperbacks
This revised edition 1999

7 9 10 8

A catalogue record for this book is
available from the British Library

ISBN 0 00 628144 3

Printed in Great Britain by
Clays Ltd, St Ives plc

To
Lindsay Grosch and Christian Vardy
– Again!

Contents

ACKNOWLEDGEMENTS

Both authors owe a great debt to their students past and present. Responsibility for the errors and omissions in this book rests entirely with the authors, however there would have been more of them were it not for the help of those who read individual chapters and offered their advice. Peter Vardy wishes to acknowledge help given by Michael Barnes SJ, Alan Carter, Bernard Hoose, Gerry Hughes SJ, Janice Thomas and Anne Vardy. Paul Grosch wishes to thank Adrian Mills and Alan Gorman for the many discussions on the nature of justice. He has also benefited from discussions with his colleagues: Dilys Wadman, Liz Stuart, Rachael Quinlan, Adrian Thatcher, Jim Little, Jon Goulding, Gordon Bartlett and Alan Cousins. He wishes to record his special thanks to Anne Littlejohn and David Benzie for their help in taming recalcitrant word-processors when time was fast running out.

PART 1

THEORETICAL
ETHICS

ONE
Setting the Scene

Ethics is central to modern life. Lawyers, accountants, doctors, nurses, the police, members of the armed forces, social workers and many others are required to study ethical issues as part of their training. Before any ethical issue can be examined, however, it is first necessary to be clear on the underlying assumptions which govern the debate and, in particular, to understand the different ethical frameworks that can be applied. Unless one is clear on the assumptions, it will not be possible to understand the viewpoints of others or challenge one's own.

Discussion of, for instance, abortion, euthanasia or sexual morality cannot usefully take place unless there has first been an examination of key issues which will include:

- When does human life begin?
- What is a human person?
- Is life an absolute good?
- Should governments seek to maximise freedom?
- Is achieving the greatest happiness for the greatest number of people the main aim of politics?
- Do you support a deontological or a consequentialist approach to ethics?
- Can a proportionate reason ever justify going against a firm moral rule?

This book is divided into two parts. The first looks at the issues in theoretical ethics underlying the debates; then, in the second part, issues in applied ethics are dealt with. The aim of this book is to present the issues clearly so that you, the reader, can make your own decisions. There is no attempt to impose a particular agenda nor to persuade you to make the 'right' answer. Indeed, the whole idea of there being single 'right' answers in ethics has come under increasing attack. Some support a radical relativism in which each person's view is as good as the next – but this carries its own problems. If this position is seriously held, then how does one condemn the behaviour of Pol Pot's regime in Cambodia, those who took part in ethnic cleansing in Bosnia, or those who carried out the massacres in Rwanda?

The terms 'ethics' and 'morality' have come to be treated as almost identical in meaning, but they have different derivations. 'Ethics' comes from the Greek word *ethikos* which relates to 'ethos' or character. It is sometimes translated 'custom' or 'usage' so it refers to the customary way to behave in society. Ethical behaviour, therefore, is behaviour that is in accordance with a virtuous character. Aristotle uses the word in this way, maintaining that virtue is happiness, and that the pursuit of virtue is the highest and noblest aim for a human being. In his book *The Nicomachean Ethics*, Aristotle maintains that a human being's highest happiness comes from philosophic speculation but that this must be combined with a life of prudence and a search for virtue. Becoming virtuous involves the individual establishing a habit of virtuous behaviour and this is directly related to a virtuous character.

'Morality' comes from the Latin word *moralis* – particularly as used in Cicero's commentaries on and translations of Aristotle. Morality is more concerned with which actions are right or wrong rather than with the character of the person who performs these actions. Today the two terms, ethics and morality, are often interchanged with particular philosophers wishing to emphasise one or another aspect.

In this book the field of ethics will be taken to cover not just those actions which are right or wrong but will also explore the fundamental principles which lie behind these actions. In addition, at least at times, the issue of virtue that so preoccupied Aristotle and many of his successors will be considered. We shall see, however, that Aristotle's approach has been subject to considerable criticism.

Ethical judgements underpin our society and hard choices face us in the years ahead as we attempt to decide

- who will have medical treatment and who will not;
- What rights a person has to restrict access to their genetic information;
- Whether genetically engineered crops are ethically justifiable;
- Whether 'living wills' by patients who are terminally ill and in great pain can justify bringing their lives to an end;
- How and for what reasons criminals should be punished;
- Whether the powers of the media should be controlled;
- Whether animals have rights.

These and many similar issues will not go away and they need to be confronted and thought through. The aim of this book is to help you in this task.

TWO

Plato – Virtue and Knowledge

Plato was born in 427 B.C. and was a pupil of Socrates. In 367 B.C. he was invited to take charge of the education of the young ruler of Syracuse – Dionysius II – who controlled the most powerful state in Sicily. The experiment failed, although perhaps more due to Dionysius' personality than to defects in Plato's philosophy. However his legacy lives on and he has had the most profound influence on subsequent philosophy.

Plato takes a more systematic approach than Socrates – Socrates' questioning method was aimed at showing those he talked to that their supposed knowledge was, in fact, shallow and vulnerable. Socrates certainly had positive views to which he tried to direct people, although he may have lacked the philosophic backing for them for which Plato argued. When the Delphi oracle proclaimed Socrates the wisest man in Athens, he came to think (after questioning many people who thought themselves wise but who, by their answers, quickly showed that they were not) that this was because he knew that he knew nothing and that 'that man was wisest who knew that he knew little'. We do not know how much of the discussions attributed to Socrates actually came from Socrates himself and to what extent Plato was using Socrates as a vehicle for his own ideas, however Plato's approach to morality certainly owes much, as we shall see, to his theory of knowledge.

i) The Euthyphro dilemma

In Plato's book *Euthyphro*, a discussion occurs between Socrates and a young man, Euthyphro, who intends to prosecute his own father because his father tied up a peasant who was involved in a dunken brawl, intending to report him to the authorities. However, the father forgot about him and the peasant died. Euthyphro is horrified and instead of dining with his father, sets out to prosecute him. The discussion centres on whether what human beings are morally obliged to do rests on what the gods command or whether the gods only command what is good independent of their commanding it. There are problems whichever route is taken:

1 If one sides with Euthyphro and claims that whatever the gods command is obligatory just because they command it, then the commands of the gods (or God) are clearly absolute. The problem with this is that whatever God commands is good just because God commands it. God could then command vicious actions which would appear to us to be wrong (such as in the O.T. when God is recorded as commanding the slaughter of women and children) and we would have to call these good just because they are commanded by God. God then becomes a supreme power figure who has to be worshipped and obeyed whatever God may command.

2 If one sides with Socrates and claims that there is a standard of goodness independent of God, then God is no longer the ultimate standard of morality. Plato and Socrates' views are the same here — Plato considered that the Forms (p. 11) provide the absolute standard of goodness and, therefore, the commands of the gods can be measured against this standard. This is attractive as it provides a reason for worshipping the gods or God (God is worshipped because God is good judged by this independent standard) but the problem is that God is no longer supreme — there is an independent standard against which God can be measured, namely the Form of the Good.

Euthyphro is effectively arguing, against Socrates, for a *Divine Command theory of ethics* – in other words he is taking the view that morality is based on what God commands or on what God wills. Paul Helm in the introduction to *Divine Commands and Morality* claims that the Divine Command Theory holds that 'God does issue commands and that these commands are to form the basis of a believer's morality'. Theologians such as Duns Scotus and William of Ockham have supported Divine Command theories of Ethics – effectively maintaining that if God commanded adultery or theft then these would then become good actions. Others have rejected this approach. Alasdair MacIntyre is a good example:

> ... We ought to do what God commands, if we are theists, because it is right in some independent sense of 'right', rather than hold what God commands is right just because God commands it, a view which depends on 'right' being defined as 'being in accordance with what God commands'.
>
> (*The Religious Significance of Atheism*, p. 33)

One can attempt to get round the problems on the first horn of the Euthyphro dilemma by saying what is good is in accordance with the commands of a *loving* God. This would then appear to rule out some of the more objectionable commands in the Old Testatment as these could not, apparently, be commanded by a loving God. However this does not solve the problem as it is then necessary to determine what it means to be loving. This is far from clear, after all even loving human parents sometimes have to hurt their children (for instance by giving inoculations). The problem thus arises as to whether what is loving depends on God's will or whether there is an independent standard of what it is to be loving – in other words the problem of the Euthyphro dilemma in relation to goodness is simply raised a level and arises again about the nature of love.

Plato opts for a standard of morality independent of God – and this he finds in the Forms (see p. 11). Plato was a realist as he held that moral statements were true or false in so far as they corresponded to an absolute moral order. His view can be rejected by maintaining that there is no absolute standard of morality – instead morality is relative. However, if one does not wish to take this approach, if one holds that there is an absolute standard of right and wrong and yet is unwilling to ascribe this standard to God, then Plato's approach must still be taken seriously. Iris Murdoch (in *The Sovereignty of the Good*) and Stephen Clark (in *The Parliament of Souls*) are two modern philosophers who take a Platonic approach.

In the *Theatetus*, Plato sets out an alternative position which he then argues against – the position is set out by Protagoras who argues that all knowledge is relative to the individual and all morality is similarly relative. If this position is accepted, then neither horn of the Euthyphro dilemma is valid – there is no absolute standard of morality at all. Protagoras' most quoted saying is that:

An individual human being is the measure of all things.

This used to be phrased 'man is the measure of all things', but the above is preferable today and is, in any case, probably a better translation. Plato sees this as referring to those things which human beings experience. Effectively Plato takes Protagoras to be arguing that things are as they seem to us that they are. There is no such thing as 'being cold' or 'being hot' independent of their relation to the observer, rather hotness and coldness are relative to the person who feels that the thing is hot or cold. 'Really cold' just means 'cold for some person x'. There is no absolute standard of 'coldness' independent of the relation. Imagine two people – a young man and a young woman. The man says:

The Mona Lisa is ugly, the United Nations is corrupt, democracy is the best political system and it is windy today

while the woman says:

The Mona Lisa is beautiful, the United Nations is trustworthy, democracy is wrong and there is no wind today.

Protagoras' view would hold that these statements do not contradict each other – rather both individuals are expressing their own point of view, their own way of looking at different things. It would make no sense to ask whether the Mona Lisa is beautiful in itself or whether the United Nations is corrupt in itself.

Plato asks Protagoras whether the same relativism holds true in the moral field. Protagoras has a problem here because he is a teacher and his role as a teacher would be undermined if everyone's judgement is equally valid. If this was the case, then Protagoras has no right to teach his own doctrine (that the human individual is the measure of all things) – because this is his point of view which is no more right or wrong than anyone else's. Protagoras' answer to this is that some men produce better results by their judgements than others – however he still has the same problem. Is there some absolute sense of what is a 'better result'? Protagoras' own view means that he must deny this, but he needs to hold this position in order to answer Plato's challenge.

Protagoras tries to argue not that what is right or wrong depends on the individual but that it depends on the state or city in which one lives. Thus he says:

> Whatever in any city is regarded as just and admirable is just and admirable in that city for as long as it is thought to be so.
> (*Theatetus*, 167C)

This is an important view with great contemporary relevance. You cannot ask 'What is good?', but only 'What is good in the United States?' or 'What is good to the Christian?' or 'What is good to the Hindu?'. If you would ask the question 'How should I live?', then the only reply on this basis is that you should live according to the rules, laws and morals of the state or society or community in which you live (this position is similar to that taken by the Victorian philosopher, F. Bradley, in his book *Ethical Studies*). On this basis, the conventions of our society rule. However, the problems in today's multi-cultural society are all too evident – which community should one choose to belong to? Whose morals should I follow? Protagoras' approach provides no satisfactory answer to these questions.

ii) The Forms and the task of the philosopher

There are many beautiful things in the world – the countryside, a baby's first cry, the first rose of summer or a sunset. These things are all very different yet they may all be termed beautiful. Plato considered that if words like 'beauty', 'justice' or 'good' were applied in so many different situations, they must all have something in common. He argued that everything that we see in the world that we call beautiful in some way participates in or resembles the perfect Form of Beauty. The Form of Beauty (as of Justice, the Good, etc.) exists timelessly and spacelessly – the Forms are neither created nor do they create. Beautiful, just or good things or persons in some way, albeit imperfectly, resemble these Forms. The Forms represent Absolute Reality as opposed to the many particular things which in some small way resemble them.

If, therefore, we were to ask how it is that two people both know a carpet is red or that two people both know that the first rose of summer is beautiful, then Plato's answer would be that since the redness of the carpet in some way resembles the perfect Form of Redness and the characteristic of the rose in some way resembles the perfect Form of Beauty, so the two people both rightly see the carpet as red and the rose as beautiful. Similarly, disputes about whether an action is good could be settled by determining whether the action can be compared with or participates in the Form of the Good.

We live in a spatio-temporal world. The whole of our world is dominated by space and time. The Forms, however, are timeless, spaceless, changeless and immutable. Plato considered that matter, the raw chaotic 'stuff' of the universe, is everlasting – without beginning and without end. The Demiurge, Plato's God, took this chaotic matter and moulded or formed it into the orderly universe that we know – using the Forms as a model. However the Universe is not perfect because the Demiurge had to work with pre-existent matter which resisted his will and also because the Universe is temporal and spatial.

The world, for Plato, is a dance of shadows – we live in the shadows brought on by time and space and our task as human beings is to see beyond these shadows. Plato puts forward three famous analogies which express this view – the Sun, the Twice Divided Line and the Cave. The last will be dealt with here although the first is also important and worthy of reference (see *The Republic* p. 274 Penguin edition):

> Imagine an underground chamber, like a cave with an entrance open to the daylight and running a long way underground. In this cave are men who have been prisoners there since they were children, their legs and necks being so fastened that they can only look ahead of them and cannot turn their heads. Behind them and above them a fire is burning, and between the fire and the prisoners runs a road, in front of which a curtain wall has been built, like the screen at puppet shows between the operators and their audience ... Imagine further that there are men carrying all sorts of gear along behind the curtain wall, including figures of men and animals made of wood and stone and other materials, and that some of these men, as is natural, are talking and some not.

Socrates then says that the bound men would only see the shadows and they would assume that the shadows were the real thing and if the curtain wall reflected sound they would assume that the shadows were talking – in other words they would take the shadows to be real. Having established this scenario, Socrates continues:

> Suppose one of (the men) were let loose, and suddenly compelled to stand up and turn his head and look and walk towards the fire;

all these actions would be painful and he would be too dazzled to see properly the objects of which he used to see the shadows. So if he was told that what he used to see was mere illusion and that he was now nearer reality and seeing more correctly, because he was turned towards objects which were more real … don't you think he would be at a loss and think that what he used to see was more real than the objects now being pointed out to him?

Socrates' point is that if someone looked directly at the light of the fire he would be even more dazzled than if he looked at the objects on the road between the fire and where he was bound. If he was then dragged out of the cave and saw the sun for the first time, he would be more dazzled still. In fact he would not initially be able to see anything of those things which he was now told were real. Gradually he might become accustomed to shadows outside the cave, then to other objects and finally he might be able to look at the Sun itself. The Sun stands for the Form of the Good – which is the highest of the Forms. Socrates' point is that the philosopher is like the man who has been untied – it is a singularly painful process to be freed from the delusion of supposed reality, from the 'dance of shadows' that represents the world as it appears to us. It is a long and painful journey out of the cave of misunderstanding before one can begin to see reality as it is. Once someone has done this, then those things that passed for knowledge and were most prized by those tied in the cave would no longer be of any importance. As he puts it:

There was probably a certain amount of honour and glory to be won amongst the prisoners, and prizes for keen-sightedness for anyone who could remember the order or sequence among the passing shadows and to be best able to predict their future appearance. Will our released prisoner hanker after these prizes or envy their power or honour? Won't he be more likely to feel, as Homer says, that he would far rather be a 'serf in the house of some landless man', or indeed anything else in the world, than live and think as they do?

The philosopher, then, is the person who has freed himself or been freed from the prison of appearance and has begun to see things as they really are. To such a person all the things that this world values so highly will be of no importance. If he or she tries to communicate them to others (who are still locked in the prison of the cave) the response will not be gratitude but rather anger or resentment. Most people will be content with the dance of shadows, they will be content with appearances and will reject the philosophic path.

Plato was preoccupied with the distinction between appearance and reality – reality is difficult to discern and one has to pierce through the shadows of appearance to arrive at the reality that lies beyond (C. S. Lewis sometimes talks in these terms and the title of the play *Shadowlands* about his relationship with his wife is based on essentially Platonic ideas). We can see from the parable of the Cave that Plato thinks the task of the individual is to leave the darkness of the cave represented by our ignorance and to come out into the light of the Sun – which represents the Form of the Good. The philosopher should be the person who has done this and who can see reality as it is.

iii) Justice and goodness

Socrates took a practical attitude to ethics – he was concerned with the question of how an individual should live in order to achieve happiness. Happiness is perhaps the best translation for the Greek word Socrates used which was *eudaimonia* but it is still inadequate as the Greek word has more to do with an individual having that which is desirable in the form of behaviour rather than simply living what he or she considers is a fulfilled life. Warm toes in front of the television screen is not an adequate understanding of *eudaimonia*! Indeed Plato and Socrates specifically reject the idea that 'The Good' can be defined in terms of pleasure. It is worth remembering that Socrates died for what he believed in which would scarcely fit with the conventional understanding of happiness.

For Plato, for a person to act justly means having the three parts of their personality in proper balance:

- *wisdom* which comes from reason;
- *courage* which comes from the spirited part of man and
- *self-control* which rules the passions.

So a person cannot be just without being wise, brave and self-controlled – and only if this balance is maintained will a person be happy. Plato's argument in favour of this last point rests on the claim that happiness depends on internal mental states. This seems an odd definition of justice (even from the individual's point of view) as it defines justice in terms of a person's mental states and not in terms of how we treat other people – although Plato would maintain that if the proper balance is maintained within each individual, then they would treat other people correctly.

Plato held that justice in the state mirrored justice in an individual (or, to put it another way, justice writ large in the state is analogous to justice writ small in the individual). In a just state the various parts co-operate harmoniously in their proper roles, just as, in an individual, the various faculties should also work together. The individual must rule himself, but state government is needed by properly trained philosopher-guardians, who are carefully educated and are not motivated by self-interest, to ensure that the proper balance essential to justice is maintained. If the majority of people live in the cave in the shadows of ignorance, they would not be in the best position to govern the state in the way it should be governed.

Plato was strongly opposed to democracy, as this gives power to the greatest number of people, because what the greatest number think may well not be correct. The mass of people are also easily swayed by rhetoric – as Socrates found to his cost when rhetoric persuaded the Athenian population to condemn him to death. Given the ease with which politicans and advertising can sway large groups of people today, Plato's suspicion of democracy should, perhaps, be given more weight than it often is, although the dangers of those who think they know best and who decide to impose their will on others are probably greater than the dangers of democracy. However, Plato still provides a challenge to our accepted western

15

liberal assumptions about government which is worthy of more consideration.

Plato's approach is élitist – most people are in the shadows of ignorance and it is the philosopher who, after much study, can pierce through these shadows to see the world 'rightly'.

On Plato's view, virtue is knowledge – Plato did not think anyone willingly acted immorally. People acted wrongly due to ignorance and he effectively denies weakness of the will. If, therefore, people could be brought to understand their error and to appreciate what was right, they would then act accordingly. This approach is based on the Socratic idea that no one would voluntarily choose what was not good for him or herself. Once one comes out of the cave of ignorance and sees the truth or what is morally right, Plato assumes that one will act accordingly. This, however, rests on a considerable error. It is perfectly possible for a person to say:

1 I know that action X is wrong, yet
2 I choose to do action X.

There could be any number of examples of this. Smokers know that smoking will seriously damage their health – yet they go on smoking. St Paul put this point very well when he said:

> For the good that I would I do not, but the evil which I would not, that I do. (Romans, 7:19)

Knowledge does not lead to virtue – and the whole of Plato's moral philosophy rests on the claim that it does.

For Plato and Socrates behaving morally or justly is always better for the individual even though this may lead to suffering and even to death. This was based on their view that the soul is a prisoner of the body and survives death and that if one does a bad act then one harms one's soul (which is one's very self) most of all. This leads to Socrates' view that it is better to suffer harm rather than to inflict it because if you inflict harm on others the person you are really harming most of all is yourself as you are adversely affecting your soul. In Plato's *Gorgias*, Socrates is portrayed as confronting Polus who holds that immoral acts can often bring an individual the greatest amount of pleasure or be in some way better for the person performing the action. Polus measures actions in terms of their material consequences for the person who performs them, Socrates measures actions by the effect they have on the soul of the individual. Effectively Socrates can be seen as saying:

> Think hard enough and you will always find that doing the right thing is best for you
>
> (Quoted in Peter Singer's *A Companion to Ethics*, Blackwell, p. 125)

However, this will be easier to accept if one first agrees with the presuppositions of Socrates and Plato – particularly those governing the immortality of the soul.

One of the gravest problems in Plato's approach is that individuals can never be sure that they have arrived at a correct understanding of virtue and the nature of the good – how does one know that one has emerged from the cave and is not still in shadow? In his own authorship Plato may have moved from seeing this process as involving the individual thinking by himself to the idea of arriving at these values by looking at the good for the community. However, no clear criteria are provided. The second major problem is that Plato's approach is far from practical and gives no guidance as to how to act in the day-to-day situations which individuals face. However Plato's realist understanding of the nature of moral claims is particularly important and still remains an important alternative to moral relativism that merits further consideration and development. As we shall see in a later chapter, an Aristotelian approach to virtue may once again be coming into vogue, but Plato's understanding remains an alternative which needs to be taken seriously.

Questions for discussion

1 What do you consider to be the most satisfactory solution to the Euthyphro dilemma?
2 Socrates considered that he was ignorant and yet he was wise. How should this be understood?
3 What are the strengths and weaknesses of Plato's understanding of morality?
4 If I hold that the grass is green and you believe the same thing, how can Plato's approach help to explain that we are both correctly seeing the same thing?
5 What point does Plato want to make in his parable of the Cave?
6 Why did Plato reject democracy? Do you think he was right to do so and why?

THREE
Aristotle and Virtue Theory

It would be difficult to begin an account of Aristotle's moral theory without first saying something about where he stands in relation to Socrates and Plato. Socrates (470–400 B.C.), as has already been suggested, is generally regarded as the founding father of western philosophy. Although Socrates never wrote anything, or at least there is almost no evidence to point to his having done so, we know of his existence chiefly through the works of the comic dramatist Aristophanes (448–380 B.C.), the writer and historian Xenophon (430–355 B.C.) and particularly through the philosophical dialogues of Plato (427–347 B.C.). Plato was Socrates' pupil for approximately ten years prior to Socrates' death, and Aristotle became Plato's pupil for roughly twenty years, studying under him at the famous Academy which Plato had established in Athens. These three, then, Socrates, Plato and Aristotle, may be referred to as the Three Greek Wise Men as, arguably, they laid the foundations for all philosophical inquiry. Although western philosophy has been described by A. N. Whitehead as merely footnotes to Plato, it is Aristotle to whom, perhaps, the greatest debt must be paid, for in Aristotle's writings we find the rigorous and systematic treatment of philosophical questions in continuous prose argument, unlike the dramatic and often poetically beautiful dialogues of Plato. Aristotle's *Nicomachean Ethics* is, effectively, the first major piece of sustained moral argument from a secular point of view.

Biography

Born in 384 B.C. in Stagyra, Macedonia, Aristotle was the son of Nicomachus, a wealthy and highly influential court physician to the king of Macedonia. At the age of eighteen Aristotle entered Plato's Academy where he stayed for almost twenty years. Disappointed at not being given the leadership of the Academy upon Plato's death, and becoming concerned for his own safety as a result of some racial hatred being whipped up against Macedonians, Aristotle left Athens and moved East. He found relative peace and security in the kingdom of Atarneus, in the Eastern Aegean. Here he married the king's niece. In 343 B.C. he became tutor to Alexander, later Alexander the Great. According to Bertrand Russell it is inconceivable that Alexander thought anything of Aristotle other than that he was a 'prosy old pedant'. Nonetheless, enjoying some political and financial support from the king, Aristotle returned to Athens in about 335 B.C. and founded his own school of philosophy, the Lyceum. However, upon Alexander's early death in a far-flung Eastern campaign Aristotle went into voluntary exile 'lest Athens should sin twice against philosophy', that is, execute him as it had done Socrates. He died in Chalcis in 322 B.C. at the age of sixty-two, and his will, which survives relatively intact, suggests that he had led a happy and fulfilled life.

His influence has been enormous for he began sorting human knowledge and inquiry into the various categories and disciplines that we know and use today. He compiled the first 'dictionary of philosophical terms' and produced major works in logic (the *Organon* or *Instrument*), in the physical sciences (the *Physics, On the Heavens*), in the biological sciences (*The History of Animals, On the Parts of Animals*), in psychology (*On the Soul*), in politics (*Politics, The Constitution of Athens*) and in ethics (*Nicomachean Ethics, Eudemian Ethics*).

Ethics

The *Nicomachean Ethics*, generally regarded as the most detailed and coherent of Aristotle's works on moral philosophy, is a collection of lectures compiled and edited by his son, also called Nicomachus after his grandfather. Consisting of ten books in all it describes the purpose of life, the divisions of the soul, and the various qualities of mind and character that are supposed to be necessary for moral conduct. It continues with a detailed description of friendship before concluding with the view that contemplation of the Good (that is, the life of philosophic reflection) is the highest form of happiness. For those not fully committed or suited to the life of pure contemplation then friendship becomes the ideal forum in which to exercise all of the virtues; the virtues being those moral and intellectual characteristics which have been fashioned by habit and education. Morality finds part of its true expression in friendship.

The purpose of life

In Book 1 of the Ethics, Aristotle makes a number of points concerning the true object or purpose of life. Firstly, he makes the seemingly obvious point that everything a person or a group does is directed towards some kind of an aim.

> Every art and every investigation and similarly every action and pursuit is considered to aim at some good (all references are to *Nicomachean Ethics* translated by J. A. K. Thomson and revised by H. Tredennick, 1976, Penguin, p. 63).

This, of course, makes complete sense. Whatever we do there is a purpose in doing it although sometimes, of course, the purpose may not seem immediately clear nor apparent. Alternatively, there may be a purpose to what we do, but we may want to object to that purpose. There is even a purpose in having no purpose! We might just want to sit and relax without having any particular aim in mind. But our purpose here is simply to enjoy doing nothing.

Secondly, there are, according to Aristotle, 'superior' and 'subordinate' aims. So, for example, writing the first philosophy essay is subordinate to obtaining the final A level or degree qualification, and sharpening the pencil or filling the ink cartridge are yet further subordinate aims to writing the essay. The point is that we do one thing in order to accomplish the aim of another more important thing, and so on, almost ad infinitum. We say 'almost ad infinitum' because there must be one overall or final aim towards which everything else is directed. For Aristotle, that final aim is the *Good*; not only the Good for oneself but the Good for all humanity.

If then, our activities have some end which we want for its own sake, and for the sake of which we want all the other ends ... it is clear that this must be the Good, that is the supreme Good ... (and) ... Does it not follow then that a knowledge of the Good is of great importance to us for the conduct of our lives? (Moreover) ... while it is desirable to secure what is good in the case of an individual, to do so in the case of a people or a state is something finer and more sublime (pp. 63–4).

Thirdly, that Supreme Good, for Aristotle, is defined as 'Happiness":

... what is the highest of all practical goods? Well, so far as the name goes, there is pretty general agreement. 'It is happiness' say both ordinary and cultured people (p. 66).

This, however, presents us with a problem. The problem is that because people differ from each other, there are therefore differing conceptions or versions of happiness. At root, according to Aristotle, there are three broad categories of people:

• those who love pleasure;
• those who love honour,
• those who love contemplation.

There are, then, lives given over to wine, women (or men!) and song; lives expressed in constant service to the community; and lives devoted to thinking. Aristotle places the life of the politician in the second category (as someone who is always trying to find practical solutions to large- and small-scale problems); the life of a philosopher inevitably falls in the third category whereas most people, it seems, would prefer to live a life of pleasure:

> the utter servility of the masses comes out in their preference for a bovine existence (p. 68).

Aristotle was nothing if not blunt! His three-part classification leads on to two further points. Firstly, the one thing that distinguishes human beings from the rest of creation is the faculty of *reason*. We share the basic function of life with both plants and animals, and we share sentience or some form of conscious life along with animals. But only humans have the capacity to use reason in order to think about the quality of their lives. Therefore, if reason is the distinguishing mark of humanity, then happiness, logically, must consist in using that reason in order to work out what a good life is, and then to live it. The second and final point is equally important. For Aristotle, and for the Greeks in general, a person is primarily a member of a group, be it a family, a household, a village or a city state. There is no such thing as a purely free-thinking individual. Our individuality is already partly decided for us by the group or groups of which we are a part. Hence, the overall wellbeing of a group is far more important then the wellbeing of any single member within it.

> For even if the good of the community coincides with that of the individual, it is clearly a greater and more perfect thing to achieve and preserve that of a community; for while it is desirable to secure what is good in the case of an individual, to do so in the case of a people or a state is something finer and more sublime (p. 64).

And that, for Aristotle, is the major reason why politicians ought to study ethics, because they have the responsibility of ensuring that the good life is lived by all members of society, and not just by some of them.

The soul

Before any description of a truly ethical person can be given, an account of the soul needs to be offered, for

> by human goodness is meant goodness not of the body but of the soul, and happiness also we define as an activity of the soul. (p. 88).

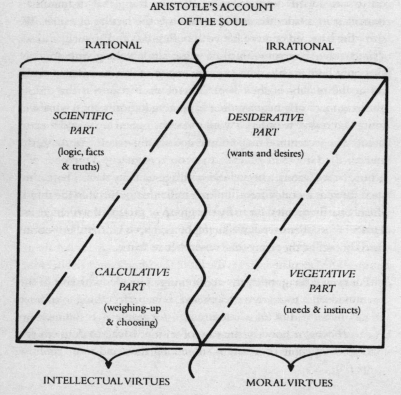

ARISTOTLE'S ACCOUNT
OF THE SOUL

RATIONAL   IRRATIONAL

SCIENTIFIC   DESIDERATIVE
PART   PART

(logic, facts   (wants and desires)
& truths)

CALCULATIVE   VEGETATIVE
PART   PART

(weighing-up   (needs & instincts)
& choosing)

INTELLECTUAL VIRTUES   MORAL VIRTUES
Cultivated through 'Instruction'   Cultivated through 'Habit'

The accompanying diagram is an attempt to simplify Aristotle's rather wordy account. As can be seen, the soul is divided into two major parts: the rational and the irrational. Whether these are actual divisions in the soul, or whether they are just helpful definitional differences is irrelevant for Aristotle. We cannot split open the person in order to examine the soul like we can a leg or an arm. Each of these two major divisions is also separated into two. The irrational part is divided into the vegetative and the desiderative. The vegetative part is the cause of nutrition and growth; that is, those basic instincts necessary for individual and collective survival, such as eating, drinking, resting and procreating.

The desiderative or appetitive part is associated with those many and varied desires and wants which can be channelled, controlled or made submissive. These are the desires not just for food (that is a need or a vegetative impulse), but for a particular kind of food – cheeseburger with all the relish plus chips and onions. The wants and desires will, of course, include all of those luxury goods and activities which are not strictly necessary for survival. The distinction is clearly between 'needs' and 'wants'; and often what we want is not what we need. I might want another pint of beer after having already drunk three, but, physiologically it is clearly not what I need.

Next, the rational part of the soul is also divided into two: the scientific and the calculative. The scientific part is the bit of the mind which can grasp invariable first principles, that is, knowledge of physics, of mathematics, of geography and so on. It is the section which houses all the facts of the world which are not up for debate or dispute. The calculative part is the bit of the mind which deliberates, considers, weighs up or thinks about things in order to make a decision about what to do, what to choose, what to make, what to buy and so on. Instead of knowing facts, it is concerned with knowing how to choose or how to come to a decision. It allows us to weigh up the pros and cons of an argument or a situation.

The fruit cake example:
It must be stressed at the outset that this is not an example used by Aristotle. However, let us suppose that the vegetative part of me needs sustenance or nutrition and growth. Now, the desiderative part of me desires cake rather than fruit. However, the scientific part of me knows the fact that, given my current waist size, fruit will do me more good than cake will. So, finally, the calculative part of my mind thinks about the advisability of cake over fruit or vice versa, and comes to a decision: How about 'fruit cake'? The scientific part of my mind will then be able to follow the precise instructions on how to make a reasonably respectable fruit cake of the health-food variety. Thus the vegetative, desiderative, calculative and scientific parts of my 'soul' have all come into play.

The virtues:

The reason why Aristotelian ethics is called Virtue Theory is because the virtues, those 'excellences' (Greek: *arete*) or qualities of mind and character, are at the heart of his argument. There are two sorts of virtues:

• *moral virtues* or qualities of character (such as courage, liberality, temperance, modesty and so on). These virtues are connected to the desiderative and hence, the irrational part of the soul. They can only be cultivated through *habit*.
• *intellectual virtues* or qualities of mind (such as wisdom, understanding and judgement). These virtues are connected to the rational half of the soul, and are to be cultivated through *instruction*.

1 Moral virtues
In Aristotle's account there are twelve moral virtues which fall between two vices: the vice of excess or the vice of deficiency. So, for example, the moral virtue of *courage* would fall between its excess which is foolhardiness or rashness and its deficiency which is, of course, cowardice.

Excess	Virtue	Deficiency
rashness	courage	cowardice
licentiousness	temperance	insensibility
prodigality	liberality	illiberality
vulgarity	magnificence	pettiness
vanity	magnanimity	pusillanimity
ambition	proper ambition	lack of ambition
irascibility	patience	lack of spirit
boastfulness	truthfulness	understatement
buffoonery	wittiness	boorishness
obsequiousness	friendliness	cantankerousness
shyness	modesty	shamelessness
envy	righteous– indignation	malicious– enjoyment (p.104)

2 Intellectual virtues

There are nine intellectual virtues comprising five main or primary virtues, and four secondary virtues:

- *Art or Technical Skill (techne)*: the practical skill of knowing how to bring something into existence. For example, knowing how to build a house or construct a bridge as well as knowing how to write a poem, paint a picture or sculpt a statue. For the Greeks all things had to meet two criteria: they had to be functional and they had to be aesthetically pleasing or decorative. Plays, poems and statues had a symbolic political, social or religious function as well as possessing what we might call 'artistic or dramatic beauty'. Similarly, houses and bridges had not only to fulfil their obvious function, but they also had to be pleasing to the eye.

- *Scientific Knowledge (episteme)*: This comprises the so-called 'facts' of the universe, that is, knowledge of all the objects in the universe as well as all the laws which govern them. Knowledge of biology, astronomy, geography and so on are all covered by this virtue.

- *Prudence or Practical Wisdom (phronesis)*: This is one of the most important virtues which helps us to balance our interests with the interests of others. This is the virtue, for example, which helps us to make the decision whether or not to purchase the colour television with stereo sound, or whether to buy the small black and white portable and give the rest of the money to Oxfam. Arguably, without phronesis the remainder of the virtues revert to being mere skills.
- *Intelligence or Intuition (nous)*: This is perhaps the basic intellectual virtue in the sense that without it probably few other intellectual virtues could get going. Arguably, without intelligence or intuition nothing else can happen in the mind!
- *Wisdom (sophia)*: This is the finished form of all the virtues. Generally speaking, one must have lived to a good age, experienced many things and learned a number of lessons before wisdom is finally cultivated.

The four secondary intellectual virtues are:

- *Resourcefulness or Good Deliberation (euboulia)*: This is a form of practical wisdom, and involves knowing where and how to enquire about something so that the best decision can be made. For example, suppose I need a new refrigerator. At the outset this seems to be a perfectly innocuous issue almost completely unconnected with moral concerns. Its relevance, however, will soon be made clear. Resourcefulness will prompt me to examine *Which?*, the popular consumer guide. This will help me to make a more informed decision about the best fridge to buy.
- *Understanding (sunesis)*: This goes beyond the ability to know external facts about the world. To understand something is to recognise all the difficulties and perplexities associated with decision-making. I might choose the best fridge recommended by *Which?*, but when I get it home it may not fit into my kitchen! In order to understand things I am obliged to deliberate over many interrelated issues.

- *Judgement (gnome)*: For a judgement to be a good one it has to take account of what is right and just for all concerned. Suppose, after examining all of the fridges on offer, after measuring my kitchen and so on, I find that my chosen fridge is called 'The Philippino Special Exploiter'. Its high quality and low price depend upon the poverty and squalid conditions of the Third World workers who help manufacture it. My sympathetic judgement will be not to purchase the fridge and perhaps to begin campaigning on behalf of the exploited workforce.

- *Cleverness (deinotes)*: the last of the secondary intellectual virtues. On its own, however, it can hardly be said to be a virtue in the true sense of the word. Cleverness unconnected with judgement can be unscrupulous. A shady second-hand car dealer may be said to be clever, but we would hardly say that he was in possession of a virtue.

Doctrine of the mean

According to the Aristotelian argument we all have the *potential* to develop these moral and intellectual virtues. However, it is likely that only a few people will be able to cultivate the potential virtues into *actual* virtues. Similarly, all acorns have the potential to become actual oak trees, but only some of them will become so. Moreover, if we are to cultivate our virtues, particularly our moral virtues, we must be aware of the doctrine of the mean. Put simply, we must regulate our emotions and responses to people and situations so that we are eventually able to conduct ourselves with dignity. We must try to ensure that we veer away from either the excess or deficiency, and so hit the 'mean' or midway point, although Aristotle is quick to mention that the midway point is not just a numerical halfway house.

For example, I have the clear capacity to feel intense anger at my computer when it fails to work. I accept my anger for what it is — a natural feeling or emotional response. However, it is my attitude towards that feeling which is crucial. I could, for example, set about my computer with a hammer in order to release my feelings. But this would be to exhibit a poorly developed virtue. On the other hand, I could simply not bother about the failure of my computer, do nothing about it and give up on writing altogether. This would be an equally poor response. The right response would be to control the anger, take the computer to a repair shop, and then hire or borrow another one for the intervening period. My feelings, no matter how overwhelming they are, should not drown my reason. Feelings are clearly important, but our virtues – our attitudes towards our feelings – are more important. What matters is what we do with our feelings so that eventually they can conform naturally to that which reason would advocate. Aristotle makes the point that children have to learn the virtues through habit. They must learn that they cannot simply give vent to all their feelings in whatever way they wish and whenever they want. Although the six-year-old may initially give vent to her emotions in the supermarket by screaming that she wants the chocolate bar, she must gradually learn that the feelings of anger and resentment at being denied it are perfectly natural. However, she must control that anger and resentment and develop a sense of patience instead. Arguably, adulthood is about learning to control and direct one's emotions. In other words, it is about developing the moral virtues.

By constantly learning through habit to control our feelings we should, according to Aristotle, begin to:

> have these feelings at the right times on the right grounds towards the right people for the right motive and in the right way ... (this is) ... to feel them to an intermediate, that is, to the best degree; and this is the mark of virtue (p. 101).

There is the obvious criticism that this approach to moral reasoning leads to a kind of blind uniformity of belief, desire and behaviour. The intention, it would seem, is to produce an automatic response in people to other people and to situations. This would perhaps be so, if Aristotle had not emphasised the importance of the intellectual virtues along with the moral virtues. Not only is it necessary for us to feel and behave in the right or appropriate manner, but we should also understand and know why it is important that we feel and act in these ways.

Friendship as the main aim of a moral life

Finally, without friendship none of the virtues – either moral or intellectual – would be of any value. For Aristotle, friendship is essential. We are social and political beings.

> Nobody would choose to live without friends even if he had all the other good things (p. 258).

A community, a society, a state, any gathering of two or more people presupposes a notion of friendship, and depends upon it. Households, marriages, partnerships, clubs, societies, etc, all depend upon sustaining a forum within which friendships can be fostered and maintained. Again, Aristotle makes the point that:

> Friendship also seems to be the bond that holds communities together ... (p. 258).

Indeed, friendship is of such primary importance that it comes before justice itself. In fact without friendship there could be no sense of justice. The lawmaker, the lawgiver and the law-enforcer all derive their rationale from acting as the supposed legally-appointed 'friend' of everyone in the community, and of ensuring that the community fosters the right conditions under which friendship may flourish.

> ... lawgivers seem to attach more importance to it than to justice; because concord seems to be something like friendship, and concord is their primary object – that and eliminating faction, which is enmity ... indeed friendliness is considered to be justice in the fullest sense (p. 258-9).

Briefly, there are three kinds of friendship, according to Aristotle: based on utility, pleasure and goodness.

- *Utility friendships* are those which are, as the name suggests, simply useful to us. Utility friends are those with whom we find ourselves in company at work, those next to us on the factory assembly line. It is convenient for both parties to engage in pleasant and friendly conversation in order to while away the time whilst doing something tedious and dissatisfying. The friendship is useful in that it is an aid to comfort. Moreover, there may be more than just pleasant mutual gain in the friendship; it may be useful for the completion of a game or a project. For example, it clearly helps if team members do actually get on with each other when a cricket or netball tour is arranged. Or the friendship may be formed deliberately to cater for plain personal need. Here Aristotle cites the elderly as a group who form utility friendships. For example, someone is needed to push the wheelchair or fetch the shopping. Or again, friendship may be sought in order to further one's own personal advantage. Here it is the middle-aged who actively cultivate utility friendships – perhaps the businessman who purposefully cultivates a friendship with a local bank manager in order to secure a business loan. According to Aristotle, most friendships in the worlds of industry, business and commerce are utility friendships.
- *Pleasurable or Erotic friendships* are slightly better than the first type. Here, friends give us pleasure, and the friendship evolves through feelings and emotions. The relationship is governed more by the heart than by the head. Friends are pleasurable to be with because they may be witty, amusing or attractive. Friendships between the young are generally of this kind. They tend to be impermanent, and are often based on sexual attraction.
- *Perfect friendships* are based on goodness and are obviously the most valuable. Here friends care more about the other person than about themselves. Moreover, it means liking or loving the other person for what she/he is, not for any incidental quality that they

might possess, such as beauty. Such friends have similar attributes, and such friendships only occur after a long while. The relationship needs time to develop. According to Aristotle, 'You cannot get to know each other until you have eaten the proverbial quantity of salt together.' This apparently is a *medimnos* or one and a half bushels. In other words, the friends need to share many meals together; mealtimes traditionally being times of social chatting, anecdote-telling and story-swapping. Finally, there are few truly good friendships for there are few truly good people.

Criticisms

According to some scholars (e.g. Ackrill 1981; Lloyd 1968; Taylor 1955), Aristotle's account of ethics is, in fact, simply a detailed elaboration of a very orthodox Greek view of aristocratic living. It is easy to cultivate the virtues when the mortgage is fully paid up, the children are looked after by a nanny, and one's inheritance pays for the daily needs and wants. Life for the Athenian (or Macedonian) aristocrat was relatively easy, being purchased with the help of a slave population and an underclass of women.

And so, from a singular and contemporary vantage point it would not be too difficult to savage Aristotle's entire system by a process of selective analysis. Firstly, he is, through modern eyes, overtly *racist*. Any non-Greek is likely to be barbarous and sub-human, and therefore, a clear candidate for slavery. Friendships of utility are the only kinds of friendships one could have with 'a foreigner'. Secondly, Aristotle appears blatantly *sexist*. He accepts unquestioningly the supposedly natural, paternalistic hierarchy of relationships in which 'man rules by merit but hands over to his wife such duties as are best suited to her'(!) (p. 276). Thirdly, he is what Singer would call *speciesist*. Animals exist on an ontological level clearly below humans and barely above plants. 'Animals have no share in happiness, being completely incapable of such activity' (p. 333). According to Aristotle, animals cannot be happy because happiness depends upon the exercise of reason in order to pursue the virtuous life. As animals do not possess reason they, therefore, are incapable of achieving any happiness. However, what we now know of animals' physiology and behaviour leads us to suspect that, to a degree, they can reason about their environment, and often do exhibit many of the signs of being happy. But, as with all issues in philosophy, it rather depends upon the meanings we wish to attach to words, in this case 'reason' and 'happiness'. Fourthly, Aristotle is *ageist* given his clear dictum that no one would want to befriend the old and the sour-tempered, the one being synonymous with the other. And fifthly, his moral theory is *élitist*, in that only magnanimous men, honourable politicians and philosophers can truly know and exercise all of the virtues, and are therefore the only ones to appreciate fully the Good Life.

However, such a critique is unfair. Aristotle was 'culture-bound' and could not have transcended all of the conceptual constraints of his time and culture. Our criticism must be tempered by historical understanding. Such a defence cuts no ice with Russell, however, who stated:

> The book (*Ethics*) appeals to the respectable middle-aged, and has been used by them, especially since the seventeenth century, to repress the ardours and enthusiasms of the young. But to a man with any depth of feeling it is likely to be repulsive ... There is ... an almost complete absence of what may be called benevolence or philanthropy. The sufferings of mankind ... do not move him ... More generally there is an emotional poverty in the *Ethics* (B. Russell *History of Western Philosophy*, p. 195).

Questions for discussion

1 Argue either for or against the view that the moral life consists in 'feeling the right things at the right times, on the right grounds, towards the right people for the right motive ...'
2 What additions, subtractions and/or modifications would you wish to make to Aristotle's list of intellectual and moral virtues?

3 Is happiness the Supreme Good? If so, in what does happiness consist?

4 How far does Aristotle's classification of friendship correspond with what we know about human relationships?

5 Is Russell's criticism of Aristotle fair? How might the criticism be rebutted?

6 Analyse critically Aristotle's theory of the soul and his doctrine of the mean.

FOUR

Aquinas, Natural Law and Proportionalism

> To disparage the dictate of reason is equivalent to condemning the command of God.
>
> *St Thomas Aquinas*

The Natural Law approach to morality has a long history. Cicero in *De Re Publica* describes natural law as follows:

> True law is right reason in agreement with nature. It is applied universally and is unchanging and everlasting . . . there will be no different laws in Rome and in Athens, or different laws now and in the future, but one eternal and unchangeable law will be valid for all nations and all times, and there will be one master and ruler, that is God . . .

However, it was Aristotle who really developed this approach and Aquinas (1225–74) built on his thought. The writings of Aristotle had been lost in the West and preserved amongst the Islamic scholars of the East. They were reintroduced into Western thought shortly before Aquinas took up his position as a professor at the University of Paris.

Aquinas considered that natural law was the moral code which human beings are naturally inclined towards. God reveals specific commands but these do not go against natural law but rather further and develop it. This reflected Aquinas' approach to theology generally by which natural theology (which was based on human reason) did not go against revealed theology (which was based on revelation by God). Aquinas said that the moral life is the life which is lived 'according to reason' and, indeed, acting in accordance with reason was the same as acting as a Christian would act. Aquinas' main difference from natural law philosophers who did not believe in God was that he considered that human beings were immortal and any moral theory and understanding of natural law had, therefore, to take account of the belief that the purpose of human existence did not lie entirely in this life.

Aquinas argued that the first priority laid down by natural law was that the self had to be preserved not just in this life but beyond the grave. If the self gave in to non-rational desires, then it became enslaved. It was possible to arrive at the natural or cardinal virtues (prudence, temperance, fortitude and justice, taken from Aristotle) by the use of reason alone. The Ten Commandments (with the exception of the command to keep the Sabbath day holy) were held to be examples of natural virtues. These natural virtues are expanded by the revealed virtues (of faith, hope and charity – derived from St Paul, cf. 1 Corinthians 13:13) and Aquinas held that the greater the extent to which these are developed by the individual, the greater will be the obedience to natural law.

The starting point for all advocates of natural law is to work out the *purpose* of human life. For Aquinas, this purpose included to live, to reproduce, to learn, to have an ordered society and to worship God. Reason is used to find out God's intention and the purpose of human existence and this will enable one to arrive at the principles of natural law.

Unlike Augustine and some of the later Christian reformers such as Calvin, Aquinas did not consider that human nature was totally corrupted. He considered that human nature, even though imperfect, was a reasonable guide to what human nature should be – since it was created by God. For Aquinas, there is no category of human beings that are in some way enslaved by a depraved nature – there is an equality of all human beings and in all human beings there is a necessary link between their happiness and their virtuous behaviour. Aquinas therefore starts from his experience of people and he expects to find natural law at work in every society in the world since all societies are made up of human beings who share a common nature. Natural law can be deduced from an examination of human nature and the ends for which human beings are created.

When we term God as good from our human perspective, Aquinas maintained that we name him as the goal of all desires or that to which all desires tend. Natural law can show all human beings what is good – religion is not needed for this and this is similar to St Paul's claim that the law is written in the hearts of all men (Romans 2:14ff). Reason can bring people to act rationally to develop the virtues. For Aquinas, 'God is good' is analytic in that it expresses a truth about God (that God is fully whatever it is to be God), but it is also synthetic as God represents the goal and destiny of all human beings, even though human beings may not recognise this. Aquinas based this idea on 'fitness for purpose' – since he held that humans were made by God for fellowship with God it follows that God, as their creator, must be the means by which human happiness will be found. Aquinas did not consider that morality was based on commands from God – a position which William of Ockham held as he considered that morality was based on revelation – Ockham held that if God commanded adultery then this would be right because of the command. Aquinas considered that if this was the case then God's commands could be irrational and arbitrary. Instead God makes human beings with a certain nature and this nature enables human beings to use their reason and their experience to understand what is right.

Aquinas considered, following Aristotle, that all men will the good. Human beings may seek some apparent good, but this is not a true good – it is only an apparent good because it does not conform to the perfection of the human nature which all human beings share. Aquinas considered that there is an 'ideal' human nature which we all have the potential to live up to or to fall away from and our moral actions are crucial in determining where we stand in this respect. If a person does something that is morally wrong, he or she will do this because they consider this to be a good although the possibility of the individual being mistaken certainly exists (examples might include smoking, drinking too much or even taking drugs). Aquinas says that: 'A fornicator seeks a pleasure which involves him in moral guilt' (Summa Theologica 1a, 19, 9). The fornicator seeks a pleasure which he thinks is a good, but this is only an apparent good as it diminishes a human being's nature.

Sin, for Aquinas, involves a falling short from the good – it means a human being becoming less than he or she is intended by God for him or her to be. To pursue an apparent good rather than the real good is to fall short of our real potential – it is to 'get it wrong' and to be mistaken. No one seeks evil for itself, it is only sought as an apparent good and therefore rests on a mistake. Hitler and Stalin did not seek to do evil – they sought what they thought were goods but they were mistaken – they strove for apparent rather than real goods. Sin is a theological word but there is no real difference between this theological idea and acting against reason. Aquinas says: 'the theologian considers sin principally as an offence against God, whereas the moral philosopher considers it as being contrary to reason' (S. T. 1a, 11ae, 71, 6, ad 5).

Since Aquinas argued that it is possible to be mistaken in which goods are chosen, it is obviously necessary to determine what is the right thing for a person to aim for. In essence, this is what discussion of natural law is about – seeking to explore what is the right good to aim for. Human beings have the ability, using their will and reason, to make deliberate moral choices (S. T. 1a, 11ae, 1, 1) which Aquinas terms 'human acts' to distinguish them from those acts performed by a person which are based on instinct. However, human reason must be used correctly, which leads Aquinas to talk of the 'right use of reason' – reason may be used to plan a murder or to decide to be virtuous, but only in the second case is reason being used 'rightly'. This obviously raises the problem of how one determines what is the 'right' use of reason when there are genuine differences of opinion as to what is good in a particular situation. A person's reason and their will both work together to help determine the choice they will make – if a person uses their reason correctly to determine what is right and then wills to do it this is, according to Aquinas, a free choice.

A person may will to make a morally wrong choice which he or she does not carry through – perhaps because the choice is not available. A man may, for instance, decide to defraud his employer of a substantial sum of money but he never gets the chance because he is moved to a new job.

Aquinas distinguished 'interior acts' and 'exterior acts' and is clear that the former are the most important – indeed morally good or bad acts are generally interior acts. An act may be good in itself but done for a wrong intention – for instance giving to charity may be good in itself but if it is done in order to attract praise then there is a bad intention ('for instance, we say that to give alms for the sake of vainglory is bad' (S.T., 1a, 11ae, 20, 1)). This does not entail that intention alone is decisive. As Copleston says in his book *Thomas Aquinas*:

> As Aquinas says, there are some things which cannot be justified by any alleged good intention . . . If I steal money from a man in order to give it to someone else, my action is not justified by my good intention . . . It is not possible to father on Aquinas the view that the end justifies the means . . . (p. 207).

In every act or proposed act, Aquinas considers that the will aims towards some end – in other words there is something which is considered to be a good (whether it is, in fact, a good or not). Aquinas needs, therefore, to establish the aim or end towards which human actions are to be directed.

Aquinas' answer is, perhaps, not unexpected. Considering that he was a Christian theologian writing from a world that was steeped in Christian thought only one final end could possibly be posited – and that is God. This raises the obvious question of those people who do not accept the existence of God and it might seem that their ends or aims would be different from those of the believer. Aquinas is by no means the only advocate of a natural law approach to morality and his understanding differs from others such as Aristotle due to his belief in a personal God. This leads Aquinas to maintain that not only do human beings in general have a purpose beyond death, but each individual also has a particular purpose which is directly related to each person's talents and abilities. Hugo Grotius claimed in 1625 (in *Prolegomena* II) that the foundations of natural law would be valid even if there was no God and Aristotle would have agreed with this, but in the absence of God the understanding of natural law would be significantly different as there would then be no life after death and thus the purpose of human existence would be changed. In addition, if God did not implant natural law in human beings then it might be argued that there was no reason why an individual should obey natural law.

Aquinas' approach is sophisticated and he seeks to address the problem of those who do not believe in God. Even such an individual would seek to fulfil his or her nature and to make the most of individual potentialities – it will therefore follow that such individuals would still incline to obey natural law, as it is in obeying this natural law that human potential is fulfilled. However, the ends that people seek are different and it may be possible to tell what ends they seek by looking at how they live – they may, for instance, look for money, power or reputation as ends in themselves and, if they do so, they will be making a mistake as to where their true happiness lies.

Aquinas does not simply assert that God is the final end for human beings – he considers alternatives. If, for instance, it is suggested that some form of sensual pleasure should be the final aim or end in life, Aquinas would reject this as it is then only the body's appetites and potentialities that are being satisfied and animals can seek the same thing. Similarly scientific knowledge cannot be the end as this good could only be sought by a small number of people who have the academic ability. Having said this, Aquinas' view that God is the final end for human beings may be regarded as an assumption and it can, of course, be challenged. However, if the assumption is accepted and if there is, indeed, a God who created the world and human beings, then it is perfectly sensible to claim (although, of

41

course, not necessarily true) that human beings were created for fellowship with this God.

It is interesting and important that Aquinas considers that all human beings share a single nature and, therefore, there should be a single aim or objective for all human beings – this justifies him in rejecting knowledge as an aim (as only some people have the ability to seek this knowledge). The one thing that every person can desire is the vision of God which is promised for the next life. It is only this beatific vision which will be fully and completely satisfying for every human being and humans can choose to seek this or to turn away from it.

The power of reason is vital for Aquinas – reason can determine what acts are necessary for the good of a human being whether this is taking food or drink or acting morally. Any act that furthers the end for human beings is morally good (whether this is eating or giving to charity). However, this is *not* to say that the acts are ends in themselves because means and ends are not separable. As Copleston says:

> . . . in the teleological ethic of Aristotle morally obligatory acts are not means to an end which is simply external to these acts, since they are a partial fulfilment of it; nor is the end something external to the agent . . . Aquinas followed Aristotle in holding that the final end of man consists in activity, and activity is obviously not external to the human agent in the sense that a picture is external to the artist . . . God is glorified by the highest possible development of man's potentialities as a rational being, and every moral act of man therefore has an intrinsic value (p. 211).

Both Aquinas and Aristotle maintained that a person can acquire a habit or disposition to either vice or virtue. Virtuous habits should be fostered by repeated acts of virtue and human beings should live without excess, according to the 'mean' (which can broadly be defined as that which is in accordance with right reason). Aquinas and Aristotle both deplored excess in any form – the classic example from Aristotle is that the brave man is neither cowardly (one example of excess) nor foolhardy (another example of excess). It might seem difficult to fit this Aristotelian notion with Christian figures such as Mother Julian of Norwich, Teresa of Lisieux or Teresa of Calcutta, and Aquinas does consider this point as he does ask whether giving one's goods away to the poor might be considered excess. His conclusion is that it would not if this action was inspired by Christ (S.T. 1a, 11ae, 64, 1, obj. 3) although it is hard to see how Aquinas could then resist a similar argument by many fanatical religious figures who claimed loyalty to Christ.

We have seen that Aquinas considers that natural law can be deduced by experience from looking at human nature and its *purposes*. Human beings have a duty to preserve themselves in existence (by, for instance, eating and drinking), to be rational and even to preserve the species. The last may seem self-evident, but it does not appear to fit well with the celibacy of priests in the Roman Catholic Church and, of course, Aquinas was himself a priest. Aquinas meets this point by saying that the need to propagate the race applies to the race as a whole:

> The natural precept about taking nourishment must necessarily be fulfilled by every individual; for otherwise he could not be preserved. But the precept about generation applies to the whole community, which not only must be multiplied corporeally but also make spiritual progress. And so sufficient progress is made if some only attend to generation, while others give themselves to the contemplation of divine things . . . (S.T. 1a, 11ae, 152, 2, ad 1).

This is a neat way of overcoming the problem, but it is not clear which 'ends' must be fulfilled by the individual and which by the group and there could be debate about the allocation between these headings. Also if only some attend to spiritual progress, does this help only those individuals or the community as a whole? This might also open debate about the possibility of only a number of individuals being homosexually inclined since only some need to be heterosexual in order to propagate the human race.

Aquinas considered that from a general principle, such as the need to propagate the species, detailed rules can be deduced such as the need for monogamy and the education of children. However, it would be possible to challenge Aquinas on the first of these – by saying that, for instance, it is not self-evident that monogamy is the best way of propagating the species. Aquinas' method is to begin with a general injunction that good is to be sought and evil avoided and then to unpack these by means of subsidiary principles (or perhaps assumptions would be a better word – although some might challenge this) that become more and more specific. It is not, however, a mere deduction of specific principles from general ones – at each stage Aquinas considers that the contemplation of human nature and its ends is required.

The problem is that at every stage the judgements being made may be challenged and there may be assumptions that govern the law that is deduced which may not be generally accepted. As an example, one might start with the general principle of propagation and then move to monogamy (although even this step might be challenged). One could then look at genital organs and consider their purpose – if their purpose is decided to be for procreation, then any use of these organs for other purposes such as pleasure (through masturbation, genital homosexuality or conventional sex using contraception) would be held to be wrong because they go against the intended purpose for these organs. However, who is to define the purpose? If, as part of the function of genital organs, one included as the purpose 'that they are intended so that two people who love each other should be able to express their love and obtain pleasure in doing so and that propagation might, when appropriate, thereby take place' then one might rule out masturbation and homosexuality, but not sexual foreplay or even adultery. Other functions might give different purposes. For instance is the purpose of a mouth for eating or for kissing or for both? Who is to decide? If kissing is part of the function of mouths, then kissing would become a good rather than, arguably, an evil. The need to make assumptions which may be challenged is, therefore, implicit in Aquinas' whole approach and weakens its effectiveness.

It may also be argued that Aquinas' approach is not holistic – it fails to consider the human being as a psycho-physical unit. To separate, for instance, genitalia out as having a particular purpose on their own without considering the whole complexity of a person's relationship to his or her body, psychology, sexuality in general, the ability of human beings as embodied persons to express and receive love and to come to their full humanity may be a diminution of human beings as people. We are not an accumulation of 'bits' – we are whole human persons and all moral judgements must take our complexity as human persons into account.

Aquinas considered that the feudal order of society of his time – with Kings, barons, knights, freemen and serfs – was the natural order. He was conditioned by his culture just as we may be conditioned by ours. It is far from easy to determine the function or purpose of different human organs or of society without being influenced by one's own preconceptions.

Aquinas believed that all human beings have a fixed, uniform human nature – this led him to maintain that there was a fixed natural law (subject to the differentiation between primary and secondary precepts above) for human beings. It may be argued that human beings do not have a single human nature and that the moral law may vary over time – in this case the whole idea of natural law may be challenged (this goes against the quote from Cicero at the beginning of this chapter). As an example, if there is held to be a single human nature then all human beings 'should' (according to their nature if it is 'correctly' ordered) be heterosexually inclined. If, therefore, someone was homosexually inclined (say due to a difference in genetic make-up) then this would be a disorder in their nature – their nature would be 'faulty' in that it was not what it 'should' be. This is one reason why Roman Catholic approaches to homosexuality tend to be clear cut – although Catholic theologians draw a distinction between an inclination which may be due to faulty genetic make-up and practising homosexuality which is due to a free decision and is therefore morally blameworthy. Against this it may be held that there is no single human nature – that some people are, for instance, homosexually inclined and others are not and this in itself is neither right nor wrong. In this case the issue may be more about how individuals should use their sexuality given their make-up rather than conformity to a specific human nature. Recent scientific studies have shown that homosexual tendencies may well be genetic. It could be (and there is no evidence for this) that in the face of an overcrowded world, nature produces an increase in those genes which direct sexual activity away from procreation. Aquinas would have difficulty coping with such a possibility.

The natural law approach to morality is much more flexible than is generally supposed. M. J. Longford (*The Good and the True – An introduction to Christian ethics*, SCM Press, 1985, p. 204) puts it like this:

> It is true that Aquinas did also appear to hold some absolute moral rules, such as the one that disallowed lying . . . but this is not what is stressed in the account of natural law . . . His overall position is that there are what are called 'primary precepts' which are exceedingly general (such as the duty to worship God, and to love one's neighbour) and 'secondary precepts' which are more specific, such as the duty to have only one husband or wife. However, the secondary precepts all have to be interpreted in the context of the situation, and it is here that the flexibility of natural law arises. At one point [Aquinas] argues as follows: 'The first principles of natural law are altogether unalterable. But its secondary precepts . . . though they are unalterable in the majority of cases . . . can nevertheless be changed on some particular and rare occasions . . .' . . . Aquinas argues, 'The more you descend into the details the more it appears how the general rule admits of exceptions, so that you have to hedge it with cautions and qualifications.'

This is an important qualification and shows that there may be more flexibility in the natural law approach than is often supposed. *It may also open the door to a natural law approach to morality coming together with situation ethics (see ch. 10) – for instance through a form of proportionalism.*

Whereas Aquinas is firm in his insistence on the primary precepts of natural law, he seems to show more flexibility when discussing the secondary precepts which 'unpack' these and sometimes modern supporters of a natural law approach to ethics do not sufficiently recognise this.

It is, perhaps, important to recognise that although many Catholic theologians today tend to support Aquinas' natural law approach, in the Middle Ages his was not the only view in the Church. It would be wrong to think, even today, that all Catholic moral theologians are Thomists – there is a real debate in the life of the Roman Catholic Church and this debate is an on-going process, although it is, perhaps, fair to say that Aquinas' legacy of the view that there is a single moral law and later theologians' opinions that the Church represents this view is still the orthodox Catholic position (put forward most strongly in recent Vatican documents such as *Veritatis Splendor* [October 1993]) – even if there is, arguably, no requirement to accept Aquinas' philosophic position if one is a Catholic.

Aquinas is suitably modest when making claims about the ability of moral philosophers to determine which actions should be performed in particular situations. He was a philosopher as well as a theologian and recognised the need for reflection. Aquinas did not think moral problems could simply be settled, a priori, by deduction – ultimately each individual has to make his or her own decision (*Ethics*, 2, c.2, *lectio* 2) and the place of conscience will be vital in this. An action is either right or wrong in so far as it fosters or undermines the good for man and Aquinas would be the first to recognise that there may be disagreements as to what behaviour will foster this 'good'. However, in spite of these disagreements Aquinas is firm in the view that there *is* an absolute natural law: Disagreements occur because of the difficulty of determining this.

At the end of the Second World War, Nazi war criminals were tried at Nuremberg according to what were claimed as universal moral laws which were closely modelled on natural law thinking. The phrase 'natural law' was avoided – instead reference was made to 'crimes against humanity', but the thinking behind the legal actions was clearly based on natural law. It is possible to develop a natural law approach to ethics which does not depend on the existence of God, but any such approach is inevitably going to involve the notion of purpose and this, in turn, is going to depend on particular metaphysical claims. Aquinas has to make assumptions at key points when developing his approach and any humanistic natural law alternative will have to make alternative assumptions (such as that there is no God or life after death) against which the purpose of human life should be measured.

Proportionalism

Proportionalism holds that there are certain moral rules and that it can never be right to go against these rules unless there is a proportionate reason which would justify it. The proportionate reason is based on the context or situation but this situation must be sufficiently unusual and of sufficient magnitude to provide a reason which would overturn what would otherwise be a firm rule. On this basis, moral laws derived from natural law or similar approaches can provide firm moral guidelines which should never be ignored unless it is absolutely clear that, in the particular situation, this is justified by a proportionate reason.

The position of proportionalism is well put in John Macquarrie's *A New Dictionary of Christian Ethics* (Blackwell, 1991, p. 392):

Perhaps the most divisive debate in contemporary Catholic moral theology concerns the existence and grounding of universally binding moral norms. The Scholastic moral theology of the manuals held that certain acts were intrinsically evil on the basis of the act itself, independent of the intention, circumstances and consequences. Revisionists maintain that the evil in acts such as contraception or even direct killing is not moral evil but premoral evil which can be justified for a proportionate reason.

The distinction between pre-moral and moral evil is central to the proportionalist position. Bernard Hoose, the leading British advocate, in his book *Proportionalism* (Georgetown University Press, 1987, p. 51), says that:

> An evil like pain, death or mutilation is, in itself, pre-moral or non-moral, and should never be described as 'moral'. It is the act as a whole which is either right or wrong, and it is the person, or the person in his or her acting, who is morally good or morally bad.

A distinction has to be made between acts which are good and acts which are right – and this distinction, proportionalists maintain, is often not made. A person may have a good intention but may be able to achieve that intention only through an act which is considered to be, in itself, evil. The proportionalists hold that it is possible for an action, in itself, to be wrong, whilst based on the actual situation in which the action is done the action may be morally right.

The American proportionalist, Philip Keane, puts the position clearly:

> When a truly proportionate reason is present in an action so that the action is morally good, the human will is clearly not morally intending the pre-moral evil in the action, even if the pre-moral evil must be done as a means to the pre-moral good. Hence proportionate reason is ultimately a more accurate indicator of what the person is actually doing in a complex human action than is the external relationship of the various pre-moral aspects of the action.

A separation is being made distinguishing the different intentions of a human being who acts:

> Part of the issue here is whether psychological intention is to be distinguished from moral intention. Surely a doctor who amputates a limb to save a person's life has to remove the limb. But does

he or she morally intend the evil in the amputation? (*Theological Studies*, 42, 1981, p. 275)

Proportionalists seek the right thing to do in the particular circumstances. Unlike advocates of situation ethics, they affirm that there are non-moral goods and evils, but they maintain that the circumstances need to be taken into account in deciding whether a non-moral evil is also a moral evil. Killing, theft or contraception (if one is a Catholic) *may* be morally good in certain circumstances. As Bernard Hoose puts it:

If what is morally good is what is morally right and what is morally bad is what is morally wrong, we shall have to revise an awful lot of our thinking in moral matters. Some of the people who burned heretics were probably morally good in such actions. Are we to assume, therefore, that the burning of heretics was morally right? Must rich benefactors seeking admiration stop giving money to the poor? Surely they should change their attitude, but continue to give their money (p. 63).

Those who support situation ethics and proportionalism both maintain that love or *agape* is the only criterion for moral goodness or badness. However proportionalists refuse to accept the view of situation ethicists that love can make a wrong action right. As Bernard Hoose puts it:

An action born of love can be wrong, while an action not resulting from love can be right (p. 63).

Proportionalists have difficulty in determining how one judges whether a given situation is sufficient to generate a proportionate reason for performing what would otherwise be an evil act. It would appear that what is needed is something like the Utilitarian hedonistic calculus to try to calculate proportionality – yet proportionalists reject this. Nevertheless it seems difficult to avoid the conclusion that the choice lies between a form of calculus and individual intuition as to the ranking of various goods. Neither position seems satisfactory. Bernard Hoose maintains that the judgement is made taking the consequences into account but without any formal method of calculation; however, this approaches a form of intuitionism which can seem very individualistic. Generally we will know that there is no proportionate reason that will justify lying, theft, etc. and the proportionalist accepts this. However the proportionalist maintains that there *may* be such reasons and that the individual will recognise the situation when it occurs. He or she weighs up the intrinsic evil of lying, theft, etc. and balances this against the consequences.

Proportionalism has for long been in use in Catholic moral thinking in the issue of Just War, but as long as it remains condemned by the Vatican (as was re-confirmed in the document 'Veritatis Splendor' issued in October 1993) it is unlikely to make significant progress within the Church in other areas. However, as has been seen earlier in this chapter, it is clear that Aquinas does allow exceptions to the secondary precepts which are the basis for moral rules in the Catholic tradition, so it may be argued that proportionalism is closer to the mainstream Catholic tradition than the rather more conservative and restrictive view supported by this Church's Magisterium at the present time.

Questions for discussion

1 What do you understand by the theory of a natural moral law?
2 Can the basis of natural law be located other than in social convention?
3 What are the strengths and weaknesses of basing ethics on natural law?
4 How might natural law be used to deal with the following ethical issues: (a) contraception, (b) abortion or (c) homosexuality?
5 On a natural law approach, how might it be argued that it would be wrong for a woman to make love after she had a hysterectomy or after her ovaries were removed?

6 Would Aquinas support the Divine Command theory of ethics?

7 'In the absence of any agreed view of human nature, natural law theory is useless.' Do you agree with this statement and, if so, why?

8 Would the natural law approach maintain that if one uses reason then one is acting morally? What would be the arguments for or against such a view?

9 Can an action be wrong yet good? How?

10 What philosophic arguments might be used to reject proportionalism?

FIVE

Kant and the Moral Law

In the history of moral philosophy, few names deserve greater prominence than that of Immanuel Kant (1724–1804). He lived a totally uneventful life in Königsberg, yet his small book *Groundwork of the Metaphysics of Morals* (1785) is of central importance for any serious student of ethics as is the *Critique of Practical Reason*. Kant says that his aim in *The Groundwork* was to establish

> a completely isolated metaphysic of morals which is not mixed with any theology or physics or metaphysics.

First, some definitions are needed: A statement is *analytic* if the predicate is included within the subject – thus 'all spinsters are female' is analytic as the meaning of the subject (spinster) includes the predicate (female). Analytic statements are *necessarily* true – they must be true because their truth depends on the way words are used and it simply would not make sense to say they were not true. The statement is also *a priori* which means that its truth is known independent of experience – we do not have to undertake a survey to determine that ' all spinsters are female' is true.

A statement is *synthetic* if the predicate is not included in the subject and therefore it firstly tells us something about the subject which we would not otherwise know and secondly it may or may not be true – for instance 'All bachelors are happy'. This statement is also *a posteriori* because it is based on experience, in other words we would have to undertake a survey of bachelors to decide whether it is true.

Kant maintained that all moral concepts have their origin a priori. Almost every statement is either *a priori analytic* or *a posteriori synthetic*, but Kant considered that statements about the moral law were very unusual in that they were *a priori synthetic* – in other words they were a priori (independent of experience) *but* they were synthetic (not analytically or necessarily true). Kant's task in *The Groundwork* is partly to explore how this unusual situation can arise – Kant seeks to establish the a priori principles by which we make moral judgements, he wishes to establish the fundamental principle of action which underpins all moral decision-making. Kant thought these principles were inherent in the universe. Unlike Plato, Aristotle or Aquinas he is not concerned with some 'good for human beings'. Kant is concerned with the fundamental principles of morals which form the basis for our moral choices. It might be thought that if Kant considered that the principles of morals were inherent within us, he would discuss psychology or human nature, but this is not the case. He considered moral principles to be an a priori given and therefore to be arrived at independent of experience.

Unlike Aquinas, Kant did not believe that morality should be founded on natural theology. He shared with Aquinas a commitment to reason as a guide to right action, although unlike Aquinas he did not bring in any assumptions which depended on belief in God as part of his approach to morality (Aquinas, as we have seen, was strongly influenced by his belief that human beings survive death and their destiny lies in God). Kant did not consider that God's existence could be proved – he rejected the cosmological and ontological arguments – however he thought that God's existence was a postulate of practical reason. Effectively Kant thought that, on the basis of morality, God's existence could be arrived at as a necessary postulate of a just universe, however this is *not* to say that Kant thought that God's existence could be proved. Part of Kant's approach to morality was that individuals should act *as if* there was a God – but this is not the same as saying that there *is* a God.

Kant's theory is *deontological* – that is it stresses duty or obligation (this comes from the Greek *deon* meaning duty). The opening words of the *Groundwork* provide a ringing declaration of Kant's fundamental position:

> It is impossible to conceive anything at all in the world, or even out of it, which can be taken as good without qualification, except a *good will*. Intelligence, wit, judgement, and any other *talents* of the mind we care to name, or courage, resolution, and constancy of purpose, as qualities of *temperament*, are without doubt good and desirable in many respects; but they can also be extremely bad and hurtful when the will is not good which has to make use of these gifts ...

The goodness of a human being's will does not depend on the results it produces since so many factors outside our control may determine the results:

> A good will is not good because of what it effects or accomplishes ... it is good through its willing alone – that is, good in itself.

In fact, the more human reason 'concerns itself with the aim of enjoying life and happiness, the farther does man get from true contentment' (5). A good will is fostered by a human being acting rationally and eliminating those inclinations and desires which tend to undermine rational decision-making. This does not mean that inclinations are necessarily wrong – simpy that they are not a reliable guide to the rightness of moral conduct.

If the development of a 'good will' is the highest task for any human being, there is one essential precondition which Kant does not argue for but considers must be assumed even though it cannot be proved – that is that human beings are free. Without freedom, there can be no discussion of morality as morality necessarily presupposes the ability to choose right or wrong. If human choices are wholly determined – if we are not free – then we are not moral agents.

Kant's method is to start by assuming that moral judgements are true. He then sets out to analyse the conditions which must be in force if these are to be true.

Kant distinguishes between two types of imperatives or commands under which human beings act:

- *Hypothetical imperatives* are imperatives that are based on an 'if', for instance: 'If you want to stay healthy, take exercise' or 'If you want your wife to love you, remember her birthday'. We can reject the command (to take exercise or to remember birthdays) if we are willing to reject the 'if' on which the command rests. These imperatives bid us do things which are a means to some end. They are arrived at by the exercise of pure reason.
- *Categorical imperatives*, by contrast, are not based on any 'if', they do not depend on a particular end and, Kant considers, they would be followed by any fully rational agent. They are ends in themselves and not means to some other end. Moral duties are categorical because they should be followed for the sake of duty only, simply because they are duties and not for any other reason. Categorical imperatives are arrived at through practical reason and they are understood as a basis for action.

There is no answer to the question, 'Why should I do my duty?' except 'Because it is your duty.' If there was any answer it would represent a reason and would make the imperative hypothetical and not categorical.

Human beings, in Kant's view, are not wholly rational – but they can strive to become so. Animals are dominated by desires and instincts and these are present in human beings as well. However Kant considers that humans also have the ability to reason and, through the exercise of reason, to act not in accordance with our inclinations but according to the demands that reason makes on us – in other words from a sense of duty. A categorical imperative is one that excludes self-interest and would be one that any fully rational agent (human or otherwise) would follow and if any command is held to be categorical, it is necessary to show that it fits under this heading.

It is not easy to separate actions done from an inclination and those done from a sense of duty – it is important to recognise that it is not the *action* which determines goodness but the intention, motive and reason lying behind the action. The businessman who is honest because it suits him or because he feels like being honest is not, according to Kant, acting morally because he is not acting rationally. The good person must act correctly, according to reason, no matter what the consequences and independent of his or her own feelings or inclinations. If a person wills to perform an act, and if this willing does not rest on a sense of duty, then it will not be a morally good action. An action which is not done from inclination at all but purely rationally, from a sense of duty, will be a morally good action. This does not mean that one *has* to act against one's inclinations, but it does mean that one's inclinations cannot determine one's moral duty.

There are, of course, particular moral rules which are categorical and which everyone would agree to such as 'Thou shalt not kill', but Kant considers these to be derived from a more general principle and he seeks to determine what this is. He arrives at a number of different formulations of what he terms 'The Categorical Imperative' on which all moral commands are based. The best known are the three that Kant includes in his summary of the *Groundwork* (79-81) and which H. J. Paton (in *The Moral Law*, Hutchinson) translates as follows:

1 Act as if the maxim of your action was to become through your will a universal law of nature.

This is the *Formula of the Law of Nature* and is saying that we should act in such a way that we can will that the maxim (or general principle) under which we act should be a general law for everyone. Kant therefore aims to ensure that we eliminate self-interest in the particular situation in which we find ourselves. Kant considers that if we will to act wholly rationally according to such a principle, then we shall develop a good will. There are, however, other formulations, including what Kant terms the *Practical Imperative* —

2 Act in such a way that you always treat humanity, whether in your own person or in the person of any other, never simply as a means, but always at the same time as an end.

This is the *Formula of the End in Itself*. Kant says that it can never be right to treat people just as a means to some end — human beings are always 'ends in themselves' and Kant describes human beings as 'holy' because of this. It can never be right, therefore, to use human beings as a means to the end of our own happiness or to treat any group of people as a minority that does not matter. This principle enshrines the idea of the equality of each and every human being irrespective of class, colour, race, sex, age or circumstance.

3 So act as if you were through your maxims a law-making member of a kingdom of ends.

This is the *Formula of the Kingdom of Ends*. Kant envisaged rational agents acting as if they were making laws for themselves based on the use of reason and, in so far as they do this, they will become 'law-making members of a kingdom of ends'. The laws adopted by all members will coincide because they are all rational and if there are disagreements then rational arguments should be able to resolve these.

It is, perhaps, significant to note the similarities between Kant's call to disinterested duty and Jesus' call to 'Love your neighbour as yourself' (Matthew 22:39). The love that Jesus had in mind was not based on emotion but on a call to right action towards every other human being (Kierkegaard, in *Works of Love*, describes this as *non-preferential love*) and this could be seen as very similar to Kant's basic position — although it should be added that Jesus's first commandment was the call to love God before anything else and this Kant rejected. For Kant, the only service to God comes in acting morally to other human beings according to the dictates of reason.

Kant considers that the highest aspiration of a human being is the development of a good will and such a good will is developed by acting rationally according to the principles laid down by the Categorical Imperative. Humans can, if they wish, think of their moral duties as if they were Divine Commands, but morality is specifically not based on such commands. If it was, it would then be arbitrary (cf. the Euthyphro dilemma p. 7).

God is largely peripheral for Kant although God is needed to underwrite Kant's trust in the fairness of the Universe – particularly the idea that, after death, the virtuous and vice-ridden will be treated appropriately. Kant has a tremendous faith in the *metaphysical fairness of the Universe* – which is strange as he wished to bar the door to metaphysics because he did not think it was possible to argue from the world of experience (phenomena) to anything beyond this. However, he had faith in the justice of the Universe and he considered that mortality was a postulate of practical reason. Kant's view can be taken as implying that if the Universe is fair, it follows that human beings must survive death as clearly in this life the virtuous are often treated very badly and those who pursue the path of vice all too often have an apparently happy and contented life.

Kant largely reduces religion to ethics – to be holy is to be moral. Religion is only valuable as a way of helping people to lead a moral life. He considered that philosophy had supremacy over theology as philosophy was based on reason without unsupported faith claims. Kant considered that religion had to operate within the bounds of reason alone and he reinterpreted the claims of Christianity so that they expressed a call to moral righteousness. Jesus was the perfect exemplar of the morally good life. As we have seen, Kant considered human beings and human reason to be autonomous and he thus rejected heteronomy (for instance using God's will as a guide to what is morally right or wrong).

Kant has a problem at the heart of his whole enterprise which is often not recognised and which he did not fully resolve. Kant considered that human beings should aim to act wholly in accordance with the Categorical Imperative – the maxim of their action would then be good. However, he recognised that many people would fail to do this and they would become corrupt as they acted from an evil, false or irrational maxim. Once a person's life had become dominated by such general principles, they would then be in bondage. The difficulty Kant had was how to explain moral regeneration or a turn around from the evil to the good when he also considered that human beings could bind themselves by their corrupt maxims. The alternatives were to either:

a) say that human beings were not bound by their corrupt maxims and Kant was quite clear that they were, or
b) to say that human beings, once bound, could not turn round from the corrupt to the good and this would have meant that the position of corrupt human beings was hopeless.

As Michalson points out (*Fallen Freedom*, pp. 125ff.), Kant's response to this was a most surprising one given the peripheral place allotted to God in most of Kant's philosophy. He maintained that it was only through the incarnation in which God became man in Jesus Christ that human moral regeneration can take place. In this one area, at this particular point (but not elsewhere) God was central for Kant, yet he did not face up to the consequences of this. It was Kant's successors, Kierkegaard and Hegel (and, following Hegel, Marx) who were to take seriously the alternatives that Kant failed to grapple with. As Michalson says:

Kierkegaard and Marx represent what happens when just one of the two aspects of Kant's account of moral regeneration is taken up and emphasised in isolation from the other aspect. As such, their positions shed light on Kant's own effort to have it both ways.

In Kierkegaard's hands, the muted Kantian appeal to grace is transformed into a full-blown 'project of thought' in which a transcendent act alone is the only antidote to our willed 'error', or sin. Contrary to our usual view of these matters, it is in fact Kierkegaard and not Kant who has the more 'rational' position here ... Kierkegaard shows the only way to offset a willed error is through a reconciling act coming from the 'outside', producing the 'new creature' ... Alternatively, Kant's more characteristic tendency to locate our moral recovery in our own efforts – however impossible he has made it for himself fully to do this – leads in some sense to Marxism• (which) ... expels the last remnants of otherworldliness remaining in the position of the philosopher ... (*Fallen Freedom*, pp. 129-30).

Kant represents a divide in the road in the history of moral and philosophic thought. The road that Kierkegaard takes firmly embraces the central importance of a personal God and the action of this God both in history and in the lives of individual human beings. Hegel takes the opposing path and rejects such a view of transcendence – Marx then takes Hegel's view further and morality becomes entirely a social construct. These issues are still very much alive and the divide is still present today.

Questions for discussion

1 Suggest two moral maxims which would give rise to contra-dictory actions. How might the differences between these be resolved?
2 Could it ever be morally right, according to Kant, to torture one person in order to get information which would save the lives of a large group?
3 Describe the difference between a hypothetical and a categorical imperative. On what grounds might someone reject an impera-tive that was claimed to be categorical?
4 On Kant's view, should the moral principles of intelligent green spiders differ from the moral principles of human beings?
5 What place does God have in Kant's moral philosophy?

6 In Kant's view, is saving the life of a child a morally good action? What are the difficulties from his viewpoint in answering this question in the affirmative?

SIX

Bentham and Mill – Utilitarianism

Utilitarianism is generally thought of as a moral theory which can best be summed up by the phrase: 'the greatest happiness for the greatest number'. However, in terms of its linguistic origins it may be more aptly described as a 'theory of usefulness', after the Latin root word *utilis* meaning useful. This, then, seems to imply that whatever is useful is moral. On a literal interpretation, therefore, my garden spade and fork are moral implements because they are useful. But clearly this is absurd. However, decisions and actions may be characterised as morally useful. Immoral decisions lead to useless or bad actions and amoral decisions are those which lead to no actions at all.

So, for example, the act of abortion is, in itself, neither good nor bad, neither moral nor immoral. However, it becomes so when we consider to what end the procedure of abortion is being used. If abortion is being used to save the mother's life and restrict an already large family in a household where the husband is unemployed, and if the abortion is conducted in a humane fashion, then its use may, on utilitarian grounds, be justified, and the act itself becomes a moral one. The greatest happiness of the greatest number, that is, of the family unit, counts over and above the future possible happiness of the single unborn child. If, however, abortion is being used by a young married woman because the pregnancy may interfere with a planned skiing trip, then clearly it is difficult to see how it could be justified, unless a cynical vision of utilitarianism were to be employed in which the maximisation of immediate happiness for the young woman and her skiing party were to count for more than the future possible happiness of the unborn child and the future long-term happiness of the prospective family. To use Singer's *Practical Ethics* (1993) argument a minor interest (the pleasure derived from the skiing trip) is placed above a major interest (the life of the child and the future possibilities of family life). Hence, we may justifiably conclude that, in this instance, abortion becomes 'immoral'.

As we have already maintained, utilitarianism has come to be largely associated with the 'greatest good or the greatest happiness for the greatest number'. Its links with majority rule in democratic politics is obvious. Here, it is assumed to be morally acceptable for there to be government by the majority without the consent of the minority. Unfortunately, all too often, particularly given the voting procedures in the democratic nations of the world, there is government by the minority without the consent of the majority!

It was David Hume (1711-76) the Scottish philosopher who first introduced the concept of utility into ethics but he is not regarded as a utilitarian. Similarly, the phrase 'the greatest happiness for the greatest number' was first coined by Francis Hutcheson (1694-1746) in a work entitled *An Inquiry into the Original of our Ideas of Beauty and Virtue*, although again Hutcheson is not considered to be a utilitarian in the strict sense.

Jeremy Bentham (1748-1832)

The theory of utilitarianism was first fully articulated by Jeremy Bentham who not only wrote about ethics but about politics as well, his most famous work being *A Fragment on Government*. Because of his interests in both ethics and politics coupled with his desire to improve the social conditions of the masses he founded a movement known as The Philosophical Radicals. Arguably many of the reforms in the eighteenth and nineteenth centuries, particularly those to do with the treatment of criminals, were the result of Bentham's efforts. Shy but extremely able, Bentham apparently began studying Latin at the age of three and received his degree when only fifteen. However, his friend and follower, James Mill (1773-1836) fathered an even greater child prodigy, John Stuart Mill (1806-73). By all accounts John Stuart Mill began with Greek at the age of three, followed quickly with other languages by the age of eight and finally completed a rigorous classical education by the time he was fourteen. By this time he had become much influenced by Benthamite thinking as his father had been before him.

For Bentham, that which is good is that which equals the greatest sum of pleasure and the least sum of pain. Hence, a right moral decision followed by a truly ethical action would be one which produced the greatest pleasure. The way in which this was to be measured was through the application of the utility calculus, sometimes referred to as the hedonic calculus. *Hedone* is the Greek word for pleasure. Hence, Bentham's version of the theory is occasionally called hedonic utilitarianism.

The hedonic or utility calculus

The utility calculus was supposed to measure the amounts of pleasure and pain according to seven criteria:

- intensity
- duration
- certainty
- extent
- remoteness
- richness
- purity.

The following example may help. Suppose you are a doctor driving to one of your patients, a young mother about to give birth. However, she is in great pain and difficulty and it looks as though she will need a Caesarian section. It is late at night and you come across a car accident down a country road. Two cars are involved and both drivers are injured and unconscious. You discover through trying to establish identities that one of them is the young pregnant woman's husband. The other is an elderly man. You don't quite know the extent of any internal injuries and are of the opinion that without immediate medical help one of them if not both may die. You are faced now with the moral decision of who to help first:

- the young mother about to give birth?
- the young woman's husband?
- the elderly gentleman?

Any one of them may die if you do not attend to them immediately.

Leaving aside what we may actually feel or believe, the application of the utility calculus may go something like this:

- Attending to the young expectant mother first is the primary concern of the doctor. The death of both mother and child is almost a certainty if he does not act now, whereas the deaths of either of the two men is not certain. Moreover, the intensity of her pain is clearly greater at present than theirs. There is a greater richness and purity in saving the life of a young child who has, in all probability, a long and happy life ahead. Therefore, the duration and extent of the pleasures experienced by two people, the mother and child, is a clear likelihood.
- Attending to the young husband is the next priority. The pleasure of a new family, its intensity, duration, extent, richness and purity are all clear probabilities. If the doctor had attended to him first and neglected his expectant wife, she would probably have died, and the intensity, duration, extent etc. of the pain experienced by the widowed husband is likely to outstrip any pleasure to be gained from continued life without his loved ones.
- Attending to the elderly gentleman is the last priority. The duration and certainty of his future pleasure is under question owing to his age. He has all but lived his life; this is sometimes known as the 'good innings argument'. According to this line, the value of his life is not now as great as the young married couple's who have

much of their lives ahead of them, nor of the young child who has
yet to go in to bat, as it were.

Some problems:

One of the problems of Bentham's theory and his hedonic calculus
was that its results were based on a *quantitative measure*. That is, how
much sheer quantity of pleasure can be gained from an action. Just
by attending to one patient, the young mother, the decision has all
but guaranteed that two people will be saved, and that the likely
number of years in which they may experience pleasure is probably
going to be a lot greater than the number of pleasurable years spent
by the elderly gentleman. Moreover, the certainty of saving either
the husband or the elderly gentleman is by no means guaranteed,
whereas the death of the young mother and her child is almost guaranteed. So, although it may be a difficult decision, the doctor on
strict utilitarian grounds would have to save the young mother and
child because the quantity of pleasure is the important issue. But, can
the quantity of pleasure actually be measured in numbers of years?
Furthermore, who will do the measuring?

The second problem is that utilitarianism relies strictly on its *predictive value*. But who can predict that the child will grow up to be happy
and productive, that the old man will soon die anyway, and that the
sum total of pleasure to be gained by the young family is going to be
greater than the old man's? The child may grow up to be a mass-
murderer, the family may then lead a collective life of guilt and misery,
and the old man may, like Bertrand Russell, have been destined to
make his major mark on political life in his eighties and nineties.

The third problem is to do with *what counts as pleasure*. Pure
emotional and bodily pleasures are clearly quantifiable. But is it just
pleasure that we wish to seek or increase and pain that we wish to
avoid or minimise? I might be prepared to suffer a great deal of pain in
order to gain a minimal amount of pleasure. The quick extraction of a
painful tooth might, on the quantity of pleasure theory, be preferable
to hours of painful dentistry involving excavating, filling and
polishing the tooth, whilst simultaneously suffering the continuing

pain of the tooth itself, all in order to satisfy some intangible desire to retain all my teeth. Or, supposing I wanted the pleasure of being thought slim, I could, like many slimming fanatics, put myself through continual painful exercises and diets in order to wear jeans one size smaller. Or, more importantly, I could forgo all obvious plea- sures of the moment, practise continuously on the piano in order to lead a precarious existence as a second-rate concert pianist combined with the dubious pleasure of fame.

John Stuart Mill (1806-73)

John Stuart Mill understood the problems only too well. Mill wanted, therefore, to define pleasure a little more carefully, and this involved shifting the emphasis from quantity to quality. Mill distin- guished between the *higher* pleasures, associated with the mind, and the *lower* pleasures, associated with the body. Clearly the two are linked. It is difficult to experience the pleasures of intellectual pursuits whilst remaining perpetually cold and hungry. But after the minimum requirements of the body have been satisfied, that is, after the lower pleasures have been attended to, then the real moral busi- ness involves pursuit of the higher goods: mental, cultural and spir- itual. Arguably, on this view, the person who eats and drinks in moderation in order to spend more time designing elegant, ecologi- cally-sound and inexpensive clothing is morally better than the person who is anxious to toss off quick, profit-making designs in order that he may then pursue the known bodily pleasures of sex, food and drink in large quantities. The higher pleasures of the mind are to be preferred to the lower pleasures of the body. As Mill states: 'It is better to be a human being dissatisfied than a pig satisfied; bet- ter to be Socrates dissatisfied than a fool satisfied.' (J. S. Mill, *Utilitarianism*, ed. by M. Warnock, 1962, Collins, p. 260).

Some criticisms:
There are still a number of problems associated with this view. Firstly, as Henry Sidgwick (1838-1900) pointed out, how in

practice do we distinguish properly between higher and lower pleasures, and how do we distinguish one higher pleasure from another? If all cultural and spiritual activities provide the same sum of pleasure and happiness, presumably it does not matter which one we choose to undertake at any time. If reading Shakespeare, playing Bach, and painting watercolours all produce the same degree of pleasure, then there is nothing to choose between them. Sidgwick understood that life is just a shade more complex than that, for every activity and pursuit, whether physical or intellectual, is both quantitatively and qualitatively different. An hour's reading of Shakespeare is just not equivalent to an hour's playing of Bach, and so on. Moreover, where do physically and intellectually demanding pursuits such as sailing, play-acting and advanced kung-fu fit into the higher/lower pleasures distinction? Is the refined eating of a carefully planned foreign dish a higher pleasure, and the eating of a takeaway beefburger a lower pleasure? The difficulties are endless.

The second problem is perhaps even greater than the first. The philosopher W. D. Ross (1877-1971) pointed to the inherent difficulties of what we might call a 'single-factor' moral theory. We cannot simply rely upon a single principle of equation such as the greatest good or the greatest happiness or the greatest pleasure for the greatest number. Life's ethical dilemmas cannot be reduced to a prepackaged, predictive calculus which balances outcomes. We experience internal conflicts between what our reason tells us, what duties we feel we ought to perform, and the need, obviously, to bring about the greatest good. Suppose, for example, you and your young son were seated next to a brilliant young doctor who, through conversation, you learn is close to finding a cure for the AIDS virus. The bus suddenly is involved in an accident and catches fire. You have just enough time to save one person before you are engulfed in flames. Who do you save: your son or the doctor? Application of the simple greatest happiness principle would undoubtedly lead to you having to save the doctor because of the number of lives ultimately he would save. The strict dictates of reason would lead to the same conclusion. However, your personal duty coupled with the moral bond of affection which ties you to your son, plus an over-riding instinct, would lead you to save your son. The saving of one's son would, using the concept introduced by Ross, be a prima-facie duty, that is, the most important duty and therefore the one that should rightly be put first. People would probably regret on one level that you saved your son and not the doctor, but it is unlikely that anyone would assume that you should have acted differently, and that your first duty, in essence, would be to your son.

Act and rule utilitarianism

A distinction can be drawn between two versions of utilitarianism:

a) ACT UTILITARIANISM holds that utilitarian methods should first arrive at specific actions which are considered to be moral or immoral and from these general rules can be deduced.
b) RULE UTILITARIANISM holds that utilitarianism should first frame general principles or rules, and from these can be derived specific acts which are not permitted.

Act Utilitarianism therefore moves from specific cases to general principles whilst Rule Utilitarianism moves in the opposite direction. In the case of Act Utilitarianism, if certain actions are conducive to the general happiness then a general rule is framed to embody these. The rule cannot, however, force us to do an action which is against the greatest happiness, as it is the actions which are the basis for the rule. Act Utilitarianism can, therefore, never justify actions we would consider to be unacceptable.

In the case of Rule Utilitarianism, the rule takes priority and does not allow exceptions – certain actions which we might intuitively regard as unacceptable could, in principle, be allowed under the general rule. Some advocates of a Rule Utilitarian approach would resist this, but the only ground for doing so would be an appeal to our intuition that certain things are right or wrong and by allowing this intuition to have priority over the general principle. The intuitions in practice have priority and this the principle of utility cannot accommodate.

Another way of differentiating Act from Rule Utilitarianism is by reference to consequences. Bentham and Mill's theories are considered to be Act (sometimes referred to as 'Classical') Utilitarianism. Under this approach the individual morally right action is defined in terms of the *consequences* of the action and the individual's motives are irrelevant. Act Utilitarians are considered to be teleologists as they measure the goodness or badness of an action by reference to the ends towards which they are directed. This form of Utilitarianism is particularly vulnerable to the charge that actions which are held to be morally right go against what may, in a wider context, be regarded as just.

Rule Utilitarianism, by contrast, determines what is morally right by the consequences of following a particular rule. Rules have to be laid down which are based on Utilitarian principles and it is then morally right to obey these rules and morally wrong to disobey them. If everyone obeys a rule which maximises happiness (for instance respecting the property of others, or treating other people with consideration) then happiness will be maximised. Any action that runs counter to this rule will then be wrong even if this action, taken on its own, may maximise the happiness of a particular group. Under Rule Utilitarianism for formulating state and international law, the function of legislative bodies is to establish rules which foster the greatest happiness principle.

Rule Utilitarianism appears to be an attractive option as a basis for morality in spite of its difficulties particularly because it emphasises the equality of all and resists the interests of particular groups being given priority over others. In the international arena this may be an important lesson to learn – why, after all, should the happiness of those in the affluent and powerful West have greater priority than the happiness of the poorest millions of the world? Rule Utilitarianism would reject such inequalities.

Whether pleasure is really the highest to which human beings can aspire may well be questioned and much will depend on whether individuals consider there is more to human life than contentment.

Mill is right to recognise that true happiness may come as a by-product of some other endeavour and in this case consideration may need to be given to the endeavours towards which human life should be directed. Is there really no difference between striving to be a good dancer, a good pilot, a good model-aircraft builder or a gentle, selfless and virtuous person? If the word 'virtuous' is held to have meaning apart from the greatest happiness principle, then utilitarianism as a theory of morality may well be a failure.

Questions for discussion

1 Do the problems of utilitarianism invalidate the theory as a whole? Give two examples in which the logical outcome of a utilitarian act may actually go against what some philosophers have called our moral sense or intuition.

2 How might it be possible to distinguish between higher and lower pleasures? How could the pleasures to be gained from playing Bach be measured against the pleasures to be gained from seeing a Shakespearian play? Give examples if you can.

3 Is it better to be intellectually aware of the world's imperfections and the sufferings of people and, hence, be unhappy or dissatisfied, or is it better to be blissfully ignorant of the world's troubles and, hence, be happy and content with life? In other words, is it better to be a Socrates dissatisfied than a fool satisfied? Is, indeed, the latter a 'fool'?

4 Invent an example which emphasises the difference between an act utilitarian and a rule utilitarian and explain the implications.

5 Is government by the majority the best political option? (For Plato, in *The Republic*, it certainly was not the best option, for the majority were unlikely to know what was in the best interests for everyone, and were unlikely to have any real inkling of the concept of justice, p. 15).

6 Do the human sciences (moral, social, political, economic etc.) have any real 'predictive power'? Utilitarianism is partly predicated on the belief that they do.

SEVEN

Post-utilitarian Perspectives

Intuitionism

Henry Sidgwick put forward a significant alteration to Mill's understanding of utilitarianism as he drew a distinction between:

1 *Psychological utilitarianism* – based on the claim that every individual seeks his or her own pleasure, and
2 *Ethical hedonism* – the claim that each individual should seek the general happiness.

Sidgwick challenged the truth of the first of these as everyone does not seek pleasure as an end. Further, even if it was true, he maintains, this could not provide a basis for ethics. Sidgwick came to the conclusion that ethics was not based on a unifying principle but rather on human intuition. Certain moral truths were self-evidently true – these were as follows:

a) *The principle of prudence* – this holds that one should prefer a future greater to a present lesser good. Immediate pleasures, should, therefore, be deferred in favour of greater pleasures to come.
b) *The principle of justice* – this holds that as rational beings we should treat others as we would like to be treated unless there is some difference 'which can be treated as a reasonable ground for difference in treatment' (*The Methods of Ethics* p. 380).

The second principle led Sidgwick to claim that it can never be right for an individual to put his own interest above the interests of the community as if everyone is treated equally it can never be right to give priority to oneself and therefore it must be right to aim for the general good. This led to the third principle.

c) *The principle of benevolence* – 'each one is morally bound to regard the good of any other individual as much as his own, except in so far as he judges it to be less, when impartially viewed, or less certainly knowable or attainable by him' (p. 382).

The principle of prudence says that each person should seek his own good and the principle of benevolence that one should seek for the good of others. The good that is sought, according to Sidgwick, is happiness or pleasure so he arrives at a utilitarian conclusion albeit one with an intuitionist starting point. Sidgwick relied heavily on common sense and self-evident truths as a basis for morality (and he was therefore to anticipate Moore).

F. H. Bradley provided a contrast to the position of the utilitarians who had a central role for the individual. The utilitarians maintain that individuals with their individual desires are primary and society is a product of an accumulation of individuals (Margaret Thatcher echoed this position when she said 'There is no such thing as society'). To Bradley it was the society or the community that was primary and the source of ethics. Bradley was strongly influenced by Hegel and his book *Ethical Studies* (particularly the chapter 'My station and its duties') sets out his position. Bradley considers that the individual discovers his moral obligation from the community in which he lives and his moral duty is derived from his society. The individual comes to fulfilment by identifying with and conforming to the norms of the society in which he or she lives – this is a moral action which the individual makes and in identifying with society's values, the individual becomes moral. The individual who stands against society is immoral and he has no time for 'stargazing virgins' – for those individuals who question the values of society and are not engaged in action. Bradley's phrase 'the concrete universal' encapsulates his desire that the individual should make real or concrete the general ethical theory, derived from society, in his or her own life. The individual should seek to identify with and be an active participant in society as a whole.

Bradley rejects utilitarianism and a Kantian ethic based on duty. He maintained that both pleasure and duty are too vague and many-faceted to serve as true ends. Instead Bradley argues that the end of moral activity lies in an individual finding his or her station or position in life and then carrying out its duties. An individual may have some choice as to which station or position in life he or she is to fulfil, but once this choice has been made then the position in which an individual finds him- or herself determines the moral obligation.

Bradley's philosophy perfectly expresses the climate of Victorian England where people were meant to live out their station in life, and hard work and obedience to the norms of society were accepted. The very idea of individuals having certain 'stations' in life (whether house parlourmaid or farmer or government minister) is today seen as an anachronism and in a multicultural society in which the values within each society let alone internationally are no longer clear cut, Bradley's approach may seem to have little role to play. Social expectations should not be the final determinate of behaviour – one could imagine a society such as that of Nazi Germany which accepted certain values but most people would want to say that this is not what makes them right.

Bradley considers that there is no answer to the question 'Why should I be moral?' In this sense he followed Kant. However, whereas Kant appealed to the categorical imperative, Bradley appeals to the good of society. Socrates rejected this move over 2000 years earlier when he stood out against the values of Athenian society and saw himself as a 'gadfly' sent by the gods to arouse the Athenians from their slumbers by challenging the moral and social status quo. Bradley could not have accepted such a challenge and might, one could suspect, have sided with the Athenian crowd in condemning Socrates to death.

Naturalist theories of ethics maintain that goodness can be defined in terms of some non-moral position. If, therefore, someone maintains that goodness can be defined in terms of pleasure or the commands of God or the good of society, he or she would be an ethical naturalist. G. E. Moore set out to refute all attempts at ethical naturalism by maintaining that 'goodness' is indefinable – no moral statement can be defined in terms of a non-moral statement. He accused those who wish to define goodness in non-moral terms as committing the *naturalistic fallacy*. Moore can be described as an ethical non-naturalist.

Moore's argument for the indefinability of moral properties can be summed up in his words:

> You can give a definition of a horse because a horse has many different properties and qualities, all of which you can enumerate. But when you have enumerated them all, when you have reduced a horse to its simplest terms, then you can no longer define these terms ...
>
> 'Good', then, if we mean by it that quality which we assert to belong to a thing ... is incapable of definition ... 'good' has no definition because it is simple and has no parts. It is one of those innumerable objects of thought which are themselves incapable of definition, because they are the ultimate terms of reference by which whatever is capable of definition must be defined ... There is no intrinsic difficulty in the contention that 'good' denotes a simple and indefinable quality. There are many other instances of such qualities. (*Principia Ethica*, p. 7).

The most famous parallel that Moore drew was with yellow. Goodness is, he maintains, just as indefinable as yellow. Both of these are simple notions which defy further analysis. This does not mean that yellow or good cannot be explained in terms of the results it produces (such as the production of pleasure) but this is not the same as saying that pleasure is what good is.

Nothing that has been said so far has actually given a reason for Moore's claim that good is indefinable – it is clear enough that he is asserting that this is the case, but assertion is not the same as argument. Moore's argument rests on examining the alternative to the claim of indefinability. He says there are two possibilities:

i) The term 'good' is a complex term about which there can be disagreement, or
ii) the term 'good' is meaningless.

In the second case, there is no such subject as ethics and although Moore thought this was in principle conceivable he rejected it as a realistic option. The first alternative Moore rejects because:

> ... whatever definition may be offered, it may always be asked ... of the complex so defined whether it itself is good (op.cit. p. 14).

If, for instance, what is good is defined in terms of pleasure, Moore is claiming that one can then ask whether pleasure is good so pleasure (or any similar potential definition) cannot be used as a definition of goodness.

Moore is not a straightforward intuitionist – in the preface to *Principia Ethica* he says 'I am not an "Intuitionist" in the ordinary sense of the term' (p. x). All Moore meant by intuition was that moral judgements were incapable of being proved – he did not mean that the origin of moral judgements lay in human intuitions. He explicitly rejected the idea that moral intuitions were infallible and this raises the problem of how true and false intuitions are to be differentiated which is necessary if moral intuitions are to be more than mere matters of opinion.

It is important at this stage to differentiate between two different types of ethical theorists:

1 *Ethical teleologists* maintain that actions are to be judged good or bad by reference to the end to which they aim, while
2 *Ethical deontologists* maintain that an action is good or bad, right or wrong, by something within the action itself.

Moore was a teleologist and he maintained that all human beings know by intuition that:

> ... the most valuable things which we know or can imagine ... are certain states of consciousness, which may roughly be described as the pleasures of human intercourse and the enjoyment of beautiful objects (p. 188).

Actions are good or bad in so far as they aim towards these ends. What is 'right' or 'good' is what causes a good result and this result should be defined in terms of the states of consciousness above. Moore is, therefore, an intuitionist about the *ends* which are sought – not about the *means* which are used to attain these ends.

H. A Prichard built on Moore's work and aimed to develop what he took to be a common-sense approach to ethics. His most important work was possibly his article entitled 'Does moral philosophy rest on a mistake?' (published in *Mind* in 1912 and reprinted in his book *Moral Obligation*). Prichard contended that moral philosophers were mistaken to look for a reason why people should act in the ways that they do. Prichard maintained that some people have clearer moral intuitions than others because their moral thinking has been further developed. He considered that ethical dilemmas could be resolved by determining which of two conflicting choices of action rested on the greater moral obligation.

Prichard differentiated between two different types of thinking – 'general thinking' was necessary in order to ascertain the situation and the facts relative to the moral decision to be made. Once this had been done, 'moral thinking' – which rested on immediate intuition and not reasoning – would indicate what was the right thing to do.

Prichard was a much clearer example of a straightforward intuitionist than Moore – his case rests strongly on personal introspection but there are real difficulties in determining which of two individuals has moral thinking that is more fully developed and he provides no clear criteria for differentiating the morally preferable course of action when faced with two or more alternatives. He is, however, at least being consistent in that providing such criteria would undermine the priority given to intuition.

W. D. Ross was influenced by Moore and Prichard. He argued that what was 'right' and 'obligatory' were just as indefinable as 'good'. Ross made use of the distinction between these terms. He defined 'right' as:

> ... suitable, in a unique and indefinable way which we may express by the phrase 'morally suitable' to the situation in which an individual finds himself (*Foundation of Ethics*, p. 146).

There are two elements in what is right – the factual situation and how this situation is viewed. Ross produced a helpful analysis of four different situations in which an individual might find him- or herself and four different senses of what is the right thing to do in these circumstances. W. D. Hudson in *Modern Moral Philosophy* (p. 94) sets these out as follows:

1 an act which is *in fact* right in the situation as it *in fact* is.
2 an act which the agent *thinks* is right in the situation as it *in fact* is.
3 an act which is *in fact* right in the situation as the agent *thinks* it is.
4 an act which the agent *thinks* is right in the situation as the agent *thinks* it is.

Ross opts for the fourth alternative and points out that any of the other three would demand that an agent should have certain knowledge of either what *is* the right thing to do and/or precisely what the situation is. In practical terms no one can have this degree of knowledge so the fourth alternative is the only viable way of judging right behaviour. It will be readily evident that the fourth alternative with its emphasis on the agent's subjective evaluation of the situation as it appears to him or her leads to a direct form of individual intuition as the determining factor in assessing right conduct.

Ross drew a helpful distinction between what it is *right* to do and what it is *good* to do. He pointed out that actions may be termed right or wrong but goodness is assessed in terms of motives and intentions. Thus it may be a right action to help an old lady across the road but if my motive in doing this is to be praised by my friends for doing this, then it is not a good action. Ross appealed to intuition both in assessing rightness and goodness.

It is significant that all moral intuitionists appeal, even though not overtly, to some ultimate sense of what is right and wrong. None of them maintains that something is right just because someone intuits that it is. No one would claim that someone can have an intuition that 10 added to 10 is 15. Similarly no moral intuitionist claims that murder is permissible for me because I believe it is. One of the central problems with any form of intuitionism is that its advocates do not show *how* I may differentiate between:

a) I believe it is right or good to do x, and
b) it is right or good to do x.

Intuitionism attempts to move from a) to b) by appealing to personal introspection and there seems little reason to maintain that this move succeeds any more in ethics than it would in any other field of enquiry. If someone asks how I know that water boils at 100 degrees centigrade in certain standard conditions or that the earth goes round the sun, I should be prepared to give reasons to justify my claim. In the same way, someone who says that she knows murder or homosexuality is wrong might reasonably be required to give reasons – failure to do so may imply that all that is being expressed is a personal opinion which owes more to education and social background (as Bradley would have said) than to any firm base for morality.

Questions for discussion

1 What is the 'Naturalistic Fallacy' and is it a fallacy at all?
2 What is the difference between teleological and deontological theories in ethics?

3 Give examples of actions which may be right but are not good.
4 What are the advantages and disadvantages of F. H. Bradley's approach to ethics?
5 What were the two ends to which G. E. Moore considered all moral activity should be directed and do you agree with these?
6 Why did Ross consider that the difficulty of knowing certain things led to an intuitionist theory of morality?

Emotivism

As we have seen there are a number of problems associated with the ethical theories which we have so far examined. Is there an objective realm of right and wrong as suggested by Plato? Does moral knowledge truly exist in the way that we say scientific or 'factual' knowledge exists? For Plato, Truth, Goodness and Beauty are eternal and immutable realities existing in the world of 'Forms' or 'Ideas'. Provided we are willing to follow the Socratic path, which takes us from this ever-changing world of 'Appearances', to the timeless realm of 'Reality' then we can be fairly certain of glimpsing The Form of The Good by which right and wrong can be properly established. To follow this path means committing oneself to a long period of education through philosophical reasoning. And in so doing we move from the ever-shifting world of opinion (*doxa*) to the ever-stable world of knowledge (*episteme*). The problems have already been addressed, and include the obvious one of how does Plato *know* that such a realm of eternal ideas actually exists? It is akin to a theological belief in God. Of course, there are many arguments in favour of the existence of such a realm, but we are still left wondering, and the sceptical position is probably the best philosophical position to adopt in relation to it.

We explored the detailed virtue theory of Aristotle. Aristotle's eyes were firmly fixed on this earth. He wished simply to observe, record and make rational sense of his findings. Consequently, for Aristotle, right and wrong was about developing those natural excellences or virtues that exist within us. Through habit and instruction we are finally able to practise the art of *phronesis* – that virtue which helps us to judge on a daily basis what to do and what not to do, what to think and believe and what not to think and believe. Again, the problems are clear to see. Is Aristotle's list of virtues accurate? Could we not draw up a completely different list of the qualities that we think are necessary in establishing what constitutes moral behaviour? Where is the notion of equality? Aren't human beings other than Greeks deserving of the same respect and moral status? Aristotle's concept of a person is rather narrow, and his idea of justice somewhat restricted.

And so it continues. Aquinas' natural law cannot meet all of the objections satisfactorily. Kant's deontological morality makes ethical behaviour, and hence, life in general, a rather dour business in which we are compelled by duty to obey a series of imperatives distilled through disembodied reason and finally enunciated by Kant. As we shall see in the next chapter on MacIntyre, the failure of the Enlightenment to provide a coherent moral theory has led inexorably to the establishment of, arguably, the bleakest moral theory of all. Bentham's and Mill's utilitarianism cannot respond adequately to all the objections raised against it, and Moore's intuitionism may be said to be deficient. Asserting that 'good' is a simple, unanalysable concept is perhaps a convenient way of avoiding the most difficult task of all – that of trying to say exactly what we mean when we talk of good and bad, right and wrong. With this historical tale of failed theories, according to MacIntyre, we are left with, effectively, no theory at all. And in a sense, that is how we may characterise emotivism – as a moral 'non-theory'.

Emotivism, as its name suggests, is the moral theory based on people's emotive response to other people, events, situations, viewpoints and principles. Emotive response here simply means a person's feelings about something. Hence, emotivism is concerned principally, if not exclusively, with how people feel about something.

So, for example, if I say that abortion is wrong all I am doing, according to emotivism, is announcing how I feel about abortion.

Even if I give a number of reasons why I believe abortion to be wrong e.g. it violates the right to life which should be accorded to a potential human being, an unborn child is made in the image of God or whatever – all I am still doing is finding other reasons which appeal to my emotions in order to support my original position. When we strip away all of the so-called rational reasons or arguments for doing A rather than B or for believing X rather than Y, at root what we are left with is just a personal preference based on feelings of approval or disapproval.

This is why the theory is sometimes referred to as 'Boo-Hurrah' Theory. To continue with our example:

Statement: 'Abortion is wrong' or 'I disapprove of abortion'
Response: 'Boo!'
Statement: 'Abortion is O.K.' or 'I approve of abortion'
Response: 'Hurrah!'

At first sight this might seem to be a rather crude and unthinking moral theory. As we have already suggested, one may be tempted to ask if it constitutes a moral theory at all. If all conduct and behaviour is simply about how we feel, if it is to do just with our psychological response to something, then how can we be sure of anything? Is the rightness or wrongness of murder, dishonesty and deceitfulness simply a matter of how I feel about these actions? Can nothing else be said about them? Can we not prove, in some rational way or other, that telling the truth is morally preferable to lying, that caring for humans is morally more justifiable than killing them, that keeping promises, respecting people's property and being loyal to freinds and partners are philosophically more acceptable than deceit, theft and betrayal? Surely we can appeal to something more substantial than just my feelings of approval or disapproval?

Logical positivism

These are important questions which need to be addressed. The problem is that, according to one particular view of philosophy, such questions cannot be answered by nor through philosophy. The particular view of philosophy which takes this position is referred to as Logical Positivism or sometimes Logical Empiricism. In order to understand emotivism properly it is important to get to grips with this twentieth-century school of analytic philosophy. The original school was known as the 'Vienna Circle' of whom R. Carnap (1891–1970), M. Schlick (1882–1936) and O. Neurath (1882–1945) were among the most famous founding members. In a seminal paper entitled 'Scientific World View' (published in 1929), the Vienna Circle outlined part of the task of philosophy: to move forward by establishing the criteria for talking meaningfully about the world.

According to Logical Positivists, philosophy, strictly speaking, is about establishing the means by which the truth or falsehood of certain propositions can be demonstrated. If a proposition cannot be established as either true or false, then, in strict philosophical terms, it is meaningless. For Logical Positivists there are, basically, three types of statements:

- analytic or logical
- synthetic or empirical
- meaningless.

Analytic statements
Examples of analytic statements would be:

- All bachelors are unmarried men
- 2 plus 2 equals 4.

These are analytic or logical simply because the truth or falsehood of the statements can be established by analysing their constituent parts. Both statements are clearly true because they both contain within themselves the means for verifying their truth. Wittgenstein called them tautologies, in the sense that 2 plus 2 means the same as 4, and 'bachelors' is simply another way of saying 'unmarried men'. Put another way, the subject of the sentence is contained within the predicate (the predicate of a sentence being everything in the sentence that comes after the subject). Hence, in the statement 'All bachelors are unmarried men', 'bachelors' is the subject, and 'are unmarried men' is the predicate. In this case the subject of the sentence is the same as the predicate. It would therefore be foolish to say that 'All bachelors are unmarried men is a false statement', unless of course, the compilers of dictionaries unilaterally decided that from now on the word 'bachelor' would have another meaning.

Most propositions of logic and mathematics are of the analytic kind.

Synthetic statements

Examples of synthetic statements would be:

- Tuesday was a wet day
- James is a tall boy
- Water boils at 100° centrigrade.

These are synthetic or empirical in the sense that the truth or falsehood of each of the statements can only be established by reference to further information. They are empirical because they have to be confirmed or verified through some form of experience. For example, to determine whether or not Tuesday was a wet day I would have to have experienced the fact myself, have known someone else who had experienced the fact or have searched through the empirical evidence, namely the meteorological records for that Tuesday. There is nothing in the statement 'Tuesday was a wet day' which automatically leads us to the knowledge that the statement is true. The predicate is not contained within the subject. Just because it is a Tuesday it does not mean that it will therefore be a wet day, unlike the fact that because Fred is a bachelor he must, out of necessity, therefore be an unmarried man.

All statements in science are of this synthetic kind. The truth of the proposition has to be tested against experience, normally through experimentation.

Meaningless statements

Having established the scope of analytic or logical statements and synthetic or empirical statements, what we are left with outside of those are, strictly speaking, meaningless statements.

Examples of meaningless statements were held to be:

- This painting of the Mona Lisa is good
- Stealing is wrong
- God exists.

When we say 'meaningless' in the logical positivist sense we don't mean that the statements are just plain nonsense which have no use in human conversation and debate. What it means is that there can be no way in which we could verify the truth or falsehood of the propositions. What each of the statements really mean is:

- I like this painting of the Mona Lisa and therefore I think it is good
- I disapprove of stealing and therefore I think it is wrong
- I happen to have a belief in the existence of something that I wish to call God.

None of these statements is logically or empirically testable. They therefore fall outside the ambit of a philosophically meaningful statement.

This tells us something about the nature of philosophy according to the logical positivists or empiricists. For the strict positivist, philosophy is essentially about epistemology or theories of knowledge (Greek - knowledge: *episteme; Logos:* words/theories). The realms of ethics, aesthetics and theology are basically outside the ambit of philosophy because they do not constitute proper knowledge. Instead, these three realms, of ethics, aesthetics and theology are basically emotive – they deal with issues that are rooted in feelings of approval or disapproval, like and dislike, preference and non-preference. They cannot be proved or disproved.

A. J. Ayer (1910-1988)

The two names most linked with a theory of emotivism are A. J. 'Freddie' Ayer, the late British philosopher, and Charles Stevenson, the American philosopher.

A. J. Ayer's *Language, Truth and Logic*, published in 1934, made an enormous impact on British philosophy and set the tone and scope of philosophical debate for many years afterwards. In the book Ayer was concerned with the 'verification' of factual statements or propositions. In other words, how might we go about proving the truth or falsehood of a statement? For Ayer, the two major routes for verifying propositions were the analytic and the synthetic. That meant that only the statements of science and logic were legitimate targets for precise philosophical analysis and investigation. Morality remained outside the legitimate arena of investigation. As Ayer says:

> We can see why it is impossible to find a criterion for determining the validity of ethical judgements. It is not because they have an 'absolute' validity which is mysteriously independent of ordinary sense-experience, but because they have no objective validity whatsoever. If a sentence makes no statement at all, there is obviously no sense in asking whether what it says is true or false. And we have seen that sentences which simply express moral judgements do not say anything. They are pure expressions of feeling and as such do not come under the category of truth and falsehood (A. J. Ayer (1934) *Language, Truth and Logic*, Gollancz, 1970 edition, p. 108).

Prior to arguing this position Ayer examines a common example of human conduct which calls upon moral judgement. The example is to do with stealing, an issue which, on a common-sense level, most people would have thought is already settled. That is, for most people, stealing *is* wrong. Deontological ethics, a classic version of which is the Decalogue or Ten Commandments, states quite unequivocally that stealing is wrong. This is an objective moral 'fact' discoverable both through reason and experience. But not so for Ayer and proponents of emotivism. For Ayer there is simply no way of verifying the truth or falsehood of the statement: Stealing money is wrong. Ayer again:

> If now I ... say, 'Stealing money is wrong,' I produce a sentence which has no factual meaning – that is, expresses no proposition which can be either true or false. It is as if I had written 'Stealing money!!' – where the shape and thickness of the exclamation marks show ... that a special sort of moral disapproval is the feeling which is being expressed (A. J. Ayer, *Language, Truth and Logic*, 1970 edn., p. 107).

However, Ayer was not centrally concerned with morality or ethical theory. His interest was, as the title of his book suggests, the same as that pursued by the Vienna Circle. Consequently his arguments concerning ethics are really only incidental to his philosophy. It is not until we come to the works of C. L. Stevenson that we find a fully articulated version of the emotivist theory.

C. L. Stevenson (1908 –)

Charles Stevenson had been working along similar lines to Ayer but his interest was chiefly centred on morality and the kind of language one could use to describe it. According to W. D. Hudson (1978, *Modern Moral Philosophy*, p. 114) two particular articles written by Stevenson in the late 1930s delineated the scope and content of the emotivist theory: 'The Emotive Meaning of Ethical Terms' (*Mind*, XLVI, 1937) and 'Persuasive Definitions' (*Mind*, XLVI, 1938). The complete account of emotivism was then described and analysed in his later book, *Ethics and Language* (1944).

Stevenson was principally interested in observing how people really do use moral terms in everyday conversation. What could be said about such conversations? Hudson sees three features emerging from Stevenson's analysis:

i) The fact that genuine agreements and disagreements occur within (them);
ii) The fact that moral terms have, so to speak, a 'magnetism';
iii) The fact that the scientific, or empirical method of verification is not sufficient for ethics.

(pp. 114–15).

The first of these features is fairly apparent in everyday moral discourse. Disagreements in ethics are, more often than not, genuine and not superficial. If A says that euthanasia is morally unacceptable and B argues the opposite then they are disagreeing on a series of very fundamental issues. The issue of euthanasia simply becomes the vehicle for such disagreements. For example, euthanasia for A might well entail belief in a particular set of doctrines and theories about human nature, natural law, objective knowledge of right and wrong, social organization, medical responsibility and political legislation. A's attitude towards euthanasia is clearly going to be coloured by his attitudes towards these associated doctrines. Each of these may conflict to a greater or lesser degree with another set of doctrines and theories held by B, and hence, B's attitude towards euthanasia is likely to be different from A's. Moreover, because of the connections with other sets of attitudes and beliefs, A and B are likely to act and behave in different ways from each other. A may feel compelled to stand outside hospitals with a placard protesting against the legalization of euthanasia, while B may campaign vigorously on behalf of the practice and lobby politicians in order to secure their support for his view. The disagreement about euthanasia, then, cannot be dismissed simply by the superficial 'boo-hurrah' characterisation of it. The disagreement is genuine in the true sense of the word because it entails acting as well as believing. The second feature simply points to the fact that moral terms have a persuasive force to them. We choose particular terms in order to substantiate our belief and to persuade others of the correctness of our belief. This view is linked to the last feature, the fact that logical positivist views of verification are inadequate when it comes to talking about moral beliefs and statements. These two things being so, according to Stevenson, all moral statements include words and phrases which have cognitive meaning and emotive meaning. So, for example, the phrase 'the technically illegal transfer of funds' and the word 'fraud' both have the same cognitive meaning, but 'fraud' has an additional emotive meaning. If I were to suspect someone of the technically illegal transfer of funds and I wished to dissuade them from continuing with the practice I am more likely to be successful if I accuse them directly of fraud. The word has a number of unpleasant connotations and assocations which the phrase does not. So often, when debating moral issues, we choose to use words which have particular emotive as well as cognitive meaning in order to persuade others to our way of thinking. Stevenson refers to this as the use of 'persuasive definitions'. The use of the word 'rape' instead of 'sexual intercourse without the person's consent' is designed to evoke a particularly strong emotional response, and hence invoke a particular moral stance. The word carries a moral force which is lacking in the plain descriptive phrase.

Emotivism as reductivism

The principal difficulty with emotivism is that if we accept it as offering the most justifiable analysis of moral discourse, then all moral debate becomes, at the end of the day, just so much hot air and nothing else. Talking about moral issues might help release our feelings, or might help us in persuading others to take our point of view, but actually we would be saying things which had no significant meaning. Now this is just plainly improbable. We not only feel that the murder of six million innocent Jews in the gas chambers in the Second World War was wrong, we also believe that we are justified in saying that we know it to be wrong. All morality cannot be reduced simply to how we feel about something. Morality involves the use of reason and the recognition that some human qualities and experiences can be demonstrated to be more objectively positive than other qualities and experiences. Put simply, it is probably an empirical fact that caring for one's children is objectively better for their welfare than neglecting them. Therefore, the rational moral response is to to care for children and not to neglect them. At root, emotivism seems too reductive. We cannot accept that such a terrible series of crimes as those committed in the Holocaust can be reduced to two simple sets of competing attitudes:

- 'I believe that killing innocent people is wrong'
- Either: a) Boo! or b) Hurrah!

Human behaviour, given its richness and complexity, arguably needs a moral account which can cope with such depth and diversity.

R. M. Hare and universalisability

The works of R. M. Hare (1919-) have sought to address the potential reductivism implicit in emotive thinking. In *The Language of Morals* (1952) and later works Hare distinguishes between descriptive and evaluative meanings, the latter being more important. As a development of Stevenson's persuasive definitions, evaluative meanings are designed partly to 'prescribe' behaviour. By arguing persuasively that 'euthanasia is wrong' A is attempting to prescribe both the attitude and behaviour that B ought to adopt. So, for example, A will hope that eventually B will join him in protesting outside hospitals rather than campaigning on behalf of the practice. Hare goes one further by advocating that on questions involving moral judgement we must necessarily move beyond our individual viewpoint and our individual preference in order to 'universalise' that viewpoint, in the belief that the viewpoint is not only good for ourselves, but good for everyone else besides. This is known as 'universalisability', and as we can see, it has a great deal in common with the Kantian doctrine of moral imperatives.

Final objection

However, for MacIntyre (1981, *After Virtue*) emotivism, including all its refinements and its sophisticated versions, is still a misconceived theory of ethics. Emotivism is a device for obscuring what really matters in moral discourse and ethical behaviour, namely the human qualities that make a life meaningful and purposeful. What qualities are these? For MacIntyre, the qualities which make for a moral life are the virtues, and the best account we have of them so far is that given by Aristotle and later expanded by Aquinas. For MacIntyre, emotivism as a moral doctrine has affected contemporary culture so much that modern life may be characterised as a kind of social emotivism in which all moral judgements are seen just simply as expressions of personal preference and nothing more. Therefore, no one is entitled to emphasise one moral position over another, because at root they are, after all, expressions of an individual attitude. The consequences of this are disturbing, according to MacIntyre:

> What is the key to the social content of emotivism? It is the fact that emotivism entails the obliteration of any genuine distinction between manipulative and non-manipulative social relations ... Others are always means, never ends (*After Virtue*, pp. 23–4).

It is appropriate that we now turn to the work of MacIntyre.

Questions for discussion

1 How far do you find emotivism a convincing account of the way in which moral issues are discussed? Try to give examples wherever possible.

2 Are all ethical, theological and aesthetic statements meaningless? Think of examples of ethical, theological and aesthetic statements and analyse them to see if they really are statements of fact, or statements of attitude.

3 What do you understand by the term 'universalisability'?

4 Is the contemporary world characterised by manipulative social relations? How far have people become 'commodified' – objects to be used by others?

5 Evaluate A. J. Ayer's account of ethical judgements and his example of stealing money.

6 List some examples of 'persuasive definitions'.

7 If a statement cannot be verified, do you consider that it is meaningless? Why?

EIGHT

MacIntyre – Virtue Theory Revisited

It would be difficult to write any text on ethics – introductory or specialist – without saying something in detail about the work of Alasdair MacIntyre. MacIntyre's *After Virtue : a study in moral theory* (1981) is probably one of the most influential and oft-quoted texts to have been published in recent years. In it MacIntyre attempts to resurrect Aristotelian thinking about the virtues, those qualities of mind and character that Aristotle believed to be so essential to living a happy and ethically justifiable life. Of course, MacIntyre is not the only one to have done this. In *The Virtues* (1977) Peter Greach has fashioned a modern restatement of the Aristotelian constellation of human qualities, but his project was far more modest than MacIntyre's. In contrast to Geach's account MacIntyre calls into question not only contemporary moral philosophy in particular, but all modern philosophy in general.

Historical approach to morality

MacIntyre argues that most contemporary moral theorizing is basically of little relevance. He claims that the works of R. M. Hare, P. H. Nowell-Smith and others are dominated by a narrow form of rationality. Their theorising, he argues, lays too much stress on reason, and too little emphasis on people and the contexts in which they live their lives. It is as if moral philosophers were so concerned to get the precise logical structure of their arguments right, and so preoccupied with analysing every moral concept, that their final ethical theories seem to be divorced from everyday human life. One can imagine rarified groups of Anglo-American philosophers arguing the toss over the precise meaning of right and wrong whilst social chaos and moral havoc is wreaked around them. Hunched in their ivory towers their analyses of ethical reasoning seem as remote and irrelevant as dissertations on phlogiston.

What is needed, according to MacIntyre, is a reassessment of the ways in which we talk about ethics. A better way of trying to understand morality, argues MacIntyre, is to adopt a narrative or historical approach. Hegel (1770-1831) and Collingwood (1889-1943), who were both concerned with the relationship between history and philosophy, provide us with better models than do Moore (1873-1958), Nowell-Smith (1914-) and Hare (1919-). Consequently, *After Virtue* traces the development of ethical or moral reasoning from its hesitant beginnings in ancient Greece through to its muddled condition in contemporary western culture.

The virtues

1. Homeric Virtues

MacIntyre traces early western concepts of right and wrong back to the world of Homeric Greece. Homer's epic poems — *The Iliad* and *The Odyssey* — provide us with the first written evidence of sustained thinking about how one ought to behave in both public and private. Scholars have argued whether these epic poems were the work of one man or many. However, recent scholarship has tended to favour the one over the many. Homer, by all accounts, was a blind poet who lived approximately in the 9th century B.C.

The Iliad tells the tale of the last days of the ten-year war between the Greeks and the Trojans. The beautiful Helen, wife of Menelaus, a Greek king, was abducted by Paris, a Trojan prince. Menelaus seeks help from Agamemnon, the Greek supreme commander. A vast Greek army is assembled and sails for Troy — a place known to have been sited on the west coast of Turkey. A ten-year war is fought on the plains outside Troy during which Hector, the son of Troy's King Priam, is eventually slain by Achilles, the principal Greek hero.

The war is brought to a close by an ingenious Greek ploy. A huge wooden horse is constructed and left outside the walls of Troy. Carefully concealed within the horse are Greek warriors. Meanwhile the Greeks pack up camp and sail away apparently leaving the horse as a gift to the Trojans. The horse is brought inside the city walls and feasting and celebrating get under way. Under cover of darkness the Greek warriors open up the gates of Troy and let in the Greek army which meanwhile has sailed back to shore. Troy is destroyed, the Trojan soldiers put to the sword and the women and children taken or sold into slavery.

The Odyssey, on the other hand, is concerned with another Greek hero, Odysseus, who has fought bravely and well in the Trojan war. It tells the story of his ten-year voyage home to his wife Penelope and son Telemachus. On the way home he encounters many dangers and undergoes many trials. Eventually he makes it home and kills his wife's persistent suitors.

These stories, along with the works of the 7th century B.C. poet Hesiod, provided the Greeks with their only written form of religious and moral education. They did not have the equivalent of the Jewish Old Testament or the Christian New Testament. Like the Hindu *Mahabharata*, arguably the world's longest epic poem, *The Illiad* and *The Odyssey* provided the moral framework for Greek culture. It described how one ought to think and act, and in what morality consisted. According to MacIntyre, the following qualities emerge which were considered essential for a human being:

- *Physical strength*: necessary to build and defend small, hilltop tribal communities;
- *Courage*: without courage, physical strength is of little value when the community is being attacked by a rival neighbouring tribe;
- *Cunning*: cunning is essential when strength fails. This is the sort of native cunning that hatches plots, plans defences and constructs treaties;
- *Friendship*: necessary for the overall survival of the community. It provides the meaning and purpose behind wanting to build and

defend the community. Friendship made the long periods of war bearable and the short periods of peace sublime. The worst crime was betrayal or treachery. Betrayal meant the possible destruction of the whole community and the meaning of life that went with that community. The person who perpetrates such a deceit deceives himself, for the community originally conferred identity upon him. So in betraying his community he betrays himself. He has, to all intents and purposes, committed moral suicide.

Consequently, honour was prized above all else, and the Greek and Trojan heroes exhibited all of these virtues, or qualities of mind and character, to the highest degree.

2 Athenian virtues

These four virtues were later changed and enriched as the small hilltop communities developed and gave way to large, complex city-states. The *polis* was established. No longer was physical strength deemed necessary, for strength was secured through sheer weight of numbers.

- *Courage* was still regarded as important, for without it there was no honour and no thought of the safety and wellbeing of anyone except oneself.
- *Friendship* was still prized, as it was looked upon as the social glue which bonded households, villages and city-states together.
- *Justice*, both retributive and distributive, was considered essential. Retributive justice simply meant that people received their just deserts, that is, the punishment they rightly deserved for wrong-doing. Distributive justice referred to the 'goods' of the *polis* being evenly and fairly distributed among the populace. Each member of the city-state should receive a just and fair share of the spoils of war, and the produce of the community, as well as partaking in, or contributing to, the various religious festivals.
- *Temperance*, self-control or personal denial was considered crucial. Without temperance, distributive justice was not possible.

Personal greed and gain would interfere with the fair share of goods. Moreover, without self-control retributive justice was impossible. Extreme punishment and excessive revenge could be exacted for the most minor offence. Disproportionate rewards could be given to the least deserving individuals.

- *Wisdom* replaced cunning. Wisdom here involved more than just the ability to use one's intelligence in a straightforward, practical manner. Devising plans to build city-states, and plots to defend them, were still deemed important. However, the growing capacity to reflect upon life and its meaning became equally prized. Wisdom involved a proper understanding of the frailty and insignificance of human life; faced with the vastness and complexity of the cosmos humility came to be recognized as a fundamental facet of wisdom.

According to MacIntyre there were four versions of the Athenian virtues:

- *Sophist*: The sophists, led by the philosopher Protagoras, saw the virtues more as a set of practical skills to be sharpened up in order to secure success for the individual. The sophists taught their students oratory, rhetoric and all the arts of debate so that their students would be able to win over their opponents in a political argument. In the eyes of the sophists the virtues became instrumental skills to be deployed in the pursuit of wordly success. Thrasymachus, the sophist in Plato's *Republic*, argues that justice is not that refined and pure virtuous form advocated by Socrates. Instead justice is simply another way of saying 'might is right!' As long as you have the means to defeat your opponent, then, to all intents and purposes, you have secured justice. If they secure a victory over you, then they have secured justice for themselves. Images of the modern sophist might be the yuppie and the cynical politician who use their skills and abilities to grab fame and fortune for themselves without considering the deeper issues of justice, temperance and wisdom.

- *Platonic*: For MacIntyre, Plato's account of the virtues, although to be preferred to the sophist version, is still unsatisfactory. The reason being that for Plato, this world in which we reside is the world of appearances rather than reality. Therefore, any virtues that we display are mere pale and imperfect reflections of the pure virtues that reside in the famous world of Forms or ideas. Any just act that we might perform is always going to be simply a poor copy of that perfect notion of justice that exists in the timeless and unchanging world of universal forms. This puts rather a low premium on the ordinary practical everyday world that we live in. Whereas the sophists overemphasised practical success in this world, Plato all but ignored it. A caricature of the contemporary Platonist might be the cultured and kindly country parson who has all but parted company from this world.

- *Tragedian*: the plays of Sophocles and Aeschylus abound with stories about the virtues and characters displaying them. However, what is different in the accounts offered by the dramatists is their recognition that the virtues do not necessarily blend in a harmonious fashion. Virtues compete and conflict, even within a single person. My virtues of courage and friendship might lead me to acts which wisdom and justice might not approve. More importantly, in Sophocles' *Oedipus Rex* and *Philoctetes* or Aeschylus' *Agamemnon*, it is understood that no matter how virtuous one might be one can never escape one's destiny. Fate is something none of us can avoid. We can cultivate the virtues all we like, but that won't prevent us from being knocked over by a bus, robbed by a thief or struck down by an incurable disease. Death and misfortune are visited on the just as well as the unjust.

- *Aristotelian*: For MacIntyre, it is Aristotle who offers the most coherent and complete account of the virtues. Artistotle's detailed understanding of how the virtues fit into the living of a good and moral life cannot be bettered.

3 Medieval virtues

With the advent of Christianity and the later development of medieval Christian philosophy, these Athenian or Classical virtues underwent some slight revision. In his commentaries on Plato, the Roman philosopher, Cicero (106–43 B.C.) discoursed on the four virtues of:

- courage
- justice
- temperance
- wisdom.

These were described, by St Ambrose (c. A.D. 340–397), as the 'cardinal virtues', and to them were added the three 'theological virtues' of:

- faith
- hope
- charity or love.

This last, charity or love, presented the Victorians especially with one or two problems. One could clearly dispense charity to the poor, or the 'great unwashed', but, heaven forbid, one could not love them! Moreover, love, for the Victorian middle classes, was a disembodied concept. The legs of pianos and tables had to be covered in case sexual passion was aroused or unseemly comparisons made; and chicken breast and chicken leg were named white and dark meat respectively to avoid any undue embarrassment. It is a matter of some wonder to MacIntyre that the word 'morality', which originally meant practical wisdom in the art of living, became exclusively concerned with highly restricted norms governing sexual behaviour.

The eighteenth-century enlightenment

For MacIntyre the destruction of moral conduct and understanding occurred during and after the Enlightenment, the period spanning the eighteenth century. Up to that point it was a matter of common knowledge and agreement that morality was closely tied to the virtues. Without the necessary qualities of mind and character, a person would be unable to live a moral life. Moreover, this was understood to be part of the natural order of things. People had a *telos* – an end or purpose. And that purpose was to become a good person. How did one become a good person? Not by arguing the finer points of right and wrong, but by cultivating the moral virtues through habit, and the intellectual virtues by instruction. Lastly, for good or ill, there was a general acceptance not just of a natural order of things, but of a divine order of things. There was a God, and one must accept the authority of the Church, whose priests were in contact with God, in order to avoid being banished from the human as well as the divine community.

The Enlightenment put an end to these modes of thinking, believing and behaving, and sought instead to isolate morality by offering a single rational reason for its existence. For Hume (1711–76) morality was simply an expression of emotion – of the passions. There is nothing logical, teleological or divine about morality. In fact morality is so reducible to human feeling alone that, 'Tis not contrary to reason to prefer the destruction of the whole world to the scratching of my finger' (D. Hume, *A Treatise of Human Nature*, p. 416). Conversely Kant (1724–1804) sought moral salvation in the power of human rationality alone. As there were clearly universal mathematical laws governing the physical world, then there must be universal moral laws governing the social world. These laws, as we have seen, were the two imperatives: the categorical and the practical.

Kierkegaard soon saw through the veil of pretentiousness that clothed human reason. In *Either/Or* (1843) he analysed two spheres of existence – the ethical and the aesthetic – whereas in other works he analysed a third stage, the religious. The ethical was exemplified by marriage and a life lived in openness and without secrecy in conformity with the values of society. Both the aesthetic and religious stages involved secrecy – the aesthetic represented by a seducer (albeit a highly sophisticated one) who departed from the ethical norms of society and chose his own path. The religious stage was exemplified by Abraham, a 'Knight of Faith' who, in obedience to God, placed himself outside the demands of the ethical by being willing to obey a command from God to sacrifice his son, Isaac (Kierkegaard's *Fear and Trembling*). Kierkegaard explores the question of whether any such action can be justified if it leaves behind the frontiers of morality – how, he asks, can one differentiate between a man of supreme faith and a madman if we no longer have ethical criteria available to us?

Kierkegaard was contemptuous of part-time Christians, those who uttered the Creed and prayers on Sundays and promptly did the opposite on Mondays. Kierkegaard wished to persuade people to decide for themselves – to decide for the ethical, the religious or the aesthetic life. In deciding, they would at least come closer to being individuals, although for Kierkegaard the 'solitary individual' was the highest category of existence and was reserved for the person who lived his or her life in relationship with God – putting everything else into second place.

Other existentialist thinkers, influenced by Kierkegaard although not faithful to him, believed that morality could be reduced to the simple act of choosing. The choice was not necessarily between leading a good or a bad life, but between choosing to choose or making no choice at all and letting one's choice be dictated by the crowd. Kierkegaard admired such a person as at least he would be an individual and would not be subsumed beneath 'peer-group pressure' and the demands of convention, but he did not think that choice alone was enough to make a virtuous man – in this he was much more sophisticated than his followers.

The virtues and human teleology had, in turn, been replaced by Hume's insistence on the passions, by Kant's narrow emphasis on reason, and finally by Kierkegaard's singular championing of individual choice. But the problems did not stop there. MacIntyre goes tilting at the utilitarianism of Bentham and Mill arguing that here was a moral rationality founded on a fiction, the fiction being the 'utility calculus'. Despite the many social, political and economic advances brought about by utilitarianism and the philosophical radicals, the 'utility calculus' was a poor foundation for moral understanding. People just do not think, work or act like that, as we have seen in chapter 6.

Bentham's and Mill's utilitarianism, along with Kierkegaard's existentialism and Kant's deontology have all been found wanting. But MacIntyre sees no good reason for accepting the moral theories that later supplanted them. He dispenses with Moore's intuitionism with the comment:

> Twentieth-century moral philosophers have sometimes appealed to their and our intuitions; but one of the things that we ought to have learned from the history of moral philosophy is that the introduction of the word 'intuition' by a moral philosopher is always a signal that something has gone badly wrong with an argument (A. MacIntyre, (1981) *After Virtue*, p. 69).

With the failure of intuitionism to provide us with a coherent moral philosophy where was one to look? The moral theory which filled the gap was Ayer's and Stevenson's emotivism. Reason, passion, choice, utility and intuition had all failed. What was left was meaningless in the strict, philosophical sense of the word. We can establish facts through science, and true or false statements through logic, but the world of value, the realm of morality is beyond fact, truth or falsehood. Instead morality is simply the expression of personal preference in a culture which has abandoned the virtues and rejected the sense of community.

In this moral vacuum, according to MacIntyre, three archetypal characters now strut the cultural stage. They are:

1 *The Bureaucratic Manager*, who matches ends to means in the most efficient manner. Manipulating others and manipulated by the system he has created, the manager examines economic resources and has no qualms about shutting down factories wholesale in order to achieve the best return for his shareholders. His area of

expertise is efficient management which, for him, has no moral dimension.

2 *The Rich Aesthete* who pursues greater and more exciting pleasures and experiences. The image here is of the ageing rock-star whose female conquests outnumber his hit records.

3 *The Therapist* who keeps the whole sorry cultural show on the road. In densely concentrated urban areas in the industrialised West we see all three characters at work. For the rich aesthete and the bureaucratic manager there are exclusive and professional therapists ready to massage them through another day. For the rest of society, who are manipulated in turn by the manager and the aesthete, there is the television therapist, the chat show host who jollies everyone along and allows them to avoid having to look too deeply at the meaninglessness and superficiality of life.

The choice between Nietzsche and Aristotle

For MacIntyre we are at the crossroads. We are faced with the stark choice of following the supreme individualist who, philosophically, represents the prototype emotivist: Nietzsche; or of following the philosopher who understood the importance of our membership of the community which conferred identity upon us: Aristotle. We either pursue Nietzsche's individual will to power or Aristotle's moral and intellectual virtues. But, in one sense, the choice has already been made, for the virtues live on in any case in the small communities we forge for ourselves. In organising jumble sales for Oxfam, parent-teacher forums in schools, fund-raising for local hospitals, and carnivals and festivals throughout the seasons we depend upon individuals and groups to exercise the Aristotelian virtues. The various practices and traditions which make up human communities, from education to medicine, and from politics to business and commerce, all depend upon people being able to develop and sustain the virtues. Without the virtues communities of whatever size simply collapse. But how, exactly, are the virtues developed and sustained in individuals and communities? The answer is a complicated one and finds its full expression in chapter 15 of *After Virtue*. Human beings and the communities they forge are governed by a narrative unity. We live our lives through a narrative structure. That is why the historical approach to morality is favoured above a purely analytical approach. Like Socrates (in Plato's *Republic*), who examines the concept of justice 'writ large' in society and then 'writ small' in the individual, MacIntyre examines the historical narrative of morality 'writ large' in western culture and then 'writ small' in individual lives. As such, a

> central thesis then begins to emerge: man is in his actions and practice, as well as in his fictions, essentially a story-telling animal ... he becomes ... a teller of stories that aspire to truth. (*After Virtue*, 1985, 2nd edition, p. 216).

Beliefs are held and intentions and intelligible actions all take place within specific practices. These, in turn, develop traditions and become established in social institutions. Such practices enable the good for ourselves and the good for others to be realised. It is a symbiotic relationship: the virtues sustain the practices, and practices continue to sustain the virtues. A rugby club is sustained by players who see the worth of the game, and the worth of the game is both ensured and enhanced by the traditions established by the club. 'The virtues therefore are to be understood as those dispositions which will not only sustain practices and enable us to achieve the goods internal to practices, but will also sustain us in the relevant kind of quest for the good, by enabling us to overcome the harms, dangers, temptations and distractions which we encounter.' (*After Virtue*, 1985, p. 219).

Criticisms

Although the case has been made on behalf of the virtues it is an open question as to whether or not it is accurate, consistent and persuasive. There are three broad sets of objections which

MacIntyre himself considers in the second edition of the text, *After Virtue*.

The first objection revolves around the relationship between philosophy and history. Frankena makes the point that MacIntyre is simply using history in order to try to settle an issue in moral philosophy. This would be like trying to settle a literary question by referring to mathematical formulae. MacIntyre's reply rests on the argument that is already in the text; that is, that the division between philosophy and history is, ultimately, an artificial one created at some point in time by those charged with establishing an academic curriculum. Edel's criticism is almost the opposite to Frankena's. Edel accuses MacIntyre of relying too much on the analytic technique to prove his case, and not enough on historical evidence. As a consequence, Edel argues, MacIntyre has rather distorted the long and complex narrative of moral philosophy in order to sustain his case on behalf of Aristotle.

The second objection is to do with the virtues themselves. Scheffler's particular criticism is that the exercise of the virtues does not assure the kind of moral life that MacIntyre maintains that it does. Scheffler argues that one could have an excellent chess player who is in possession of all the virtues necessary for the practice of chess-playing but still be a vicious individual. MacIntyre maintains that it would be a contradiction in kind to talk of an excellent chess-player who exhibits all of the virtues, and yet can still be a vicious individual who is more concerned with, say, fame, money and prestige than with the quality of the game. For such a person, external rewards are of primary concern, whereas for the truly virtuous person, the internal rewards of playing the game of chess well are sufficient. Wachbroit offers, arguably, the semi-postmodernist objection that an emphasis on the virtues still does not and cannot refute moral relativism. Are the virtues the same in all cultures? Are the practices, traditions and cultural purposes roughly the same in all cultures? Clearly not. MacIntyre replies using the standard, 'best so far' argument: Aristotelian moral theory is the best theory so far … adherents are rationally entitled to a high measure of confidence in its epistemological and moral resources (*After Virtue* p. 277).

The third set of objections is to do with the relationship between moral philosophy and theology. Stout maintains that MacIntyre's account of the virtues does not do justice to the long medieval tradition which interpreted Aristotle by way of Scripture and theology. The point is that it really does make a difference that God exists and that the natural virtues have their origin in divine virtues. MacIntyre concedes the point and partly redresses the balance in his later text *Whose Justice? Which Rationality?* (1988). Here the relationship between theology and philosophy is explored in greater detail.

A final objection not addressed by MacIntyre is that offered by Richard Bernstein in *Philosophical Profiles* who simply points out that MacIntyre has placed too much faith in the wisdom of the 'ancients' (i.e. Aristotle) and has rejected too quickly the inquiries of the 'moderns' (i.e. Kant, Bentham, Mill etc.). For Bernstein there are 'truths' to be found in both ancients and moderns.

Questions for discussion

1 What objections would you wish to raise in response to MacIntyre's theory? In what ways might Bernstein's criticism be valid? Can the so-called 'moral disaster' be attributed solely to the Enlightenment?
2 Are there any other 'virtues' that Heroic society may have deemed important?
3 In what ways may pre-Enlightenment morality have been more restrictive and constraining than post-Enlightenment morality?
4 Might there be characters in the contemporary world other than the manager, the aesthete and the therapist? If so, what are they? What reasons can you give for suggesting them?

5 Which Aristotelian virtues are necessary for the maintenance of a rugby club/Oxfam branch/educational institution/hospital/political party (or any other social/professional community)?

6 Is modern culture best described as 'emotivist'?

NINE

Virtue Ethics

The background

As we have seen, MacIntyre is an important advocate for what has become known as virtue ethics. However, he is by no means the only, nor indeed the first virtue theorist in modern moral philosophy. Arguably, it was the Cambridge philosopher Elizabeth Anscombe who, in a seminal article entitled 'Modern Moral Philosophy' (1958), first began to place a heavy question mark over the dominance, during the post-war period, of three groups of moral theories – deontological or Kantian ethics, utilitarianism, and meta-ethics – and to suggest instead that virtue ethics might provide a much firmer foundation for reasoning about moral dilemmas. All three theories have been dealt with, respectively, in chapters five, six and seven, although meta-ethics, and its converse, normative ethics, need a special, further mention before contemporary virtue ethics can be properly explored.

Normative ethics and meta-ethics

One way of examining moral philosophy is to divide theories into normative and meta-ethical. Normative theories are those which are supposed to guide, govern or prescribe human behaviour in order that such behaviour becomes 'normal', or so that it can approximate the norm. On this view most ethical theories, from virtue ethics and deontological ethics to situationism and utilitarianism, are normative. They attempt to isolate either character traits or rules and principles, or to describe particular circumstances along with appropriate responses, or to analyse certain goals and future states of affairs, all with the aim of helping to normalise human behaviour so that it becomes, as it were, more morally justifiable. For Aristotle and MacIntyre we should all develop the moral virtue of courage so that we are able to act in certain, partly prescribed ways in times of stress, conflict or war. For Kant, we should all obey the categorical imperative to tell the truth or to keep our promises on every single occasion simply because the moral law obliges us so to do. We would, according to Kant, be illogical and irrational if we didn't obey that law. Arguably, nothing could be more prescriptive than this; hence, it has a tendency to make morality not just flexibly normative but rigidly uniform. For Bentham, Mill and, more recently, Singer we ought to assess all the possible outcomes of an action, say, the spending of excess cash on either an additional private pension scheme or a significant donation to Oxfam, and determine which action would benefit the most people. Goal-orientated behaviour, intended to maximise the greatest happiness for the greatest number, would, it is argued, lead to a more normalised view of moral activity.

Meta-ethics, on the other hand, is not at all concerned with guiding or prescribing human behaviour so that it becomes more moral. Instead, it is wholly concerned with simply analysing the language that people use when they discuss any moral issue. Emotivism is probably the best-known meta-ethical theory in that it focuses exclusively on the language being used and the meanings being suggested, and not at all on the rightness or wrongness of the character of the person, or the principles and purposes followed. It is called meta–ethics, because it is the kind of analysis done after or beyond the ethical discussion. The Greek word *meta* means 'after' or 'beyond', as in Aristotle's famous treatise *Metaphysics*, meaning, effectively, 'the book that comes after the earlier book entitled *Physics*'. The two related meanings – after and beyond – are instructive. First, it means that any meta–ethical analysis can only take place after the actual ethical debate has run its course, in the same way that the *Metaphysics* could only come after the *Physics* had been written, read and understood. (It is, of course, generally known that Aristotle's treatises were, for the most part, lecture notes copied up and put into some sort of order by others.) Second, it means that meta-ethical analysis takes place somehow beyond the ethical debate and should rise above it. It should remain uncontaminated or unaffected by any of the points, principles or arguments being made in that debate so that detached, uncommitted and unprejudiced comments can be made about how and why the debate followed the linguistic pattern that it did. It is sometimes said that such meta-ethical analysis is a type of second-order philosophy, dealing in a clarificatory way with first-order activities.

1 *First-order activities* – e.g. gardening, driving and playing golf, as well as talking about the best ways to do one's garden, drive one's car or play the game of golf.
2 *Second-order activities* – e.g. clarifying the terms, explanations and arguments people use when they talk about the activities they engage in, without in any way supporting the so-called best ways to do such things (as gardening, driving and playing golf).

So, for example, three surgeons might be discussing the pros and cons of how best to treat Alzheimer's disease, the degenerative brain disease which results in the loss of memory, identity and human purpose. Surgeon A claims that the newly discovered method of using tissue from discarded human embryos and injecting it into the brains of Alzheimer sufferers offers the best hope for the future. Surgeon B, although confirming its clinical success, claims that the practice has such a potentially immoral side to it, that it cannot be condoned. He argues that there is the real possibility of poor people being financially induced by rich people to deliberately conceive and produce embryos which could then be aborted. The tissue from the aborted foetuses could subsequently be freeze-stored and later used if they (the rich people) were ever in the unfortunate position of suffering from the disease. Lastly, Surgeon C acknowledges the possibilities outlined by Surgeon B but claims that as long as

111

sufficient legal safeguards are built into the whole process, further research and practice ought to be permitted. They cannot all agree. Surgeon A wants as few safeguards as possible. As a geriatric specialist, working from an act-utilitarian position, he is concerned with the maximisation of quality of life for all of his ageing patients. Surgeon C, working from a rule-utilitarian position, wants far greater restriction placed upon the procedure's use, in the interests of possible foetuses who may be conceived and then terminated for purely mercenary ends. Surgeon B, working from either religious or secular deontological principles, wants the procedure banned altogether, despite his deep regret at there not being an equally successful clinical alternative, although there are treatments which are, unfortunately, less medically efficacious. They decide to speak with the resident philosopher on their ethics committee (all hospitals are required to have ethics committees, although there is no obligation for them to invite philosophers to become members). The philosopher herself may, of course, be persuaded of the overall benefits of normative ethics, and hence, may advise following one of the two broad routes, the deontological or the utilitarian, offered by the three surgeons. She may, however, be more persuaded of the meta-ethical view and her task then would simply be to try to clarify the language used by the doctors, refine the arguments for and against each position, and than retire again to olympian detachment without recommending any route at all. She will claim that the surgeons are involved in the first-order activity; she is there simply as a second-order clarifier.

Virtue ethics

Now, virtue ethics is a normative theory, but it differs from most other normative theories in that it focuses on a person's character and not on the actions they may undertake nor on the principles which they may be dutifully obliged to follow. In summing up what is known as the 'Being vs Doing Debate' (a debate outlined originally by Bernard Mayo and William Frankena), Robert Louden says:

'the central question is not "What ought I to do?" but rather "What sort of person ought I to be?" (R. Louden, 1984, 'On Some Vices of Virtue Ethics', in *American Philosophical Quarterly* 21, reprinted in R. Crisp and M. Slote, eds, 1997, *Virtue Ethics*, Oxford, Oxford University Press, p. 205).

As has already been claimed, MacIntyre is a modern and extremely important proponent of virtue ethics. In reviving a clear interest in Aristotle's corpus of moral philosophy he has done much to underline the absolute relevance of human character over abstract principles. However, as was suggested at the beginning of this chapter, it is Elizabeth Anscombe to whom much of the credit must go. In her paper 'Modern Moral Philosophy', which first appeared in the journal *Philosophy* 33 (1958), Anscombe controversially claimed three things:

1 modern moral philosophy (as it was then conceived in 1958, comprising utilitarianism, deontological ethics and meta-ethics) should be 'laid aside' until an adequate understanding of the psychology of moral reasoning was attained
2 the concepts of 'moral obligation and moral duty' should be abandoned until psychology has done its work
3 most modern moral philosophers, irrespective of the particular position they claim to hold, are largely all saying the same things. In other words they are all equally misconceived as to the true nature of ethical reasoning or moral theorising. Anscombe mentions two philosophers in particular, P. H. Nowell-Smith (*Ethics*, 1954) and R. M. Hare (*The Language of Morals*, 1952). Both may be said to be the prime exemplars of the meta-ethical approach.

Morality and history

Anscombe was in part interested in the historical development of ethical reasoning and made the significant point (a point developed later by MacIntyre) that Aristotle's conception of moral wrongdoing was given a legal boost by the Judaeo–Christian interpretation of it. What exactly does this mean? Well, it seemed quite clear that Aristotle (as we have already seen) was concerned with a purely secular and natural account of moral behaviour or conduct. (Conduct is a better word as it suggests much more than mere observable behaviour, as the English philosopher Michael Oakeshott argued in his masterful work *On the Theoretical Understanding of Human Conduct*, 1975.) Aristotle's account was secular in that he sought not to ground ethics in religion or a divine being. It was natural – or, more properly, naturalistic – in that he believed that human character developed, or failed to develop, along certain natural lines, and that his description and analysis of it was justified on empirical grounds. In other words, his account was derived from observing people individually and collectively and coming to reasoned judgements about their overall conduct. This was how people naturally conducted themselves, or how they believed they ought naturally to conduct themselves. Most people, thought Aristotle, were neither, in Greg Pence's phrase, 'moral monsters' ('Virtue theory', in P. Singer, ed., 1991, *A Companion to Ethics*, p. 252) nor moral heroes or heroines. Instead they were somewhere in between; in following the doctrine of the mean they were for the most part good, but sometimes they lapsed a little, especially when the intellectual virtue of *phronesis* or practical wisdom failed them momentarily, or when a moral virtue such as friendliness was not practised sufficiently often. However, this occasional lapse in character, this 'mistake', 'missing the mark' or 'going wrong' (Anscombe, 1958, reprinted in Crisp and Slote, p. 30) took on a sinful air and a legal edge when the Judaeo–Christian and the Roman notions of law and guilt were added to it.

Human nature and/or human action?

Once the idea of a moral law was established, along with the later Enlightenment idea of a pure realm of secular reasoning being appealed to, the way was open to remove morals and ethics from their embeddedness in particular human individuals with particular characters to their universal existence as rational propositions. Plato and Aristotle talked of an unjust man as someone who, more or less, performed unjust actions, but the point was that the focus was primarily on the character or the soul of the person; it was only secondarily focused on the actions of that person. Who you are is, ultimately, more important than what you do, but, of course, people can only begin to know who you are by virtue of what you do. It is (almost, but not quite) a circular argument, in which the first definition (identity) is dependent upon the second definition (action), and thus fulfils the condition of the ancient dictum: 'know them by their deeds'. But the principal issue is that we are interested primarily in the human flourishing of the person, not what possible actions he or she may undertake. For example, in a marriage, the partners love each other for who they are, not simply the sum total of loving actions in which they each engage. Now, one partner may behave or act in all kinds of loving ways, but this is no real guarantee of actual love of, or concern for the other, despite the fact that it might, of course, be a fairly good indicator.

In modern moral philosophy, argued Anscombe, the idea of the unjust man – the person – has all but disappeared, and the concern for *who* he is has been completely substituted by a detached consideration of *what* he may do. Actions have replaced persons, behaviour has been separated from people, and doing is elevated above being. Instead of concentrating on the deeply problematic issues of human flourishing, moral personality, and the complex relationship between character, identity and conduct, there has been, among moral philosophers, a preoccupation with the tedious drafting of legalistic propositions to which one ought to assent, the abstract calculation of future goals to which one may or may not subscribe, or the pedantic clarification of moral terms, explanations or arguments which one often deploys, 'it can be seen that philosophically there is a huge gap ... which needs to be filled by an account of human nature, human action, the type of characteristic a virtue is, and above all of human "flourishing" ' (Anscombe, 1958; source: Crisp and Slote, pp. 43–4).

Philippa Foot's argument: Virtues as beneficial

The Oxford philosopher Philippa Foot has also been a tireless proponent of virtue ethics. In her *Virtues and Vices and Other Essays in Moral Philosophy* (Oxford, Blackwell, 1978) she examines the claim that virtues, those *aretai*, human excellences of mind and character, are in a very real way necessary for our future well-being or flourishing. In a slightly amended extract from her book (reprinted in Crisp and Slote) Foot argues that 'First ... virtues are, in some general way, beneficial' (p. 164). However, she readily concedes that this is too wide a claim to be of much philosophical use. Lots of things are beneficial to people: clean air, unpolluted water and healthy food for a start. So, what else might make something a virtue and another thing not? Foot then examines the possibility that a virtue is connected with human will which covers 'what is wished for as well as what is sought' (p. 166). However, as both Aristotle's and Aquinas's accounts of the virtues demonstrate, virtues are sometimes 'moral' (to do with character) and sometimes 'intellectual' (to do with mind and knowledge). In which camp does the will sit? Foot takes the example of the wise person and argues that there are (at least) two parts to wisdom, both of them involving the will.

Goods and their value

There are certain ends or goals which are good, and the wise person knows the relative value of each particular good. Moreover, such ends or goals are usually both intrinsically good, or good in themselves, and extrinsically good, or good for the sake of something else. The wise person directs her will to these goods, and not to others. So, for example, it is good to get to know my neighbour because I value his friendship for its own sake. It is pleasurable for us both to discuss politics and sport whilst walking the dog or enjoying a meal. It also happens to be good for the sake of something else; he is a director of a premier-league football club and can get me tickets for the World Cup. However, if I am a wise and virtuous person I will know that the former (intrinsic) good – my neighbour's friendship for its own sake – far outweighs the latter (extrinsic) good – my neighbour's ability to secure World Cup tickets for me.

The means to achieve such valued goods

There are certain good means to certain good ends; in other words, the wise person will know how best to achieve the goals she wishes to achieve. Again, if I am wise and virtuous, I would know and appreciate that there are particular and acceptable means of attaining certain goals, and unacceptable means of attaining the same goals. I direct my will towards these means and not to others. I could, for example, gain my neighbour's friendship through deceit and cunning simply in order to obtain some World Cup tickets. I could wine and dine him for a few months, take his children along with mine to a number of local football games, and generally make myself agreeable to him before expressing mock surprise and wonderment at his offer of scarce and important tickets. Indeed, my neighbour might never know that secretly I am not at all bothered about him as a person; I am simply interested in whatever it is he can do for me. However, this would mean that I would make two fundamental mistakes in the exercise of virtue. First, I would be substituting purely extrinsic goods, or external ends (the tickets) for the twinned combination of intrinsic and extrinsic goods, internal and external ends (the friendship itself and the tickets). Second, the means I would have to employ in order solely to gain the tickets would be empty of value, deceitful, emotionally fractured and Janus-faced. The Roman god Janus had two faces, the one looking in the opposite direction to the other. Whilst joking, smiling and conversing in a friendly fashion to my neighbour, I would simultaneously be congratulating myself on my duplicitous performance, and mentally ridiculing him for being 'gulled' so easily. The benefits here, derived from the means, would be very shallow indeed.

Virtues and skills

Part of Foot's argument is to do with wanting to distinguish virtues from arts and skills, neither of which may fully engage the will. Foot uses the example of the good speller who makes a calculated error and contrasts it with the just man who makes a deliberately unjust 'mistake'. The good speller may say that he deliberately made a mistake in order to make a point, and that this would in no way damage his reputation as a good speller. However, if a man, renowned for his just dealings, were to imprison someone quite unjustly and then say that he was doing it in order to make a point (however important that point might be), his reputation for justness would suffer irreparable harm. Good spelling is a skill; justice is a virtue.

Virtues as correctives

Second, 'virtues should be seen as correctives' (p. 171). This is akin to Aristotle's orginal thesis that training is the basic groundwork of virtue ethics, which is why the moral virtues need to be nurtured and developed through constant habit, and particularly in early years through enforced habit. Human beings are like warped pieces of wood which need careful and continuous straightening. The ship-wright knows that planks of wood left out in the open without any kind of restraining device will soon bend and warp and will eventually become useless – or no good. If, however, they are placed in some kind of restraining cramp in order to keep them straight and true, then eventually when weathered they will be most useful – or good. The old scriptural injunction 'Spare the rod and spoil the child' encapsulates a similar argument, although the idea of corporal punishment or physical beatings is now, thankfully, an outmoded piece of psychology. But the underlying theory is still the same: If you fail to correct the child early on in life and simply let him do what he wishes – to go unrestrained in anything – then he is more than likely to grow into an unpleasant and somewhat self-regarding individual.

One of the problems, however, is to do with what may be called the relativity of virtue given the context. Take the following examples partly derived from Foot:

a) The rich person who is compulsively avaricious but who, with difficulty, always manages to refrain from stealing

b) The rich person who is a hard-working and effective businessman who finds little or no difficulty in refraining from stealing

c) The poor person who because of what he sees as the injustice of vast material inequalities is sometimes driven to the point of stealing but never does so

d) The poor person who, irrespective of massive wealth differences, simply never considers stealing as an option.

Who is the most virtuous? Or are they, given the fact that none of them actually engages in theft, all equally virtuous? Aristotle claims that a truly virtuous person is one who thinks, feels and does the right thing on the right occasion. Therefore, on this count, B and D are more virtuous than A or C. However, A and C clearly demonstrate a greater level of personal courage and self-restraint on this issue than either B or D, and so on this count they may be said to be the more virtuous.

Essentialism and core virtues

Pence talks briefly of essentialism in virtue ethics. In referring to the work of Edmund Pincoffs (*Quandaries and Virtues*, 1986) Pence reflects on the possibility of isolating 'core virtues' (p. 255) which would be the irreducible list of basic virtues or qualities of mind and character that would contribute to the maintenance and flourishing of any human culture, irrespective of geography and climate, or political and social structure. Unfortunately, what those precise virtues are is never made explicit, but presumably they would not be far removed from the cardinal virtues of courage, justice, temperance and wisdom, orginally laid down by Plato, further enhanced by Aristotle and added to by later Christian philosophers. (These have been fully rehearsed in the chapters on Plato, Aristotle and MacIntyre.) In this sense, the list of core virtues would be considered essential for any meaningful group or society to be able to emerge and sustain itself. But this form of essentialism ignores cultural differences so that what might be conceived of as a core virtue in one culture may not be viewed as a virtue at all in another. As the early example in the analysis of MacIntyre showed, strength was clearly (and obviously) seen as a core virtue in ancient Homeric times when small hilltop, tribal communities regularly fought each other either for survival or for supremacy. Being able to draw on only a few warrior tribal members, the sheer physical strength of key individuals was prized above many other qualities. However, by the Athenian period, some five to seven hundred years later, abnormal body strength was not seen as particularly important, as the comparatively vast number of available fighting troops was sufficient to counterbalance any single show of individual brawn. In any case brain more than brawn began to count more significantly.

Sexual difference: Male and female virtues?

A more interesting and certainly more contemporary example of essentialism can be found in Slote's discussion of a feminist reappraisal of ethical reasoning. Slote, a clear defender of virtue ethics, briefly examines the feminist attack on standard (deontological, utilitarian, and meta-ethical) moral philosophy, focusing specifically on Carol Gilligan's *In a Different Voice* and Nell Noddings's *Caring: A Feminine Approach to Ethics and Education*. Although neither Gilligan nor Noddings claim to be advocates of virtue ethics, their theories, especially Gilligan's, rest upon certain essential qualities – or virtues – exhibited by moral agents. Their interest for Slote is their analyses of differing male or female ethical characteristics. Gilligan claims that moral philosophy has always been male-centred, largely because most moral theories have been written by men. And that 'men tend to conceive morality in terms of rights, justice and autonomy, whereas women more frequently think of the moral in terms of caring, responsibility and interrelation with others' (Slote on Gilligan, p. 256).

Consequently, men are more given to abstract theorising and the distillation of universal rules and principles, whereas women are more taken by individual cases where compassion and care for agents and victims are of prime importance. The result of this is what may be called a dual essentialism:

- male virtues: rights, justice, autonomy, individualism, principles, universals
- female virtues: care, compassion, interdependence, community, cases, particulars

Interestingly, Gilligan has, since writing *In a Different Voice*, denied that there is any fundamental link between being a woman and necessarily adopting a caring perspective (see Postscript to Anette Baier, *What do Women Want in a Moral Theory?* in Crisp and Slote, p. 227). What, therefore, began as (at least) a two-pronged argument (i) ethics is currently not about caring, but should be; and (ii) women are concerned with care, but men are not, is now reduced to a single-pronged argument – ethics should be more about caring. And indeed, no-one, presumably, would want to deny that it should.

Multi-aspect theories

Finally, it cannot have escaped most people that in the messy work-a-day world in which we live we do not, even as moral philosophers or critically thinking ethicists, rigidly subscribe to nor systematically apply a carefully considered and well-chosen moral theory, however accurate, correct or true we may believe that theory to be. We recognise the value of drawing up broad rules and principles which, generally speaking, can apply across a wide range of cases. Telling the truth and keeping our promises are largely good and justifiable commands. Equally, however, we acknowledge that there may well be many cases in which the utilitarian approach will justify us in overturning those very same rules. Moreover, we know that in judging moral issues, a person's character is as important as the act they have undertaken. In courts of law, judges weigh up a defendant's character testimonies given by defence witnesses before sentence is passed. A person of 'good character' who does something completely out of character is generally given a lenient sentence, whereas the person of dubious character who performs an act seemingly in keeping with his past bad habits is often given a much harsher sentence. An act of aggression committed by a persistant liar, drunkard and brawler is viewed with greater approbation than a similar act of aggression committed by a previously kind, considerate and temperate individual. Principles, acts and agents all tend to merge with each other in the busy world in which we live. Hence, Virginia Held, in *Rights and Goods: Justifying Social Action* (Chicago, University of Chicago Press, 1984), argues that we ought to be thinking more along the lines of meshing different theories when trying to understand and respond to specific issues. Complex moral dilemmas demand complex moral theories, and as no one single theory seems to fit the universal bill, as it were, then perhaps we ought to be a little more creative and imaginative in our moral reasoning. Every moral issue comprises innumerable aspects which need to be taken into account; a multi-aspect theory may, therefore, assist us in clarifying carefully and in detail what, arguably, we ought to do when faced with such an issue. In the second part of the book we examine some of these complex moral dilemmas.

Questions for discussion

1 Compare and contrast normative ethics with meta-ethics.
2 How is it possible to draw a distinction between 'being' and 'doing'?
3 What are 'virtues' and how might they be distinguished from 'skills'?
4 Does it make sense to talk of 'masculine' and 'feminine' virtues?
5 Give examples of ethical issues which might give rise to a 'multi-aspect' theory.
6 How, if at all, does modern virtue ethics differ from the virtue ethics of Plato and Aristotle?

TEN
Situation Ethics

Bishop John Robinson in *Honest to God* said that:

> There is no one ethical system that can claim to be Christian
> ('*Christian Morals Today*', p. 18).

Whilst this may be true, Christianity has traditionally been dominated by natural law thinking and Situation Ethics arose out of this
background. Bultmann claimed that Jesus had no ethic – by this he
meant that Jesus did not put forward any form of moral theory.
Situation ethics can be summed up in two quotations:

> There is only one ultimate and invariable duty, and its formula
> is 'Thou shalt love thy neighbour as thyself'. How to do this
> is another question, but this is the whole of moral duty (William
> Temple).

> The law of love is the ultimate law because it is the negation of
> law; it is absolute because it concerns everything concrete ... The
> absolutism of love is its power to go into concrete situations ...
> (Paul Tillich).

Joseph Fletcher, an Anglican theologian, developed the situation
ethics approach and his book by that name was the classic treatment
and was published in 1966 (by SCM Press). However, he did not
pioneer the basic ideas of situation ethics, which had a longer
history. This chapter draws heavily on Fletcher's book.

At the beginning Fletcher tells the following story: A friend of his arrived at St Louis in the USA just as a presidential campaign was ending. The cab driver who drove him was clearly involved in the battle and said: *'I and my father and grandfather before him, and their fathers, have always been straight-ticket Republicans.'* *'Ah,'* said Fletcher's friend, *'I take it that you will vote Republican as well?'* *'No,'* said the driver, *'there are times when a man has to push his principles aside and do the right thing.'* This cabbie, Fletcher claims, is the hero of his book.

Fletcher claims that there are only three possible approaches to ethics:

1 The legalistic – i.e. ethics based on unalterable laws,
2 The antinomian – the lawless or unprincipled approach, and
3 The situational approach.

Take an example. According to Catholic moral theology, abortion is immoral and can never be permitted. *However* the principle of double effect means that a surgical procedure may be acceptable even if the indirect result is the death of the foetus. For instance, if a pregnant woman has cancer of the uterus and where the cancer is spreading then it is permissible for a surgeon to remove the uterus even if, as a by-product, the foetus has to die. In this case abortion is *not* the primary intention, but as it is an inevitable by-product of the primary objective it is permissible.

This principle becomes more difficult when different situations develop. If a pregnancy occurs in the Fallopian tube the woman will die, so Catholic moral theology allows the removal of a Fallopian tube even if the by-product is the death of the foetus. Medical technology today makes it possible to remove the foetus without damaging the Fallopian tube. This is attractive as it does not damage the child-bearing ability of the mother. However the doctor *cannot* remove the foetus as this then becomes the primary objective so, morally, the doctor would have no choice but to take the more severe surgical choice – remove the whole tube. It is at points such as this that the basic natural law approach begins to seem questionable.

The problem with this principle if it is applied in a straightforward sense is that almost any evil effect can be allowed provided the main purpose of an action is held to be good. On the basis of the principle, it might be argued to be acceptable to kill a hundred thousand Iraqi women and children in order to avoid the deaths of one hundred Americans. Who is to decide what the good is that will justify the 'indirect' evil?

A central issue is whether God has laid down firm and unalterable rules or whether human beings need to make their own moral decisions. If the latter position is taken then this seems to leave moral decision-making firmly in the situation ethics camp with the natural law approach undermined. It appears that everything is now relative and dependent on the circumstances that the individual has to face. On this basis, it is the *consequences* of an action which will determine which action is right or wrong – this comes very close to the situation ethics approach which denies any absolutes.

The four working principles

Situation ethics rests on six fundamental propositions and four working principles. Fletcher sets out the working principles as follows:

i) **Pragmatism**
To be right, it is necessary that a proposed course of action should work. This seems reasonable, but, of course, it immediately forces us on to the next question – what is the aim towards which it must work? Fletcher claims that the norm or end by which the success or failure of any thought or action is to be judged is *love*.

ii) **Relativism**
Supporters of situation ethics reject the use of words like 'never', 'always' and 'absolute' as they believe that circumstances can always throw up exceptions. Relativism does *not*, Fletcher insists, imply that anything goes – to be relative, one has to be relative to something and

situation ethics maintains that it should be relative to love. As Fletcher puts it, it *'relativises the absolute, it does not absolutise the relative!'* Human beings are commanded to act lovingly, but how this is to be applied will depend on the situation.

Jesus attacked the Pharisees' insistence on following the Torah or Jewish Law — Christians cannot and should not lay down any law. When they do, they become once more like the Pharisees.

iii) **Positivism**

There are, Fletcher claims, only two ways of understanding religious knowledge or belief:

a) Theological Naturalism — in which *reason* leads to faith or the propositions of faith from human experience. Natural theology is the best example of this giving rise to the claim that God's existence can be proved.

b) Theological Positivism — in which faith is accepted on a voluntary basis. Reasoning takes place within faith rather than as a basis for faith — this was St Augustine's approach.

In Christian thought, the supremacy of Christian love is established by the decision to say 'Yes' to the faith claim that 'God is love'. Faith comes first. Situation ethics depends on a free decision by individuals to give first place to Christian love — this, therefore, rests on a fundamental value judgement which cannot be rationally proved. If someone says 'Why should I love?' then there is no answer to this question. A person has to see for themselves that this is the most important thing of all.

iv) **Personalism**

Situation ethics puts people in first place. The supporter of the natural law approach asks what the law says, the situationist asks what is the best decision to help human beings. The Christian is committed to love people, not abstract principles or laws. Because God is held to be personal, so morality should be person-centred as well.

Fletcher claims that it is not the unbelieving who invite damnation but those who do not love, who do not make themselves into people who can love. This necessarily results in action on behalf of persons.

Conscience

Situation ethics claims that there is no such thing as conscience which should guide human action – at least if conscience stands for intuition or God in some ways speaking to human beings. Conscience is simply the term used for attempts to make decisions appropriately according to the particular situation. Fletcher considers that Aquinas' definition of conscience comes closest to the truth 'reason making moral judgements' – but it is in no sense a separate faculty.

The six fundamental principles

1 Situation ethics holds that nothing is good in and of itself except for love. Actions are good if they help human beings and they are bad if they hurt people – there is no other criterion.

What is right in one case may be wrong for another – for instance stealing a pistol from a man who intends to use it to murder his wife may be right. No act is 'right in itself' – it all depends on the circumstances in which the act is done. Love decides which actions are good and which are bad.

St Augustine says that in order to know whether a man is a good man, *'one does not ask what he believes or what he hopes, but what he loves'* (Quoted in *Situation Ethics*, p. 63).

Natural law holds that suicide and lying are *always* wrong regardless of circumstance, even though loving concern may be the motive. Faced with the problem that the law may condemn something done from love, a wide range of theories has been produced to make sense of the position – these can be avoided by simply saying that no actions are intrinsically wrong in themselves.

2 Jesus and St Paul replaced the Torah, the strict Jewish Law, with the principle of love. Even the Ten Commandments are not absolute – Bonhoeffer in his *Ethics* considered the command against killing to be absolute and he uses this to reject euthanasia, yet Bonhoeffer himself was executed for trying to kill, or murder Adolf Hitler. Supporters of situation ethics would maintain that this may well have been right.

Christian love is not based on desire – it is self-giving love or *agape*. Agape does not depend on being loved in return. The command of love calls individuals to a high level of personal responsibility. Natural law denies the demands of love, but natural law has the great advantage that people can be told what to do – it brings us back to the Christianity of the Grand Inquisitor (in Dostoevsky's *The Brothers Karamazov* – see the discussion on this in *The Puzzle of Evil*, HarperCollins 1992, by Peter Vardy). The Inquisitor says that Christ must not come back again with his offer of freedom and individual responsibility – the Church has now subdued people under a new set of rules and will not allow Jesus to free them again. Situation ethics aims to widen freedom and responsibility because it believes human beings can cope with this.

Albert Schweitzer was, Fletcher claimed, right to say that 'the good conscience was an invention of the Devil' – this is because people think they can have a good conscience just by refraining from doing things, whereas love makes it a positive duty to go out to people in need.

3 Love and justice, Fletcher claims, are the same, for justice is love at work in the community in which human beings live. Justice is – or should be – working out the most loving thing to do taking the interests of all those in the community into account.

4 Love wills the good for the neighbour, whether individuals like others or not. Søren Kierkegaard talked of the need for Christian love to be non-preferential – in other words love cannot be selective or have favourites. Christian love is a matter of attitude not feeling – Christian love is not erotic. Christian *agape*, real Christian love, desires the good of the other, not one's own good. Bultmann said:

In reality, the love which is based on emotions of sympathy or affection, is self-love; for it is a love of preference, of choice, and the standard of preference or choice is the self (*Jesus and the Word*, p. 117).

Christian love is above all *practical*. Jesus makes clear that our neighbour is anybody when he says 'Love your enemies ... for if you love those who love you, what reward have you?' – Christians even have to – or at least are meant to! – love their enemies.

An *agapeistic love* says 'I will give, requiring nothing in return' and Fletcher contrasts this with *a mutualistic ethic* which says 'I will give as long as I receive' which is the common form of love in friendship, but it carries the consequence that it is a love that depends on the actions of the person loved, it is not unconditional.

5 Only the end justifies the means, nothing else. Love can and does justify anything but love really must be the end that is sought, it is never a means to something else. Fletcher here seems to be close to a form of utilitarianism but he substitutes 'love' for 'happiness' and all the difficulties of utilitarianism may arise.

6 Love's decisions are made in the circumstances of each situation. Dostoevsky's Grand Inquisitor wanted to do away with freedom and to impose law because he recognised that people cannot cope with freedom – freedom is too heavy a price to pay as people who are genuinely free cannot be controlled. Yet he also recognised that freedom was what Jesus came to bring. Situation ethics depends on the claim that the Inquisitor was wrong and that individuals can cope with freedom.

Moral laws are continuously supported in theory and ignored in practice – this is not because people are fundamentally evil but because the laws fail to take account of the situation. Nowhere is this more the case than in the sexual field where Churches tend to lay down blanket rules and prohibitions which tend to be based on natural law thinking. Fletcher says:

Jesus said nothing about birth control, large or small families, childlessness, homosexuality, masturbation, fornication, premarital intercourse, sterilisation, artificial insemination, abortion, sex foreplay, petting and courtship. Whether any form of sex (hetero, homo or auto) is good or evil depends on whether love is fully served (*Sitatuon Ethics*, p. 139).

Some theologians claim that people do not want to grapple with moral ambiguities, instead they want certainties. Situationists would say 'Of course, they want the Grand Inquisitor – they cannot handle Jesus' gift of freedom'.

Fletcher claims that it is a mistake to generalise. You can't say 'Is it ever right to lie to your family?' The answer must be 'I don't know, give me an example.' A concrete situation is needed, not a generalisation. '*It all depends*' may well be the watchword of the situationist.

Is a girl right to have sex with a man for money? The situationist will say 'It all depends'. If the money is to be used to buy a new dress the situation is different from if the money is to be used to stop the woman's family from dying of starvation.

Christian love is a *responsible love* – yet responsibility can be frightening. The individual has to judge carefully the particular situation in which he or she finds him- or herself and then make the decision as to what is the most loving thing to do taking all factors into account and not simply accepting convention. This is not at all easy.

Situation ethics was condemned by Pope Pius XII in 1952 (14 years before Fletcher's book was written) as

an individualistic and subjective appeal to the concrete circumstances of actions to justify decisions in opposition to the natural law or God's revealed will.

Pius XII was right that situation ethics is opposed to natural law, but this only invalidates situation ethics if natural law is first accepted as correct. As for the Pope's reference to 'God's revealed will', supporters of situation ethics would say that God revealed his will most fully in Jesus Christ and it was he who insisted on the primacy of love.

Situation ethics is very individualistic and it is far from easy in some situations to decide what 'love' requires. If there are *no* rules this can make murder of an unwanted granny 'loving' in the relative's eyes. Specific criticisms of this position include:

1 It is not easy to determine the consequences of actions and this the situationist needs to do. As an example, it may seem 'loving' to a parent to advocate that a daughter who has 'carelessly' got pregnant should have an abortion without being able to judge whether the long-term heartache this might cause makes it the 'right' or 'loving' course in the long run.
2 Humans tend to look at situations from their own points of view and there is a real danger of selfishness creeping in under the banner of 'love'.
3 Actions are not necessarily as dissimilar as Fletcher seems to suggest. Theft, adultery, lying, stealing, etc. do not necessarily become good just because they are done from a loving motive.
4 Situation ethics can lead to crossing boundary lines that are dangerous to cross – for instances once one accepts that euthanasia can be justified in certain circumstances, one may have entered dangerous and uncharted waters.

Situation ethics also tends to bring together two positions which need to be kept distinct – i.e. that which is *morally good* may not be what is *morally right*. The moral goodness of an action may depend on its motive or intention – a person may be considered to have done an act which is morally good because he or she did it in good conscience and taking account of all the known circumstances and yet, objectively, this may have been a wrong action (for instance stealing or lying to save a life). Situation ethics refuses to make this distinction and instead considers what is morally good is also what is morally right – this has obvious dangers.

However, situation ethics can provide a corrective to taking the natural law approach too literally. Perhaps what is needed is a middle way – this some Catholic theologians are seeking under the heading of *proportionalism* (see chapter 4). Proportionalism holds that there are certain moral rules and it can never be right to go against these unless there is a proportionate reason which would justify it. The proportionate reason would be grounded in the particular situation, but the situation must generate a reason which is sufficiently strong to overturn what would otherwise be a firm rule. On this basis, moral laws derived from the natural law or similar approach may be firm guidelines which should never be ignored unless it is absolutely clear that, in the particular situation, this is justified by a proportionate reason. This approach may well bring together supporters of natural law and situation ethics in the future and there is certainly fertile ground for development in this area.

Questions for discussion

1 Is it right that actions should be judged by their consequences?
2 What does it mean for an action to be loving? How might love be defined?
3 What are the principal dangers of situation ethics and do they outweigh the possible advantages?
4 How might a supporter of situation ethics decide whether capital punishment was right or wrong?
5 What does it mean to talk of conscience?
6 If a woman could save the life of someone she loved by going to bed with a fat, old man in a powerful position and if no other option was available, would it be right for her to do this and why?
7 What is proportionalism and what are its advantages?

ELEVEN

Justice and Morality –
Rawls and Nozick

The nature of justice (Latin: 'right' or 'law') has been the concern of philosophers since Plato first wrote *The Republic*. The principal concerns of philosophers have been twofold: firstly, how to define justice, and secondly, how to devise a system so that justice is able both to operate and be seen to operate in the community. There are a number of ways of classifying theories, one of the most common being to divide them into those theories that emphasise the primary importance of the individual, and those theories that stress the primary importance of the community. Theories of individualism are based on the assumption that the good of the individual comes first, and the good of the community, second; whilst communitarian theories are based on the assumption that the good of the community must come before the good of any single individual within it. Clearly, common sense points to a compromise position, neither purely individualist philosophies can survive nor can purely communitarian philosophies. That is not in dispute. It is not a question of 'either/or': either individualist or communitarian theories and practices, but more a question of 'both/and', and how much of each? For Aristotle, it is the intellectual virtue of prudence, or practical wisdom, the balancing of one's own interest with the interests of others, that provides us with the capacity to balance the rights of the individual with the responsibilities towards the community. What is in dispute is the *extent* to which the needs and desires of the individual should override those of the community, or vice versa.

Individualist theories

At root an individualist theory assumes that society is merely a collection of individuals living their lives separately and purposefully from each other, and only really coming into contact with each other whenever a bargain has to be struck. It may be an emotional bargain such as: If I love you, will you love me, and therefore, if I ask to marry you will you accept? (Indeed, in the USA 'marriage contracts' are becoming increasingly popular, in which material goods jointly owned are already divided up in the contract should divorce or separation occur in the future.) Or it may be an economic bargain: If I give you two thousand pounds will you sell me your second-hand car? Or it may be a political bargain: If you vote for me I will ensure that you pay less in income tax and that more policemen will be deployed on the streets. And so on. In a famous speech by a former British Prime Minister, Margaret (now Lady) Thatcher, it was maintained that 'There is no such thing as society. Instead there are individual men and women and families.'

Arguably, a full-blown individualist philosophy of justice began with Thomas Hobbes (1588–1679) in his principal work, *The Leviathan, or the Matter, Form and Power of a Commonwealth, Ecclesiastical and Civil* (1651). For Hobbes there are two basic conditions which characterise man in his natural state:

i) continual fear; and (thus) the life of man is solitary, poor, nasty, brutish and short; and
ii) contention, enmity and war.

Moreover, for Hobbes, we are all competitive beings who desire to get one over on our neighbour. To hit the winning tape first is the primary impulse in humankind, and to think any differently is to subscribe to the 'absurd ..., repugnant ... and ignorant' writings of Aristotle (*Leviathan*, ch. 46, p. 669). Given this particularly glum picture of humanity, what can be done to secure at least a tolerable existence? The answer is the 'social contract', a set of laws designed to ensure maximum freedom combined with personal security. Effectively, the contract is based on a minimalist theory of rights in which the individual is understood to be morally bound only by the 'Don't harm me, and I won't harm you' doctrine.

This individualist theory received its major articulation in John Locke's *Second Treatise on Civil Government* (1689). Leaving aside the many obvious differences between the two thinkers, it may be said that in both their works primacy rests with the individual rather than with the community. Locke's account rests on two principles: the right to self-preservation for the individual, and the right to property bought, held or acquired by the individual. The underlying moral obligation is a simple one: we each have a moral right not to harm another. But that, effectively, is the extent of our moral obligation to others, as determined by Nature. The modern version of Locke's theory is to be found in Robert Nozick's famous text, *Anarchy, State and Utopia* (1974). Singer (1993, pp. 226-7) makes the same point in a chapter devoted to examining the moral relationship between the First and the Third World.

Communitarian theories

On the other hand, the communitarian theory assumes that society is rather more than merely the sum of its parts. Moreover, it takes as its starting point the view that being an individual is only made possible if society recognises the concept of individuality in the first place. The tradition of communitarian thinking is rather longer than the individualist tradition and arguably began with Plato's *Republic* and *Laws* where the good of the whole of the city-state is placed above the good of any single individual. It is continued in Aristotle's *Ethics* and *Politics*. The theories of Marx (1818-83), Hutcheson (1694-1746), Rousseau (1712-78) and others all could be counted as communitarian in principle. The underlying argument finds its recent expression in Alasdair MacIntyre's *After Virtue* (1981), but it may be said to find its most complete and detailed articulation in John Rawls' *A Theory of Justice* (1971). Aside from obviously resting on the first moral obligation that lies at the heart of the individualist theory, that is, we are under a moral obligation not to harm another, it also rests on a rather loosely formulated second moral obligation: to assist those who are worst off in society. Or put another way, we are all under an equal moral obligation to assist those who are worse off than ourselves. (Interestingly, Singer (1993) extends this thesis by arguing that those of us who live in the affluent First World may be accused of the moral equivalent of murder, as our luxurious but exploitative lifestyles are contributing to the death of millions in the Third World.) Rawls' theory is also referred to as a liberal theory in that despite the moral obligations set by these two principles, the maximum amount of freedom should rightly be accorded to the individual.

1 Justice as entitlement: Robert Nozick

Patterned and unpatterned theories

According to Nozick in *Anarchy, State and Utopia* (1974) there are two sorts of theories to do with social justice: firstly, 'patterned' theories such as Marxism, utilitarianism, egalitarianism and so on. They are patterned in the sense that they impose a particular pattern or order upon social reality which for Nozick has no formal pattern as such. Patterned theories, it is argued, close off the normal, practical and pragmatic way that people engage with others, live their lives and shape their futures. They just don't work in reality. Patterned theories suffer from the age-old criticism: Fine in theory, but what about the practice? Experience counts for more than formal learning. Countries run along strict Marxist lines, so the argument goes, will inevitably collapse sooner or later because a semi-utopian order placed upon communities does not take proper account of human nature. Human nature isn't ordered and neatly patterned, why should we expect societies to be so?

On the other hand, there are 'unpatterned' theories, of which Nozick's is claimed to be one of the best. All I am doing, argues Nozick, is just taking full account of reality as we find it, and trying to explain the concept of 'justice' in those terms. I am imposing no set pattern or order on society or communities, merely reporting what I see and trying to make sense of it in a theoretical way. As a consequence, the theory is quite persuasive, inasmuch as it claims to be descriptive and not prescriptive.

Entitlement

Nozick defines justice in terms of 'entitlement'. I am entitled to what I have, or to what I earn, or to what I acquire, as long as I do it legally, or in the way in which my society or community defines as legal. Moreover, you are equally entitled to what you have, earn or acquire, so long as you do so legally. And there is the end of the matter. It is clearly a theory which emphasises the importance of property or material goods. All goods — material (food, dwellings, transport, etc), and cultural (ideas, entertainment, etc.) — are, in Nozick's terms 'holdings'. Now, according to Nozick there are three main principles at work in a just society, and these principles apply to the just distribution of all 'holdings'.

- First principle: Just acquisition (the legal procurement or purchase of goods or holdings)
- Second principle: Just transfer (the legal selling or transferring of goods or holdings)
- Third principle: Rectification (the resort to law if the acquisition or transfer of goods or holdings has been illegal).

If all of the principles are adhered to then everyone is legally entitled to what they have got. We may not like the fact that a person can make millions of pounds or dollars by being a cigarette manufacturer, a good-looking but rather wooden television actress, an international weapons dealer, or even by being an image-hungry politician, but as long as the money or goods or holdings are acquired and transferred legally, then the society is a just one. This is what constitutes justice. We have no moral obligation to anyone except ourselves, and provided we live by the rules of society then we are morally safe.

As we can see, Nozick's theory is a clear example of the individualist position. In law we are all under a clear injunction not to harm another. This is a minimum position, but it is a moral position, and it is all that is required of us. We are under no moral obligation to assist anyone else, although it may be rather nice if we did so now and again.

2 Justice as fairness: John Rawls

The original position

John Rawls' theory is rather more complex. In *A Theory of Justice* (1971) he argues from what he refers to as the 'original position'. Let us assume, for the sake of argument, that people are on a desert island and they know that they will never be rescued. There are both men and women, and so they know that they will have to build a society for themselves and their children and future grandchildren. In fact, they know they will be responsible for laying the foundations of a vast community which will grow and develop. They agree to lay down certain principles which will be fair and just not only for themselves but for future generations. They will have to construct what in philosophy has come to be known as a 'social contract'. This is a contract binding on everyone both present and future which acts as a kind of moral, political, legal and economic template for all decisions which will affect society.

What would we have to assume about the people on our desert island? Well, for Rawls, we assume that people are:

i) self-interested. Egoism and self-preservation are natural conditions
ii) equal to one another in their ability and freedom to make suggestions on how society should be constructed. In a natural and original state it will be assumed that no one will have prior claim to power over anyone else.

iii) rational. Each person has the capacity to think through in a reasoned fashion the social contract that they are about to construct.

iv) all have access to general facts about human nature and affairs. Most importantly,

v) all are ignorant about their own particular futures in the society they are about to agree upon and build.

This last condition, known as the 'veil of ignorance' is crucial. If no one is able to have prior knowledge about his or her future position or status in the society, then benevolence or compassion is ensured. For no one (being self-interested) would wish to help build a society that may leave them helplessly abandoned or so disadvantaged that there would be no way of securing future hope, advancement or self-fulfilment. As Rawls says:

> The combination of mutual disinterest and the veil of ignorance achieves the same purpose as benevolence (*Theory of Justice*, p. 148).

Principles of liberty and difference

Assuming these things about the people in our original position, a social contract is agreed which is built upon two principles:

- *principle of liberty* (people must be allowed the freedom to pursue the kind of life they would wish to lead provided it does not directly or indirectly harm another)
- *principle of difference* (it is assumed that people are different, and will have different aims or goals in life. Therefore, the social contract must be sufficiently flexible to allow differences to manifest themselves).

Given these two principles it is clear that some form of inequality will ensue. In this, the theory is similar to Nozick's. However one wishes to organise society there will always be some form of material or cultural or physical inequality, marginal though it may be. It was once suggested by a famous economist that if we all agreed on the equal distribution of goods today, by tomorrow we would all be back in the same position of inequality. For example, suppose that everyone at 1.00 p.m. on Wednesday would each receive from the combined total of a country's resources exactly the same by an agreed process of redistribution, then by 1.00 p.m. on Thursday there would probably be the same degree of inequality as now prevails. In the 24 hours some will have saved what they have, others will have gambled it away, others will have spent the bulk of it, others will have put it on the stock market immediately and trebled it, and so on.

Maximin rule of game theory

So, given that inequality is an inevitability, we must choose the distribution pattern that most favours the least well off. This is known as the 'maximin rule of game theory': select the strategy in which the worst outcome is none the less better than the worst outcomes of all other possible strategies. Take a simple game such as snakes and ladders. We ought to devise the rules so that irrespective of who finally wins the game, everyone else has been able both to participate fully and has been given an equal opportunity to win. So, for example, it is better to say that everyone begins on their first throw of the dice, rather than only those who throw a six can start. So irrespective of who gets the six, who gets the five, who gets the three and so on, everyone gets involved in the game at the outset. For the worst outcome of this strategy is that the poor person who, by chance, never throws the six, also never gets the opportunity to participate in the game at all. However, if just throwing the dice ensures getting a game, then even if the person comes last in the game (the worst outcome), at least they have had the opportunity to participate fully in it.

Suppose we translate the snakes and ladders game into real life. If the 'throw a six to start' rule was part of the game it would be equivalent to, say, the large inheritance of wealth which allows the beneficiary to get an early start in the all-important 'game of life'.

The element of choice and meaningful participation is automatically given to the early starter. It seems fairly obvious that the child of wealthy and titled, land-owning parents has before her a greater set of human possibilities to realise her potential than does the child of an unemployed single black parent living in a run-down part of an inner city. The latter might never get to throw a six and start the game, whereas the former has had the six already thrown for her.

The social wage

The purpose of the Rawls 'maximin' game strategy used in politics and economics is to give all people the opportunity to play on a relatively 'equal playing field'. The recent social commentator, Bill Jordan (*The Common Good*, 1989) has advocated a basic wage or a social wage available to everyone as a right. This is not a new idea, of course, and can be found, for example, in Bertrand Russell's visionary essay entitled 'The World As It Could Be Made' (in *Roads to Freedom*, 1918). For Jordan this social wage would be sufficient for a person to maintain a decent standard of living. Anything earned above and beyond it would then be subject to a progressive income tax. That is, the more you earn as an individual, the more you assist the community in helping those who are unable to earn much or, indeed, anything at all. According to Jordan this would afford everyone the opportunity of feeling and being part of a wider community. It would then give them an incentive to participate lawfully in a society which they see themselves as having a direct stake in. Rather than excluding the unemployed, and the 'travellers' from mainstream society, it would be a way of including them in a morally dignified manner.

We can see then that there is an in-built concern for those worse off than oneself, and that there is an in-built moral obligation to consider carefully the plight of those who will inevitably come off worse in the serious game of life. Indeed, under the veil of ignorance it may be us who, in the future, become worse off. At root it is a simple matter of 'There but for the grace of God, go I'.

We are therefore under a moral obligation, it is argued, not only not to harm another, but also to assist those who are worse off than ourselves. Or at least, if we do not assist those who are worse off than ourselves, then the onus is upon us to come up with a good argument or justification why we should not do so.

Questions for discussion

1 Suppose you are stranded on a desert island with a small group of survivors from a shipwreck. What principles would you establish, and what kinds of rules and regulations for communal living would you draw up?
2 Is it possible always to balance the interests of self with the interests of others?
3 Is it morally justifiable simply to obey the laws governing present society and do nothing else, as Nozick's theory seems to suggest?
4 Are people naturally competitive or naturally co-operative? Alternatively, are people governed by both impulses in equal measures?
5 Is it morally less reprehensible to steal from a bank or a large corporation than from an individual or family home?
6 Argue the case both for and against establishing a minimum 'social wage'.

PART 2

APPLIED ETHICS

TWELVE

Abortion and Personhood

Imagine that your father or mother or someone else whom you loved was seriously ill with Parkinson's disease and you were able to take an unwanted female egg, fertilise it, grow it in an incubator for four weeks and then use the foetal tissue to cure him or at least relieve his symptoms. Would you do so? This and many related issues will be affected by your attitude to the abortion debate. There are also many issues in medical ethics which will be affected by your definition of what it is to be a person and whether or not it is right and proper to carry out medical research on fertilised or unfertilised human eggs.

The abortion issue generates strong feelings yet all too often people have not probed the philosophic assumptions lying behind the debate. There are two central issues:

1 Whether the foetus is a person or potential person, and
2 Whether the foetus has rights and, if so, how these are to be balanced against the rights of the mother.

i) Stages in development

Some initial definitions may be helpful:

Conception to 14 days	–	Pre-embryo
14 days to 8 weeks	–	Embryo
8 weeks onwards	–	Foetus

This is important, as often the language of the abortion debate gets heated and the issues are obscured by the language. Take the following syllogism:

MAJOR PREMISE	–	Killing people is wrong
MINOR PREMISE	–	A baby is a person
CONCLUSION	–	Killing babies is wrong so abortion is wrong.

This seems very simple. However, the first premise can be questioned – sometimes killing people may be right, for instance in a just war or in self-defence. The second premise may also be questioned – the very use of the word 'baby' anticipates the argument. The crucial issue is *whether* a pre-embryo, an embryo or a foetus is a baby or not. This sort of approach is far too superficial – more detailed analysis is required.

ii) Person or human being

A distinction may have to be drawn between a person and a human being. Are all human beings persons? Some moral theologians would question this – for instance a baby born without a brain may be human because it is made up of human tissue but it would not be regarded as a person. It might also be argued that on some definitions dolphins or whales with a relatively high level of intelligence should be regarded as persons worthy of respect in the same way as human persons – after all few would deny that if extraterrestrial beings visited our planet they should be treated as persons even though they might not be human. To reject such claims might render one vulnerable to the claim of being 'speciesist'. How, then, might we define what a person is?

Jack Mahoney in his book *Bioethics and Belief* points to characteristics such as rationality, ability to make free choices, continuity, being an autonomous centre of sensations, experiences, emotions, volitions and actions as being amongst the criteria for personhood.

Michael Tooley in an article 'Abortion and Infanticide' comes to the conclusion that if a being lacks consciousness of self and has no self-conscious feelings about its own future existence it is not a person at all. The problem is that such factors do not apply to babies immediately after birth and yet many people would want to affirm that full-term babies are clearly persons. Some other way of approaching the problem is needed. The following are some of the criteria that have been suggested for personhood:

a) Relational factors
The relational aspect of personhood means that a human being only becomes a person when accepted as such by others. Personhood, therefore, can be a matter of social convention – by a family giving a baby a name they make it into a person with a recognised autonomy of its own. This, however, seems a very loose criterion – some people do not name their babies until well after birth and there seems clear evidence that a woman who has seen the foetus in a well-formed state and has listened to its heartbeat may consider it a person well before a woman who has not had these experiences. Also there is no absolute claim being made here and much will depend on the mother or father's outlook – a determined effort not to regard a foetus as a person would easily be possible.

Relational factors may indeed be important in later life, but in the first twenty weeks of a foetus' life they do not seem very helpful.

b) Biological development and viability
Many attempts have been made to draw a dividing line at a particular point in the foetus' development and to say that before this point the foetus is only a bundle of tissue with potential and after this point it is a person. The problem is that there is no easy way of drawing the line. One could, of course, say that until the main organs are formed the foetus is not a person – but which organs are essential and at what stage of development? Some people say that the crucial stage is when there is movement (often about sixteen weeks) and they may be related to the mother's recognition of the foetus' independent

147

existence for the first time, but again the experiences of mothers differ widely. Others may hold that before the cells in the fertilised egg become differentiated any talk of personhood is inappropriate – but this leaves open the question of what degree of differentiation is necessary for the award of personhood status.

Mary Anne Warren in the chapter 'Abortion' in Peter Singer's *A Companion to Ethics* (Blackwell) argues that 'birth, rather than some earlier point, marks the beginning of true moral status' (p. 313). Warren rejects the idea that a foetus is a potential person as 'If a foetus is a potential person, then so is an unfertilised human ovum with enough viable spermatozoa to achieve fertilisation; yet few would seriously suggest that *these* living human entities should have full and equal moral status' (p. 311). However, Warren's argument that birth is the crucial point is vulnerable – a foetus of 34 weeks is quite clearly viable and if aborted is likely to live outside the womb and may actually have to be killed or left to die. On Warren's criterion abortion up to the time of natural birth could be argued to be permissible and this seems questionable – surely a foetus that is capable of surviving outside the womb is entitled to moral rights? Once this is admitted, the problem of drawing a line to determine at which point moral rights are to be conferred again raises its head.

Another possibility is that a foetus is viable when it can exist independently of the mother – but what does this mean? It is now possible to keep a 21-week foetus alive in some of the best teaching hospitals but only in an incubator and with intensive care. Does this make such a foetus 'viable'? Even a full-term baby is only 'viable' if given considerable care. There is evidence that within five years or so it may be possible to grow a foetus entirely independently of the mother's body – on this basis the 'viability' line becomes even more obscure.

John Gallagher in 'Is the human embryo a person?' asks us to recognise that change is gradual. If at a certain time the embryo is X and at another time it is James, then in between there is a time when it is partly X and partly James. At different points there may be more X and less James and there is no single point when we can say '*Now we have James*'. Drawing lines, therefore, is not really practical.

Perhaps none of these traditional approaches will do and it may be that there is one key issue in this whole debate and it is often neglected:

iii) Ensoulment

Many people are dualists – in other words they consider that a human person is made up of a body and a soul/mind which is separate. Plato was a dualist and he believed that a soul survived death and, indeed, the soul existed before the human person was born. Descartes was another dualist who considered that the soul and body interacted – through the pineal gland at the back of the head. This has had a profound effect on many religious thinkers – sometimes leading to a negative view of the human body and the view that humans should subjugate their material bodies and develop their minds which represented the 'higher self'. The negative views on sexuality and bodiliness in general that such an approach engenders are obvious.

If you are a dualist, then a human person consists of a soul and body. The crucial issue, then, is when the soul becomes implanted. Some religious believers maintain that the soul is implanted by God. Augustine maintained that the soul was implanted at 46 days although he condemned the killing of both formed and unformed foetuses, whilst Thomas Aquinas maintained that souls of girls were implanted at 90 days and souls of boys at 40 days. This, of course, led to the idea that abortion was not a problem provided it was carried out before the soul was implanted. Indeed Aquinas maintained that if you hit a pregnant woman and she aborted then you had not committed murder if the foetus was earlier than 90 or 40 days. Aquinas maintained that in the early stages there was only a vegetative soul, then subsequently an animal soul and finally the foetus was only a human person when a human soul became implanted. At each stage the previous form, animal and vegetative, is discarded and a more perfect one introduced until the conceptus possesses a human form.

In the 17th century, however, the Catholic Church affirmed that ensoulment took place from the moment of conception. This is highly significant. If a soul is introduced the moment fertilisation takes place, then clearly the fertilised egg is a human person – at least in embryo. This had led to a very strong Catholic attitude against abortion and against embryo research as in both cases such measures are held to involve killing persons. Catholic teaching gradually developed between the 17th and 19th century to the point where all abortions were prohibited except where they were a side effect of some other procedure – for instance the removal of a cancerous womb or, as we saw in the chapter on situation ethics, a pregnancy in the Fallopian tube. Here the main purpose is not the abortion, rather it is a by-product of the main purpose. The argument that the cancerous uterus should be removed rests on the principle of double effect. This holds that some actions are so evil that they could only be permitted if some other aim was sought. In the case of removal of a cancerous womb, the key factors were held to be:

1 The action itself was seen as good (removal of the cancerous uterus)
2 The intention is upright (removing the womb to save the mother's life)
3 The killing of the foetus is a true by-product as the womb would be removed whether or not there was a foetus present.

This is an attractive and important idea but the principle of double effect does not really permit abortion – rather it permits actions where the by-product of the action may be an abortion if the action in itself is absolutely necessary (this last phrase has led some Catholic theologians to deny that it is right to remove a cancerous uterus if there is a foetus present unless the mother's life is in immediate danger. We have here a form of proportionalism being introduced – although this is not always recognised). The central problem remains as to whether the firm Catholic stance against abortion can be upheld, and here the issue of ensoulment is vital.

There are many problems with the idea that a soul is implanted at conception, not least that a fertilised egg or zygote may split into two and then these two come together again. If this happens and there is a single soul, has each part of the split cell a separate soul and, if so, then what happens when the two halves come together again?

Not all Christians agree with the idea that the soul is a separate something implanted at conception. Christianity has traditionally affirmed the resurrection of the body – of the whole person. Perhaps, then, the soul is a part of human personality which grows with the person. Gilbert Ryle in *The Concept of Mind* maintained that all talk of a soul rests on a *category mistake*. He asks us to imagine our showing a cricket team to a foreigner – we might point out the batsmen, the wicket keeper, the bowler and the fielders and he might see and understand all these. However, he might then say: 'I have seen all these things, but where is the team spirit?' This question, Ryle holds, rests on a category mistake. 'Team Spirit' is not something apart from the team – similarly the soul should not be looked on as something separate from the person as a whole.

One might imagine someone saying: 'Paul Grosch has no soul' – this would not mean that he is missing something but rather that he is not fully a person as he treats others as if they were robots. Ensoulment may, therefore, be one of the key issues in the debate.

If:

1 You are a dualist and believe that a separate soul is implanted at birth, then clearly embryo research or abortion in most circumstances will be wrong as you are killing people. This will, broadly, be the Catholic position, although Catholic theologians will often deny that they are dualists – yet Aquinas maintains that the soul can separate from the body and go to purgatory pending reunification at the last judgement so there are strong dualist overtones in their approach.

2 If you reject dualism and believe that 'a person is a person', then the line between being a human being and a person may be more difficult to draw and deciding on the status of the embryo or

foetus may be more difficult. The right to life must still be respected, but the issues become more complex and subject to dispute. The Protestant Churches tend to adopt this view and to be more open to other factors which may affect the decision.

Those who do not believe in God would probably reject the dualist position but would then face the problems set out in 2 above.

This, however, is only part of the debate. Even if an embryo or foetus *is* regarded as a person, its rights must be balanced against those of the mother.

iv) Conflicting rights

If the embryo or foetus is regarded as a person, how does one balance its rights against the rights of the mother? Beverley Harrison in an article 'Our right to choose' argues forcefully for the rights of the woman. She maintains that abortion cannot be discussed in isolation from the psychological and social position of the woman. The history of women has been a history of male domination and oppression. Women have often been restricted to the role of being mothers and have often been given limited freedom in deciding whether to fulfil this role. The woman has to go through the pain and difficulty of labour, the woman has to care for and support the child and it is the woman's decision that should be paramount. Permitting abortion is seen by many feminists as a way of emancipating women from a form of slavery to their bodies – a slavery that is often used by men to 'keep them in their place'.

Harrison says:

The wellbeing of the woman and the value of her life plan should always be recognised as of intrinsic value.

Harrison supports this by saying that:

A good society is one that assures the existence of basic conditions needed to pursue an individual's own life plan.

She cites the example of Italian women who have used this argument to convince a majority of Italian women that they should have sole rights over their own bodies. Her second argument is a utilitarian one and maintains that an action is only wrong if it causes suffering or reduces happiness and this is not the case with abortion.

Harrison does not, however, give a clear account why one should not take the happiness of the embryo/foetus into account in the equation. It is true that the woman's position must be respected, but opponents of abortion say that no such rights can over-ride the rights of another person to life and a foetus or embryo is a person. Conflicts may also possibly arise with the happiness of the father which also needs to be taken into account as well as the perspective of society as a whole. Certainly the woman's rights must be recognized, but her rights cannot be considered in isolation.

It should also be recognised that there may be alternative ways of freeing the woman – for instance by providing child-care services or helping her to go back to work more quickly. The woman's problems *do* need to be addressed, but abortion is not necessarily the best way of doing it. This is really important – abortion is *not* an isolated issue. For instance in Ireland the social stigma attached to an unmarried woman who gets pregnant is so great that *this* can force her to choose an abortion. Sometimes the Churches are partly responsible for this and they need to look at their own role in this wider context.

There is an important defence of abortion based partly on the argument from individual rights. Judith Jarvis Thomson, in a celebrated paper entitled ' A Defense of Abortion' (originally published in the journal *Philosophy and Public Affairs* Vol. 1 No. 1 1971), proposed the following analogy. Suppose you were to wake up one morning, having been kidnapped by the Society of Music Lovers, only to find that a famous violinist had been plugged into your blood supply because his kidneys had failed. You are asked to support him for at least nine months. According to Thomson, although it might be very considerate of you if you agreed to the request, you would be under no moral obligation to do so. The same is true of pregnancy. The woman's right to life and her right of ownership of her own body are of greater significance than the right to life which may be accorded to the unborn foetus. In a second, but related, analogy Thomson distinguishes between the Good Samaritan and the Minimally Decent Samaritan. The former would, it is suggested, agree to the continued unselfish support of the violinist. The latter probably would not. What makes her a MDS, however, is the fact that should the violinist miraculously continue living after being unplugged she should not, of course, request his immediate murder. Many have tended to dismiss Thomson's argument, Singer amongst them, as a feminist rights issue, rather than as a feminist reappraisal of the abortion debate. As Thomson states:

> ... while I do argue that abortion is not impermissible, I do not argue that it is always permissible. There may well be cases in which carrying the child to term requires only Minimally Decent Samaritanism of the mother, and this is a standard we must not fall below. I am inclined to think it a merit of my account precisely that it does not give a general yes or a general no. It allows for and supports our sense that, for example, a sick and desperately frightened fourteen-year-old schoolgirl, pregnant due to rape, may, of course, choose abortion, and that any law which rules this out is an insane law. And it also allows for and supports our sense that in other cases resort to abortion is positively indecent. It would be indecent in the woman to request an abortion, and indecent in a doctor to perform it, if she is in her seventh month, and wants the abortion just to avoid the nuisance of having to postpone a trip abroad (source: J. Rachels, ed. 1979 3rd edition, *Moral Problems*, p. 149).

However, there are some logical conclusions of Thomson's argument which she probably would not have intended. Allocating to individuals absolute rights over their bodies and giving them complete ownership of the same can lead to some unintended logical outcomes. For example:

a) A person would be morally free to mutilate themselves in order to increase their income as a beggar, or
b) A man could insist on his sole right as to what to do with his body even if this involved rape.

It is wrong to concentrate on rights alone, responsibilities must also be taken into account. A woman's life plan must certainly be considered, but it must also be recognised that actions have consequences. If I sign a contract I cannot then get out of it because its implications affect my life plan; similarly if a man and woman make love, there may be implications that cannot simply be ignored.

In her book *Beginning Lives*, Rosalind Hursthouse criticises concentration on women's rights alone as she believes that this may obscure the issue that abortion may actually be wrong. To say

It is no longer a moral issue, it is a rights issue

obscures the fact that it may indeed *be* a moral issue – it may actually be *wrong*. Critics could, of course, reply that there is no absolute standard of right and wrong. To say that morality is relative is an attractive position, but it may also be flawed. Perhaps, for instance, the Nazi killing of homosexuals, Poles, disabled people, Gypsies and Jews was absolutely *wrong* – this is not just a matter of Anglo-Saxon morality judging an alternative system, but an appeal to a higher perspective, a claim to an absolute morality. It may be that a similar claim may be justified in the case of abortion – although the problem then arises as to how one justifies this claim.

A woman's views *must* be taken into account, it *is* her body that has to be used, the feminists are right that her life plan *will* be affected, but these are not the only considerations. Above all, it needs to be recognised that actions have consequences and sometimes individuals have to pay the price for actions which they later

155

regret. I may sign a contract to sell a house and then regret doing so because I receive a higher offer, but the fact is that I have signed the contract – the same may be said about the consequences of intercourse. Certainly it seems unfair that the price for this should so heavily fall on the woman and there is no doubt that the father's responsibilities must also be recognised. The heavy burden the woman has to bear seems inequitable, but perhaps this alone cannot be the last word.

If a woman is four months pregnant, then to destroy this foetus because she wants to be slim for a planned holiday; because she discovers that she is carrying a female child (as happens more and more frequently in parts of China, India, Egypt and other countries); or because she feels she is too busy to have a child seems difficult to justify. This does not mean that abortion will always and everywhere be wrong – just that the issue is complex and that it is important to be clear on the philosophic assumptions that underlie the different positions.

Where there is doubt, it may be right to err on the side of life and favour the less selfish position and, therefore, to oppose abortion except in the most exceptional circumstances – but in a way the definition of what are and are not exceptional circumstances is what this whole debate is about.

Questions for consideration

1 Is there any difference between a human being and a person?
2 What are the strengths and weaknesses of a dualist understanding of human personhood?
3 Has a woman sole rights over what to do with her own body? What are the problems in maintaining this position?
4 How could the rights and obligations of a woman considering abortion be balanced? What factors might be taken into account?
5 Why might it be held that talk of a human being having a soul rests on a category mistake?

THIRTEEN

Euthanasia and Medical Ethics

Does a person have total freedom to do as he or she likes? Clearly the answer must be 'no' if the use of these rights will hurt others – but what if it does not? Suicide used to be the only crime you could be punished for if you failed to carry it out. Nowhere is this issue clearer than in the case of voluntary euthanasia. Does a person have the right to bring his or her own life to an end? When one gets old and is in great pain and discomfort, some people may well feel that they have had enough and that death would be a welcome relief. Should they not in these circumstances have the right to ask doctors to bring their life to an end or at least to be given pills which they could freely take themselves which would make them drift off into a deep sleep followed by death?

An example will illustrate the problem:

Monsignor Thomas O'Brien, an 83-year-old pastor emeritus of Manhattan, suffered a massive stroke so that he could not swallow, speak or take nourishment. He had pulled out a nasogastric feeding tube some fifteen times, therefore a New York judge ordered a feeding gastronomy. This was a direct insertion tube into the stomach. Monsignor O'Brien was examined by four psychiatrists who testified that he was able to make rational decisions affecting his life. However, State Supreme Court Justice Edward Greenfield would not order a discontinuance of a life-support mechanism as he believed that Monsignor O'Brien had not clearly indicated he wished to end his life and it was against his theology and faith. Monsignor O'Brien died after the gastronomy was in place.

St Thomas More, who went to the scaffold because of his loyalty to the Pope and his refusal to accept Henry VIII's position as head of the Church of England, claimed in his book *Utopia* that euthanasia for the terminally ill was a major ingredient in the life of an ideal society and Hume, Bentham and Mill all challenged the previously accepted view that euthanasia was always wrong.

The Roman Catholic Church produced a 'Declaration on Euthanasia' in 1980 and defined euthanasia as:

... an action or omission which of itself or by intention causes death (p. 6).

However it is not always clear which actions 'cause death'. It is important to distinguish here between:

1 Where doctors give drugs the main purpose of which is to bring relief from pain and, as a side effect, these drugs cause earlier death.

Here the intention is not to bring an early death and there may not be any moral problem. The Roman Catholic Church's 'Declaration on Euthanasia' maintains that if death is caused because of the cumulative effect of drugs administered to relieve pain, then that is not euthanasia and is morally permissible as 'death is in no way intended or sought, even if the risk of it is reasonably taken' (p. 9), and

2 Where doctors are requested for drugs whose purpose is to bring death.

The issue of voluntary euthanasia (as opposed to involuntary euthanasia which is the killing of those who cannot decide for themselves, such as senile people or badly retarded or malformed babies) arises in the second case. However, the difference between the first and second cases may not always be clear – who is to define the 'main purpose' of drugs? On the basis of this distinction, much will depend on the state of mind and intentions of the person giving the drugs and this is not easy to determine, even for each individual. Few of us can readily decide what our true motives are. Also it is one thing to say that a doctor does not *intend* to cause death, but if she knows that death will result from the treatment that she is giving, is this lack of intention of sufficient moral importance to render the act permissible? At the least there seems to be no clear line here.

At first sight, the case for voluntary euthanasia seems strong. Surely the individual should have the right to make his or her own decisions as to when life should be ended? Some definitions may be helpful:

- *Death* – A person is dead once the heart and lungs stop. If these are kept going artificially, a person dies when brain activity ceases.
- *PVS* or *Persistent Vegetative State* occurs when the higher brain functions are either damaged or permanently destroyed. If they are permanently damaged, the question is what further care the patient should be given. If the higher brain functions are only damaged, then the patient may be in a coma and may recover. The Catholic Church respects the right of the individual to die with a minimum of pain. The use of pain-killing drugs is clearly right and the Church recognises that *Extraordinary* means to prolong life may be inappropriate: *Extraordinary Treatment*, however, is above the ordinary and need not be given in some circumstances – for instance resuscitation of a patient who has no chance of surviving very long, even though the technology is available. However, this is not to sanction euthanasia.

In Washington, a referendum was held in 1991 saying that a doctor should be allowed to administer 'aid-in-dying' to a terminally ill patient if requested to do so, but this is radically different from ceasing extraordinary treatment. Once the principle of helping someone to die is accepted, then the *cause* of death is the treatment rather than being a by-product of the treatment. This is a crucial distinction in the whole debate on euthanasia. Euthanasia is illegal in

Holland but there is a working arrangement whereby doctors who keep to certain guidelines will not be prosecuted. 'Help' here means that assistance can be given which actually brings about death. There are two key issues in this debate which are closely parallel to 1 and 2 above:

a) Should doctors have to use extraordinary means to preserve life if there is no possibility of a reasonable quality of life being achieved by the individual?

b) Should doctors be allowed to bring a life to an end if the quality of life has deteriorated to such an extent that it is intolerable to the patient and if the patient, while sound of mind, requests this?

Once the process of dying is under way, the problem is deciding on appropriate treatment. The final judgement is generally best left to the patient or to those who know him best, but the doctors and nurses have decisions to make as well. The first issue is not very difficult – few would argue that 'extraordinary means' should not need to be used if there is no possibility of a reasonable quality of life and if the patient clearly wills that there should be no further treatment. In this case, natural events take their course and failing to use extraordinary means does not cause death. However, even in this case there may be ethical debate – for instance if a patient is in a hospital, should he or she be allowed to refuse treatment which he or she may consider is extraordinary? Who is to decide what is extraordinary and what is not?

The Roman Catholic Church has moved to address this issue by employing a notion that has been referred to elsewhere (see chapter 4) – that of proportionalism. The issue is held to be whether the proposed treatment with its accompanying pain, discomfort and risk is proportionate to the benefit that is likely to ensue. No treatment is, on this basis, right or wrong in itself – instead the benefits to be gained from it must be weighed against its costs to the individual. A major operation with great pain and discomfort might well be appropriate for a 17-year-old girl with cancer who may have a long life ahead of her but not for an 85-year-old man as, although the two operations and the discomfort they caused might be the same, the potential benefits in the two cases are not equal. Although the Catholic Church would be unlikely to acknowledge it, we have here a form of situation ethics being applied to measure the rights and wrongs of actions.

There is debate as to whether it is right to call the refusal to use extraordinary means to prolong life euthanasia at all. Some would hold that the word euthanasia necessarily involves an action to bring about death and not taking action is not the same thing at all.

Dr Jack Kevorkian of Detroit has invented a machine called the 'Mercitron'. This allows patients to kill themselves painlessly at the flick of a switch. He advertised for customers and in June 1990, in Dr Kevorkian's old camper van, Janet Adkins used the Mercitron to escape from Alzheimer's disease (source: *The Economist*, November 13, 1993). Dr Kevorkian has been called a 'serial killer' in the US Senate and the Michigan State Board of Medicine has suspended his medical licence. The Catholic arch-diocese of Detroit was sufficiently alarmed that in November 1993 it placed a full page 'Statement on Euthanasia' in the local press. Dr Kevorkian maintains that religion and medicine should be completely divorced. However there is a fundamental philosophic divide between the Church and the doctor – summed up in his answer to a question as to what he thought happened after death. He gave the simple reply 'You rot'. Clearly one's attitude to euthanasia or to the Mercitron may be different if human destiny continues after death or if death is the end.

The Mercitron's distinctive feature is that it allows a person to bring his or her own life to an end – doctors do not have to do anything. However, the issue it raises is very similar to b) above. At first sight, if we are to respect persons and they are free to make their own decisions, then active euthanasia (defined in terms of doctors taking action to bring death about as opposed to passive euthanasia which only involves refraining from treating a terminal condition) in clearly defined circumstances seems reasonable. However, various arguments can be put forward against such euthanasia:

i) If you are a religious believer and consider that life is a gift from God, then you may well argue that your life is not your own. Only God has the right to take life and you have no right to put an end to it early. Even great suffering can have spiritual value and the decision to 'opt out' of suffering is not one that a human being should be allowed to make. Also, even in the last moments of a person's life there may still be tasks to perform and an individual's faith can affect others and lead them to God – to 'opt out' of the struggle before it is over may well, therefore, be considered to be wrong.

If we take the example of Monsignor O'Brien, he could not possibly have guessed the publicity that his dying would generate – yet now it is a standard text-book example. Similarly we may not be able to see how our example will affect others.

ii) If euthanasia is legal, an old person may feel pressurised to die because they feel they are a nuisance to their children or surviving relatives. Imagine that you are being cared for by your daughter and you are incontinent and unable to move easily, you may well feel that you are a burden to others and have a duty to die. This, it may well be argued, is unacceptable in a civilised society.

iii) Euthanasia may leave the door open for elderly people to be quietly disposed of against their will. Supporters of euthanasia argue that this is not the case as one could have tight legal safeguards which would permit euthanasia only if clear consent had been given by a person in front of independent witnesses when he or she was of sound mind.

iv) The development of the hospice movement has had an important influence on the euthanasia debate. Hospices are dedicated to helping people die with dignity – they are experts in pain relief. If such facilities can be developed and their availability extended, then the need for euthanasia because of extreme pain may be eliminated.

v) 'The Wedge Argument' (or slippery slope argument) maintains that euthanasia is the thin edge of the wedge – that once one accepts this principle, the door is open for all sorts of other procedures and abuses including infanticide. The argument is that euthanasia involves crossing a line and once this line is crossed the consequences are unforeseeable. The euthanasia debate is strongly influenced by the idea of the quality of life of a human being – if a person's quality of life has permanently and irreversibly altered so that life is solely a burden, why should they not put an end to their life? Much is, of course, going to depend on one's religious attitude and the safeguards against abuse.

The slippery slope argument may not be as convincing as it first appears. As Helga Kushe puts it in the chapter on Euthanasia in Peter Singer's *A Companion to Ethics* (Blackwell, p. 302):

> ... in the Netherlands a 'social experiment' with active voluntary euthanasia is currently in progress. As yet there is no evidence that this has sent Dutch society down a slippery slope.

Having said this, euthanasia even in the Netherlands is still new and the long-term effects are hard to determine. It has been argued that it was the programme of euthanasia for handicapped and retarded children that started the Nazis down their extermination programme of Jews, Gypsies, homosexuals, Poles and others.

There is a significant difference between the case of abortion and euthanasia. In the latter case we are talking about the right of a sane and sensible person to make a free decision about his or her own life and to have help in carrying out that decision. This seems to be fundamentally different from the abortion case where the foetus has no one to protect it. The foetus cannot protect itself and therefore society must take very strongly its duty to care for that which cannot care for itself. You may or may not agree with euthanasia, but the central issues may be ones of human dignity and human freedom as well as one's religious assumptions.

In the end, the attitude to the question 'What is a person?' is going to partly determine the answer to many other questions ranging from abortion and euthanasia to life after death and human rights issues and these can even run into questions of immigration and help for the poor.

Euthanasia is one amongst a number of issues facing the medical profession including not only advances in DNA manipulation techniques, the possibilities of breeding animals to provide human organs but also the allocation of scarce resources. In every country in the western world the demand for health care is increasing faster than the ability of the country to finance the cost and this means that difficult choices have to be made. Is it better to save a single life through a highly expensive surgical technique or to improve the quality of life for a large number through a simpler procedure? A utilitarian market might point to the latter approach, but it can be argued against this that surgical techniques that may be expensive today may become much cheaper and therefore more widely available tomorrow, so balancing utility considerations is not easy.

Dr Kevorkian's activities have led to a debate about the purpose of medical care for the elderly. Is the purpose to keep people alive at any price? There are also financial factors at work – we live in a world in which the resources that can be devoted to medicine are limited and a very large proportion of these resources are used in the last two weeks of a patient's life. It can be argued that if the purpose of medical care includes to provide a painless death for someone for whom there is no hope and who knowingly and after taking advice wants to bring life to an end, then this may be a humane step and it may also release resources which could be better used to relieve suffering in younger people.

John Harris in *The Value of Life* (1985) explores the problem of how to choose between patients. Assume that there are two patients in a hospital – both critically ill. Due to lack of resources, one patient has to be transferred to another hospital many miles away – however the journey will jeopardise the patient's recovery. Which patient should be transferred? If, say, one patient was a two-year-old infant and the other an eighty-year-old man, the scales might tip in favour of the infant. According to Harris, two arguments tip the scales:

1 The 'fair innings' argument. The eighty-year-old has already had a long life and it would, therefore, be morally more acceptable to give the infant the chance, and

2 The 'quality of life' argument. Upon recovery, the infant is likely to enjoy a much more active and varied life style than the grand-parent.

Both these arguments suffer from the problem of whether one life can be intrinsically more valuable than another. Is age the only determining factor and what other factors might be admissible? To deal with this sort of difficulty, some providers of health care have introduced what are known as QALYS or Quality Adjusted Life Year Schedules. A QALY is a unit of measurement intended to determine the cost and effectiveness of a range of medical treatments from drugs to surgery. However this idea itself raises problems – is it preferable to achieve a high quality of life for five years or a lower quality of life for fifteen years? How does one balance the one against the other? Also there is the standard utilitarian problem – is it better to achieve higher QALYS for a small number of patients or lower QALYS for a large number? Issues of finance are also raised – should people who have more money be entitled to better medical treatment than those who have less and should a leading politician have better medical care than a refuse collector? Approaches such as QALY measurements tend to raise more problems than they solve – which is not to say that the attempt to address these issues is not worthwhile, but it does show how much will depend on presuppositions and that there is no simple utilitarian calculus which will solve such dilemmas.

These issues also affect the euthanasia debate as it can be argued that, when medical resources are limited, it is wrong to allocate scarce funds to someone who has had a long life when this will diminish the resources available for, say, ante-natal care. One of the problems of the modern world is that hard choices have to be made and, it must be admitted, philosophers have not been very successful in showing how these choices should be resolved.

Questions for consideration

1 If a doctor gives heavy doses of a drug to relieve pain, is there a moral difference if he intends these drugs to cause the death of the patient or if he simply knows that the patient will die from the drugs?

2 Should a healthy sixty-year-old woman be allowed to refuse to have a blood transfusion even if she will die if she does not have the transfusion? What factors might govern the moral acceptability or otherwise of her decision and why?

3 In what ways might one's attitude to euthanasia be different depending on one's religious outlook?

4 What is the moral difference, if any, between euthanasia and suicide? How should the two be differentiated?

5 What factors might be the most important in determining that a person's quality of life is so low that it could be terminated? What are the risks of such an approach?

6 Imagine you are a doctor and you can choose either to prolong the life of an eighty-year-old woman for three years or to give hip transplants to six forty-year-old women who at present cannot walk. Which would you choose and why? Would your choice be different if the eighty-year-old woman was your grandmother – if so, why?

FOURTEEN
Just War

Was it right for the western European Powers to go to war against Iraq in 1990 following the invasion of Kuwait? Was it right for the Allies to refuse to intervene militarily in the Bosnian conflict in 1993? Was it right for NATO to bomb Yugoslavia in 1999? The lives of millions of people are affected by warfare and the issue as to the morality of war is a vital one. With modern methods of warfare, military activity can no longer be confined to the combatants – civilians and civilian installations are inevitably affected and this needs to be taken into account in modern accounts of when war can be regarded as just. Just War thinking has to take into account developments in military thinking and technology and the spread of war to civilian populations. However, although the problems are modern the origins of the debate as to whether it can be right to wage war and in what circumstances have a very long history.

The Old Testament

The Old Testament clearly recognised the importance of war and Israel was called by God to fight against its enemies. Rules were laid down for this warfare – for instance the Levitical code in the Old Testament exempted newly married men from service in the army (Deuteronomy 24:5) and if one of the Israeli tribes were not invited to take part in a war they felt left out (Judges 8:1). Under King Saul there was a standing army (1 Samuel 14:52) and in 1 and 2 Samuel there are constant references to King David's armies and his foreign mercenaries. Warfare was fierce and cruel, thus:

At the same time we captured and destroyed every town and put everyone to death – men, women and children. We left no survivors (Deuteronomy 2:34).

Joshua spared no one, everyone was put to death. This was what the Lord God of Israel has commanded (Joshua 10:40).

A radical alteration took place in thinking about war following Jesus' teaching. For the first 250 years after Christ, violence of any sort was believed to be wrong and against the basic commandments of Jesus – Christians did not resist even when taken to the lions. However this did not last. The Emperor Constantine decreed that Christianity should become the religion of the Roman Empire in A.D. 313. In around A.D. 410 Rome, which had controlled most of the known world, was facing defeat at the hands of the Visigoths and the neighbouring tribes.

Non-Christians in the Roman Empire saw the weakening of Rome's power and its vulnerability as being partly due to the reluctance of Christians to fight. St Augustine responded to this challenge. By now the situation had changed – the Emperor was Christian and so was a large part of the Roman state so fighting for the state seemed much more reasonable. Augustine turned to the Hebrew Scriptures and had no difficulty in finding texts to support the use of war. To begin with, in the Hebrew Scriptures if God commanded war then it was right for war to take place and since the Roman Emperor was held to be appointed by God, it was right for Christians to go to war in the interests of the state. Augustine put forward two conditions under which a war could justifiably be waged:

1 It had to have a legitimate authority, and
2 There had to be a just cause.

Augustine saw the purpose of war as being the punishing of wrongdoing and the bringing about of peace. He considered that it was permissible to fight and even to undertake torture and the killing of innocents in order to bring peace about. However he also considered that it was essential that war should be waged without love of violence, cruelty or enmity.

St Thomas Aquinas in the 12th century added a third condition to the two put forward by Augustine:

3 There has to be a right intention.

However these traditional criteria are not enough. After the First World War, Germany might well have claimed that it had legitimate authority, a just cause and a right intention for going to war. The Allies had bled Germany dry after the First World War under the provisions of the Treaty of Versailles and had made the country an impoverished nation, destroying the Weimar Republic and leading to the great inflation of the nineteen twenties. The theologian Reinhold Niebuhr wrote in 1942 that the sins committed by Britain, France and the USA after the First World War were the seeds that helped to produce the desire for an Aryan race and hence the rise of the Nazis.

After the First World War, there was a turning point in just war theory due to the advent of the League of Nations (succeeded by the United Nations after the Second World War) and the Geneva conventions.

The immediate problem arises that both sides in a conflict may claim legitimate authority and right intention, so the crucial factor becomes establishing a just cause. At the Nuremberg trial after the Second World War, the difference between two problems became more clearly established:

a) When is it right to go to war – *Jus ad Bellum* and
b) How should war be fought – *Jus in Bello*

In 1983, one of the most comprehensive statements on just war conditions came from the Catholic bishops in America in which they took this distinction into account. This set out conditions for a just war to be undertaken:

Conditions to be met for *Jus ad Bellum* (when it is right to go to war):

1 There must be a just cause
2 War must be declared by a competent and legal authority
3 Comparative justice – the justice of the claims of both sides must be compared
4 There must be a right intention in going to war
5 War must be a last resort
6 There must be a reasonable probability of success, and
7 There must be reasonable proportion between the injustice suffered and the death and suffering of war

The conditions to be met for *Jus in Bello* are:

8 Proportionality, and
9 Discrimination

Because this is such a detailed analysis it is helpful to examine these in turn.

Conditions for *Jus ad Bellum*

1 *Just cause.* The Catholic bishops said that 'War is permissible only to confront a real and certain danger, i.e. to protect innocent life, to preserve conditions necessary for decent human existence and to secure basic human rights.' However determining which basic human rights should be taken into account is very difficult and leaves the door wide open for one country to go to war with another to obtain a 'decent human existence' for its people.

2 *Competent and legal authority.* Augustine and Aquinas held that any authority declaring war had to have been legally appointed and that no private individuals or private armies were justified in going to war. However any government may hold that it has 'competent

authority' – it may be that, in the future, the only competent authority which would be acceptable is the United Nations, but this is not the case at present.

3 *Comparative justice.* This involves comparing the justices of the claims of both sides in a conflict – this seems to be a weak condition as almost always there may be justice on both sides of a dispute. The trouble is that if any country admitted this, the war would not take place as once you see the opponent's point of view, you may be unwilling to fight him.

4 *Right intention.* Augustine did not make right intention one of the conditions for going to war, but he did apply this criterion to the actual combat by soldiers. The soldier must feel no enmity to his enemies and must maintain a virtuous inward disposition whilst killing. He did say that a nation wages war to bring about peace and this might indirectly be held to mean that right intention must be present. Again this condition is difficult to justify – Mussolini claimed right intention when invading Ethiopia and this was sanctioned by the Bishop of Milan as the invasion was 'opening the gates of Ethiopia to the Catholic faith and Roman civilisation'.

5 *Last resort.* All alternatives to waging war must be exhausted before war can be waged – for instance all possibilities for negotiation and for mediation must first be explored before war is resorted to.

6 *Probability of success.* The reasons given by the Catholic bishops for including this factor is '... to prevent irrational resort to force or hopeless resistance when the outcome of either will clearly be disproportionate or futile'. In other words it is wrong to wage war unless there is a reasonable chance of success. One problem with this may be that it can lead to the build-up of forces before war commences in order to guarantee success.

7 *Proportionality*. The criterion of proportionality requires that the damage inflicted to and by both parties must be proportionate to the good that is expected to result. As an example, one side cannot drop a nuclear bomb on the capital city of another due to aggravation over a fishing dispute. Taking proportionality seriously has the great advantage of seeing the effects of warfare on human beings. In *The Ethics of War*, Barrie Paskins and Michael Docknill claim that wars fought in defence of national honour must be viewed with suspicion as if one weighs the value of human beings against national honour, the former should always have priority. It is always important to maintain a clear view of one's own and one's enemies' humanity.

The doctrine of proportionalism in ethics is, possibly, one of the most important ideas for the future as it brings together acceptance of the importance of a natural law approach to ethics with a recognition that consequences have to be taken into account – it holds that a proportionate reason may be necessary in order to overrule basic moral principles but it leaves the door open for these principles to be overruled. This approach is often rejected by traditional Catholic theologians but it is significant that it has always been an important part of the just war debate – it has also been an integral part of the principle of double effect (see page 124).

Conditions for *Jus in Bello*

Jus in Bello deals with how a war should be fought. In a Vatican statement entitled 'Gaudium et Spes', the following point is made:

> ... any act of war aimed indiscriminately at the destruction of entire cities or of extensive areas along with their populations is a crime against God and man himself. It merits unhesitating and unequivocal condemnation (Article 80).

There have been a number of attempts to rule out certain weapons for use in war. Perhaps the first was the Second Lateran Council which forbade the use of crossbows, bows and arrows and siege machines. However these restrictions only applied to wars between

Christians – no restrictions were imposed on warfare with non Christians. These attempts to restrict weapons have continued down to the present day with agreements about chemical and biological weapons as well as restrictions on certain nuclear weapons. Even nuclear weapons are not necessarily always evil – if nuclear weapons were absolutely wrong then even their use in defence would be ruled out. However recent developments in nuclear technology (for instance in battlefield nuclear shells) mean that the after-effects of such weapons have been greatly reduced and some chemical or biological weapons can be even more terrible than nuclear ones.

Robert Holmes in *On War and Morality* holds that the justice of waging war and conduct in war cannot be separated:

> Unless one can justify the actions necessary to waging war, one cannot justify the conduct of war and the pursuit of its objectives and if one cannot do this one cannot justify going to war.

In the Nuremberg trials after the Second World War, it became necessary to make a distinction between the reasons for waging a war and the way the war is conducted. Two criteria set limits to how war should be waged:

8 *Proportionality*. Proportionality applies, as set out above, to the justice of waging war but it also applies to just conduct of war. The way warfare is conducted may be out of proportion to the reasons the war is waged. It would, for instance, have been unacceptable for Britain to drop a nuclear bomb on the capital of Argentina after Argentina invaded the Falklands – such action would be clearly disproportionate.

9 *Discrimination*. This is particularly concerned with discrimination between the killing of innocents and those fighting in a conflict as well as the treatment of prisoners of war. The Geneva protocols 1 and 2 of 1977 limited the use of starvation as a means of warfare because it does not discriminate and it may well be that 'carpet

bombing' of cities by Allied planes in the Second World War or German submarines trying to sink Allied ships bringing food to Britain violated this principle. If the difference between different categories of people in a country are ignored, then the country claiming to wage a just war will find this claim undermined by the charge of itself being immoral in the conduct of the war. It would then become a state against which a just war should be waged.

The issue is not whether the accidental killing of innocents in war is wrong as this would no more show that war was wrong than accidental deaths in aeroplanes would show that flying was wrong. The issue is the division between accidental and intentional killing of innocent people. In the 1983 Pastoral Letter, the Catholic bishops say that 'The lives of innocent persons may never be taken directly, regardless of the purpose alleged for doing so.' They say that when a response is made to aggression, it must be made against the aggressors and not against innocent civilians who through no fault of their own are caught up in the conflict.

The problem is that it is far from clear who are the innocent. In the 17th century, the theologian and philosopher Hugo Grotius maintained that if in a situation of war, State A is justified in waging war against State B then all members of State A from the generals and soldiers to the civilians are considered to be innocent. The problem with this view is the implication that all members of State B could therefore be considered to be non-innocents.

Holmes draws a distinction between people who are guilty, and those who are non-innocent. Guilt implies a direct and purposive action on the part of the offender. Holmes divides members of the offending state into five categories:

1 Initiators of wrongdoing (government leaders)
2 Agents of wrongdoing (military commanders and combatant soldiers)
3 Contributors to the war effort (armament manufacturers, military researchers and taxpayers)

4 Those who approve of the war without contributing in any significant way, and

5 Non-contributors and non-supporters (e.g. children and those who refuse to obey the laws, including the insane).

Objections to just war theory

Holmes maintains that the very fact that there are held to be conditions in which a just war may be waged makes wars possible. He maintains that since the fifth century and the time of Augustine justification for war has been taken and used by nations to sanction their own wars. He argues that there may be a correlation between discussion of just wars and the outbreak of war. Holmes maintains that if no conditions had ever been held to justify war, then wars would not have taken place. However many wars are waged by non-Christians and by people who have never engaged in just war discussions so Holmes' claim seems debatable at the least.

In 1987, George Weigel challenged the approach taken by the American bishops. He said that instead of rejecting the very idea that wars could ever be just and considering the possibility that Christian thinkers from Augustine onwards could be wrong, the Catholic bishops had merely tried to justify their own position by setting out slightly more complicated conditions. These conditions, as we have seen, are far from clear cut and may themselves provide a justification for the aggressor – so much depends on the individual viewpoint being taken.

In the Gulf War in 1991 and in NATO attacks on Yugoslavia in 1999, efforts were made to minimise civilian casualties. The 'cleverest' weapons – such as Tomahawk cruise missiles – were used against Baghdad and Belgrade to keep down the risk of casualties. Laser guided weapons were used and the civilian casualties were thus reduced, but sometimes things went wrong as when Tornados attacked a bridge and one of the missiles went out of control and hit a residential area. Also American aircraft attacked a command and control centre and afterwards found that women and children were taken shelter on the site at a higher level to the control centre.

A bigger problem in modern warfare arises with the attacks on civilian installations such as power stations which do have a partially military role as they provide power to military and civilian facilities. In the Gulf War, the consequences of air strikes on these positions were to effectively bomb Iraq back fifty years and the suffering and deaths that have been caused since the war have been very great indeed.

Rarely in just war theories is the policy of tyrannicide considered, but it could be argued to be an attractive option. If Hitler or Saddam Hussein had been assassinated, then great suffering by millions could have been avoided. If the death of one man who is held to be wicked would be likely to save the lives of millions, can it be justified? Certainly Bonhoeffer thought the answer was in the affirmative in the Second World War when he took part in a plot to assassinate Hitler.

The *pacifist* possibility also needs to be taken seriously. Once Augustine had opened the doors to Christians fighting, the issue of those Christians who did not want to fight had to be addressed. According to Eusebius of Caesarea pacifism could be justified by a high way of life. Lay people could get married and fight in wars whilst the clergy could not marry and could not even participate in just wars because they had a higher, i.e. more 'spiritual' way of life. The Monastic movement (with the notable exceptions of movements such as the Knights Templar) reflected pacifist tendencies but there was no provision for lay people to be conscientious objectors.

Augustine and Luther said that Jesus ruled out *malitia* (hatred) not *militia* (fighting). In the Middle Ages, a number of Christian groups were pacifist but they were very small in relation to institutional Christianity. Erasmus defended humanistic pacifism and the historic 'Peace' Churches such as Quakers, the Mennonites and the Brethren have taken a firm stand on this issue, but it has always been a minority view and the main Churches have often seen justification in the use of war.

The strongest argument against just war theories is the high moral standards they assume by the parties to the potential war. To adhere to the just war conditions, a state has to maintain an almost impossibly high moral standard as *any* breach of the conditions lays the state open to the sort of challenge it itself is fighting against. The very fact that innocents may be killed in a conflict can infringe the rules of proportionality and discrimination.

The idea that Christian teaching on just war should be taken back to pre-Augustine days has been put forward by Walter Wink. In an article 'Is there an ethic of violence?', he argues that two statements can be made regarding the New Testament approach to violence:

i) Jesus and the entire tradition of the Early Church up to the time of Constantine practised non-violence (although against Wink, St Paul may have sanctioned the use of violence – see Romans 13:1, 2 and 5 and also 1 Peter 2:14).
ii) Oppressive violence is always evil – it may be necessary as the lesser of two evils, but it can never be a good in itself.

Wink therefore considers that Augustine's introduction of just war teaching led in the wrong direction. The idea that wars are sometimes necessary is an odd idea in the moral arena. Ethics demands free choice and yet necessity denies choice – there may be reasons for waging war but, Wink maintains, they can never be *just* reasons as justice is defined by applying fairness and bringing about equality on both sides – and war certainly does not do this.

Conscientious objection when related to war falls under two criteria:

1 Conscientious objection on the grounds of Pacifism – the Quakers are one religious grouping which adopts this position in all cases, and
2 Conscientious objection in particular cases on the grounds that just war criteria have not been met. It has traditionally been held that a Christian has the duty to refuse to take part in an unjust war or to commit certain acts in a war, although this only applies in the clearest cases. Generally *'Obedience to orders'* protects soldiers from guilt in cases of doubt.

The problem is, of course, that if all warfare is rejected, this also means rejecting the possibility of taking up arms to protect innocent people against a cruel and vicious government. If Britain had not gone to war in 1939, it is arguable that Hitler's tyranny would have continued and extended across Europe. If Israel did not have an efficient fighting machine, then it would have been wiped out early in its modern history.

The UN may well provide the way forward in terms of fair application of the just war criteria, but it can only work if it is truly an unbiased body and not one that is dominated by the wealthy nations of the world – as is sometimes the case at the moment. The issue of wealthy versus poverty-stricken nations may well provide the basis for war in the future and the possibility of religious wars is still real – Muslim fundamentalism is a potent force and the concept of a *just war* may have little to say to anyone who believes in a *holy war*. Justice and religious conviction do not always go hand in hand.

Questions for consideration

1 If the people in country S are starving to death for lack of food and those in country M have a huge surplus of food, could it be just for S to go to war with M if all attempts to obtain relief through negotiation have failed?

2 Why has modern military technology been helpful in the practical application of just war theory?

3 Would Jesus have been for or against warfare? What reasons would you give to support your answer?

4 Who do you think are the innocent people in warfare? Give reasons for the categories you choose.

5 How might the whole idea of a just war be rejected?

6 What are the advantages of the United Nations in the application of just war theory? How might this organisation make a difference in the future?

FIFTEEN

Crime and Punishment

Jesus said that his followers should forgive their enemies and give to those who harmed them. He said that they should 'turn the other cheek' and said that only those without sin (which, by implication means no-one) was fit to throw the first stone which was the punishment for adultery. Yet such commands have traditionally been ignored in so-called Christian societies – all of whom seem to accept that punishment is morally acceptable.

Any society has people who break the rules – whether this involves breaking the speed limit, parking illegally, theft, insider share dealing or murder. Society protects itself by locking away certain members who are seen as a threat, it seeks to deter people from committing crimes by inflicting punishments and it seeks to punish those who commit the crime. However there is a wide range of opinion on which punishments should be inflicted and what the aim of these punishments are. The backgrounds to most theories of punishment lie in religious beliefs although modern theories tend to be divorced from any religious underpinning.

Nowhere is the idea of crime and punishment clearer than in the religious field where theistic religions tend to maintain that obedience and worship of God brings rewards after death and disobedience brings punishment. This raises the issue of whether it can be held to be fair or just for God to punish people in hell. There are four separate theses involved in the idea of hell as a punishment:

1 The punishment thesis: the purpose of hell is to retributively punish those who deserve it

2 The no-escape thesis: that it is impossible to get out of hell once one has been sent there
3 The anti-universalism thesis: not all people will go to heaven, some will be sent to hell
4 The eternal existence thesis: hell is a place of conscious existence (Quinn and Taliaferno, *A Companion to Philosophy of Religion*, Blackwell, 1996, p. 562).

There seems little alternative to the idea of hell as retribution. Some have held that the wicked are annihilated after death but this does not overcome the problem because it implies that it is better to cease to exist than to exist and be punished. Yet in this life many in western society reject capital punishment for exactly the reason that they think it better for some to live and to be punished than to be killed. To do away with the idea of hell by denying the anti-universalism thesis would involve saying that everyone goes to heaven and no-one goes to hell. This does not overcome the problem either as, if Mother Teresa, Nelson Mandela and Hitler, Stalin or Pol Pot are to be treated the same, then the idea of this life having a religious and moral purpose is seriously undermined. Theologically, therefore, the idea of hell seems to be necessary if there is to be any idea of life after death. The most logical purpose for hell would appear to be retribution. Alternatively it may be held that heaven and hell (if they exist) are the places where we would be most at home given the choices we have made and the type of people we have become in this life.

History – St Thomas Aquinas

It is easy to assume that modern discussions of issues such as crime and punishment are 'right' but there is a radical cultural relativism in most writings on the subject. St Thomas Aquinas was probably the single most influential theologian within the Roman Catholic Church and his views have been enormously influential, yet today most people would look back on his ideas with some revulsion.

Aquinas considered that it was morally acceptable for vengeance to take place if the purpose was to stop evil. Since some people are without virtue, they can only be stopped from committing evil acts by fear of the consequences – the government has a duty to act on behalf of God in inflicting pain and punishment on evildoers which includes depriving them of life, health, possessions and freedom. Aquinas therefore holds that punishment should terrify more than the sin attracts. Bernard Hoose summarises Aquinas's position clearly:

> In principle, Aquinas writes, a healthy well-functioning limb cannot be removed without doing harm to the whole body ... However, the whole man is himself part of the whole community. Suppose, then, that a limb is removed as a penalty to restrain him from sinning ... the community as a whole will benefit. Therefore, Aquinas continues, just as a public authority may execute a man for certain major faults, it may remove one of his limbs for a lesser fault ... one who has authority over another may resort to beating that person. Thus ... a father may legitimately beat his son and a master may legitimately beat his slave ('Received Wisdom', in Chapman, 1994, p. 114).

In spite of the influence that Aquinas has exerted over Catholic theology and moral philosophy, most people today would reject his views on punishment as they would reject his approval of the feudal structure of society and of slavery. Times have moved on and we have become wiser with the passing of the years. Having said that, Aquinas could claim considerable biblical support for his ideas, for instance:

> He who spares his rod hates his son, but he who loves him takes care to chastise him (Prov. 13:24).
> Withhold not chastisement from a boy; if you beat him with the rod, he will not die (Prov. 23:13).

In Deuteronomy, God is held to instruct that rebellious teenagers should be dealt with firmly:

> If a man has a stubborn and unruly son who will not listen to his father or mother, and will not obey them even though they chastise him, his father and mother shall have him apprehended and brought out to the elders at the gate of his home city, where they shall say to those city elders, 'This son of ours is a stubborn and unruly fellow who will not listen to us; he is a glutton and a drunkard'.Then all his fellow citizens shall stone him to death. Thus shall you purge the evil from your midst, and all Israel, on hearing of it, shall fear (Deut. 18:18–21).

One can imagine what reaction such a suggestion would meet today! Freud has claimed that punishment of children is frequently due to the parent or other adult taking out on the child his or her own fear of certain 'crimes' which they have fought to master in themselves, or else the sexual pleasure that may come from administering the punishment. The best example is possibly masturbation which was most severely punished by some fathers and priests, possibly because they had difficulty themselves coming to terms with something they felt guilty about. Some public school teachers enjoyed smacking the bare bottoms of young children in their care, possibly even finding sexual release in so doing (T. P. Morris, 'Punishment' in 'Crime and Punishment', *The New Encyclopaedia Britannica*, 1985, Vol. 16, pp. 859–60).

The Church of England's Book of Common Prayer contains a prayer which asks God that '...those in authority may truly and indifferently administer justice, to the punishment of wickedness and vice and to the maintenance of thy true religion and virtue'.

However, it is John Stuart Mill's definition in his essay 'On Liberty' which underlies many contemporary attitudes: 'The only purpose for which power can rightfully be exercised over any member of a civilised community against his will is to prevent harm to others. His own good, either physical or moral, is not a sufficient warrant' The last sentence is important but is regularly ignored in our society. It is against the law and punishable not to wear seat belts or to take drugs, it is a criminal offence to use the service of a prostitute or to be a prostitute, to help someone to commit euthanasia or even to look at certain types of pornography. In some societies, homosexual acts in private are illegal. All these activities may harm the individual more than other members of society.

There are three main theories which lie behind the idea of punishing criminals. These are:

1 Utilitarianism or the theory of the greatest good for the greatest number of people. This treats punishment as an evil in itself but considers that it is justified by the greater good for the whole community that results from the punishment. On this view, punishment produces desirable consequences either because it deters people from committing crimes or because it prevents offenders from committing further offences.

2 The retributive theory is based on the view that the offender has freely committed a wrong act and therefore has brought on themselves the appropriate punishment. On this view, the suffering of those who have committed crimes is not bad in itself – only the suffering of innocents is bad.

3 Therapy or reformation of the wrongdoer. This would see the main aim of imprisonment to be to change the views, outlook or conditioning of the offenders so that the same offences do not reoccur. One of the clearest examples where this approach could be taken is with sex offenders, many of whom have had difficulties in their formative years and may need psychological help and counselling to overcome problems which cause them to offend (cf. Peter Vardy's *The Puzzle of Sex*, HarperCollins, 1997). Similarly junior offenders are sometimes confronted with those individuals whose property they have damaged in order to bring them to see the effects of their action, with the aim that once they see this they will not re-offend.

A major problem with the utilitarian theory is that it can justify punishment of someone who is innocent on the grounds that this would benefit society as a whole. It could be that a tribal or religious riot in a country in Africa could be prevented by convicting and punishing someone who is innocent as this scapegoat could diffuse the tension in the community that may have arisen because of a criminal act (such as rape, arson, etc.). However the utilitarian could reply to this by saying that such punishment would not be justified in the long term because it would undermine the administration of justice. Whatever the short-term benefit that might come from the punishment of an innocent person, the harm that would result if and when the truth came out would more than outweigh any such benefits. Deterrence is a crucial part of this approach to crime and punishment. The most often quoted example of this is that of the eighteenth-century judge, Sir Thomas Burnet who sentenced a man to death for stealing a horse. The man replied, 'It is very hard my Lord to hang a poor man for stealing a horse', to which the judge replied, with some wit, 'You are not to be hanged for stealing a horse, but so that horses may not be stolen' (Patrick Pringle, 'Hue and Cry. The Birth of the British Police', quoted in Hoose's 'Received Wisdom'). The point is clear – punishment is intended to deter criminals and others for resorting to crime. One problem is that it is not at all clear that prison or other punishments do deter. Many criminals feel that they will not be caught and therefore do not seriously consider the issue of punishment. There has been no clear evidence linking increases in sentences to reduction in the crime rate.

It is far from clear what influence prison has on the prisoners. Some may, of course, be reformed, but in many cases prison can be a place where homosexuality and lesbian behaviour is rife, where drugs are available and where people can learn to become more effective criminals. Prisons may, indeed, be 'schools for crime' in which contacts are made and techniques learnt.

Lord Devlin in 'The Enforcement of Morals' maintains that a recognised morality is as necessary to a society as a recognised government. A society is held in existence by its moral codes such as those governing marriage and property and if these break down society itself breaks down – a society is, therefore, morally justifiable in enforcing a moral code in order to protect itself. H. L. A. Hart accuses Devlin of failing to distinguish between what he terms 'universal values' (such as 'Thou shalt not murder') and a morality of variable tastes and conventions of which, for instance, much sexual morality would be a good example. Hart maintains that a society can only enforce universal morality and not its own, relative morality which may depend on culture and time. If Devlin's view is accepted, then the law could be used to enforce, for instance, institutions such as marriage, the family, adultery, divorce or monogamy, and these would become matters for the criminal courts.

The retributive theory has the advantage that it only punishes for acts freely committed, for instance an accidental act is not punished. However, the problem with this approach is that the purpose of punishment is not to reduce crime and this raises the question of why one is punishing at all. Some who support the theory of retribution respond to this problem by saying that the criminal takes advantage of innocent citizens by refusing to accept the rules of the society in which they live. This seems to be the view taken by Pope Pius XII when he said:

> The punishment is the reaction, required by law and justice, to the crime: they are like a blow and a counter-blow. The order violated by the criminal demands the restoration and re-establishment of the equilibrium which has been disturbed. It is the proper task of law and justice to guard and preserve the harmony between duty on the one hand and the law on the other and to re-establish this harmony ... (Pope Pius XII, December 1954, from 'Catholic Documents' Xl to XX, Salesian Press, 1955).

Society depends on mutual acceptance of the rules, so criminals have to have their rights forcibly restricted in order to restore a fair and even balance (cf. C. L. Ten, 'Crime and Punishment', in *A*

Companion to Ethics, Peter Singer, ed., pp. 368–9). However, the person who is wronged in, for instance, a murder is the person who is murdered and it seems clear that one reason for punishment is to stop further crimes being committed, so this amended version of the retributive theory seems to be defective. As Ten says:

> The retributive theory allows people to be punished without reference to the social consequences of punishment ... suppose that ... punishment significantly increases the crime rate rather than reduces it, mentally unstable persons might be attracted by the possibility of punishment. Punishments might embitter and alienate criminals from society and increase their criminal activity. If utilitarianism had these and other bad effects, utilitarians would renounce punishment in favour of some other and more effective means of dealing with offenders (op. cit., p. 369).

Attempts have been made to combine both the utilitarian and the retributive approaches by having a mixed theory. This holds that the aim of punishment for crime is the utilitarian one of preventing or reducing crime. Thus the aim must be constrained by the view that only those who have voluntarily broken the law should be punished and that their punishment should be proportionate to the offence. Failure to punish such people who threaten society would mean there would be additional innocent victims.

In Phoenix, Arizona, an elected sheriff has introduced 'Tent City'. This houses over 1000 men and 1000 women in tents out in the searing heat with temperatures over 100 degrees. They are in chain gangs and have no privacy, showers are communal, they wear pink socks and underwear. This is done because they do not like the colour and to shame them. In 1997, Amnesty International said that the punishment there is dehumanising. It also says that Tent City is a severe environmental hazard and guards have been accused of using excessive force. Most of the people in these tents have prison sentences for less than a year. The sheriff is supported by 80 per cent of the local population who clearly approve of these methods and he is seeking to run for higher office. Observers from many police forces around the US and the world have come to look at his methods which he sees as the way of the future.

The *lex talionis*, 'law of retribution', is often appealed to by those who hold to a retribution theory. This maintains that the punishment should equal the crime (e.g. 'an eye for an eye', see the quote above). Capital punishment thus becomes the appropriate remedy for murder, enthusiastically embraced by many Christian groups in America. However, this principle suffers from considerable problems. It does not, for instance, take into account the mental states, background or intelligence of those committing the offence. Also it is not easy to apply this law exactly, for instance in cases of theft where the perpetrators have no money. Also, crimes differ. For instance, the killing of a husband by a wife who has been beaten and abused by him in a domestic quarrel and the killing of a bank guard by armed robbers are both killings, but the latter is surely in a different category from the former.

The *lex talionis* points to the moral acceptability of capital punishment. Such punishment is held to be a good deterrent and to be a fitting punishment for those who commit murder. One of the key problems with capital punishment is the number of innocent people who have been convicted for murder. Long gaol sentences at least allow the possibility of the error being discovered and rectified but capital punishment is so final that innocent people are likely to be killed. What is more, it makes acceptable what is considered unacceptable. It is precisely because killing is regarded with such horror that a severe penalty is proposed, but if the penalty itself leads to the state carrying out killings then, it may be argued, this forces the state down to a low moral level. It may be held that capital punishment is the most effective deterrent, but there is little clear evidence for this and, in any case, few murders are committed by people who weigh up the likely consequences. A life sentence in prison can be every bit as severe a deterrent as capital punishment.

Because the retributive theory leaves no space for attempted reform, the situation can arise that after the designated period of retribution (in prison, or in a US chain gang) the offender can be released to offend again. There have been many instances where sex offenders have served their time and then been released, only to almost immediately commit the same crime for which they faced retribution in the first place.

Punishment can, however, also be seen as fulfilling a third role, namely a therapeutic or reformatory role, and to be intended to stop offenders repeating their offence. This is an attractive picture as it concentrates not on the instinctive but perhaps primitive reaction of 'an eye for an eye' but on stopping offenders offending once more. Many people pay lip service to this approach but, in practice, prisons' are rarely the best places to reform people. For instance, in many British and other prisons the conditions are appalling and can dehumanise people. Instead of building up offenders and providing them with a feeling of responsibility and self-worth, it can operate in the opposite direction by degrading those concerned and destroying any respect for civilisation or decent behaviour. All too frequently prisons are filled by people who should not be there. Bernard Hoose gives an example from the US where a young man was imprisoned for a year for possessing marihuana. He was placed in a room with 12 others and they sexually assaulted him every hour for 48 hours (Bernard Hoose, 'Received Wisdom', p. 133). This is hardly the atmosphere conducive to reform.

It must also be recognised that prison is a very expensive way of protecting society from offenders. The cost of locking people up is exceptionally high and on a purely cost-benefit analysis, it is very often not good value. The British Conservative Government in 1995 cut back many education and training programmes in prisons because these were considered to be a luxury. Michael Howard, the then Home Secretary, delighted Tory Party conferences by spelling out the strictness of the punishments proposed for offenders. This doubtless appealed to the middle class and secure members of society who support the Conservatives, but it showed no insight into, understanding of or interest in any sound and rational approach to the administration of justice.

The 'short sharp shock' type of punishment, for instance the kind that puts young offenders into a semi-military regime, is as likely to alienate those who suffer it as to deter them, and this sort of programme has no component which aims at reformation or help for those involved. Indeed, it is precisely the provision of education and training which might enable prison inmates to earn a living in society, yet it is precisely these provisions which were severely curtailed by certain Governments. This is a good example of political decisions being taken to appeal to a certain group of voters rather than to do what is equitable, just and effective for society.

There seems to be no single, adequate philosophical basis for punishment. Each system points out the weaknesses of the other, yet it is undoubted that society does need to protect itself against those who refuse to accept its rules. The debate is, therefore, likely to concentrate on the forms of punishment rather than whether punishment in itself is acceptable. A new issue in the ethical debate is raised by some evidence that certain criminal tendencies may be inherited.

Inherited criminal tendencies

If it can be established (and at present the evidence is not conclusive) that criminal tendencies are based on genetic factors, then the whole arena of the debate about crime and punishment will be changed. In particular the problem of whether human beings are free when they act will arise. They may, indeed, be doing what they want to do, but what they want to do may be determined by their background and nature. If this could be established, then the whole retributive basis of punishment would be radically undermined and the way could be open, for instance, for genetic screening of foetuses to eliminate criminal tendencies. This, in itself, would raise very worrying ethical issues about what it is to be 'normal' and would radically undermine the whole basis of religion and morality, both of which depend on the idea of human freedom. Kant maintained that freedom cannot be proved but is nevertheless a necessary postulate of any morality.

The evidence for a genetic link between criminality and certain genes has not yet been established – but even research into this issue is contentious. Reiss and Straughan put it this way:

> … it may be that as we learn more about DNA we will find that there is a genetic component to many human traits. Certainly much human behaviour has a significant genetic component. If you present a Border collie puppy (bred to round up sheep) and a Newfoundland puppy (bred to rescue drowning sailors) with, for the first time in their lives, a collection of scattered tennis balls and a large bowl of water, the Border collie will often attempt to round up the tennis balls and the Newfoundland will jump into the water.

Similarly, it seems likely that a considerable amount of human behaviour is genetically determined – but the issue is how much this is the case. Human beings are incredibly complex and our actions, to the extent they are determined, are influenced both by our nature and our nurture – in other words, both by our genes and also the environment in which we grow up. Even these two factors, when taken together, may only influence rather than determine behaviour. One problem is that even discussing the issues is controversial and raises difficult issues:

> In 1992, a conference on genetics and crime was cancelled amid angry accusations and counter-accusations. The conference called 'Genetic factors in Crime' was planned for October 1992. A brochure introducing the conference stated that 'genetic research holds out the prospect of identifying individuals who may be predisposed to certain kinds of criminal conduct'. A key figure opposing the conference was psychologist Peter Breggin (who) maintained that the … children of inner-city schools would be tested for biological markers, such as low levels of 5-hydroxytryptamine, that allegedly make people more likely to be violent. Most American inner-city schoolchildren are

black (*Improving Nature* by Michael Reiss and Roger Straughan, Cambridge, Cambridge University Press, 1997, pp. 212–3).

The problems are obvious as the motives of the testers may be called into question. It could be that there is an implicit racist agenda in place which could seek to find 'evidence' that black children are more prone to crime than white. Much would depend on where the tests were conducted, what criteria were used for selection and other factors. It could even be the racism that is genetic!

Having said this, if a link could be established between criminal activity and genetics, then this would raise the issue of whether there should be mandatory genetic alteration of people who have these genetic traits. This would be an affront to personal liberty. On the other hand, the criminal justice system precisely does impose punishments and sanctions on people and sometimes even seeks to alter their nature (for instance in the case of paedophiles so that they do not reoffend), so the issue is not as straightforward as it might first appear. What is obvious is that much work remains to be done and, even if a tendency towards crime is detected, this is a long way from the claim that human actions are determined by the gene pool.

Perhaps it is a mistake to look for a single justification of punishment. At the least, in the modern arena, punishment should seek to protect society, to deter crime but also to prevent the criminal reoffending. Unless all three elements are present, then any theory may be impoverished and may be morally flawed. Too great a concentration on reforming the criminal may be just as bad as too great a concentration on the victim. Many criminals come from unfortunate backgrounds and the sociological influences of environment and culture need to be taken into account. Some criminals undoubtedly need help and, in today's world, much crime is drug related with people being forced into crime in order to maintain a habit which they are not capable of giving up on their own. Similarly, lack of jobs and opportunities can tempt young people to crime and whilst this cannot, by itself, be an excuse for criminal behaviour, it is nevertheless a factor that should be taken into account. It is often the refusal to wrestle with complexity that leads to simplistic and inadequate solutions.

A society that accepts injustice for the poor, that tolerates high levels of unemployment and a sense of hopelessness amongst some sectors can hardly be regarded as a just society. When 'justice' is appealed to as a means of safeguarding the interests of the 'haves' against the 'have nots', then any idea of morality or fairness must be subject to real question. Plato held that the wealthy should not be paid more than six times as much as those who are poor. In Europe, America and other societies the differentials have grown much larger than this. In South America, a small number of wealthy people control most of the land and the poor are kept in order by the force of the law. Any challenge to the rights of the rich is then punished as a crime. The moral basis for any such system must be considered to be dubious.

Questions for discussion

1 Is it morally justifiable for people to be sent to hell? Give your reasons.
2 Was it morally justifiable for Pontius Pilate to condemn Jesus to death in order to prevent a riot?
3 Discuss the strengths and weaknesses of utilitarianism as a basis for punishment.
4 'An eye for an eye, a tooth for a tooth.' Evaluate this statement.
5 Does retribution have any role to play in deciding on punishment for crime?
6 Can there be justice in punishing criminals if the State is unjust?
7 Assess the arguments for and against capital punishment.

SIXTEEN

Human Rights

We have seen in the chapter on Rawls and Nozick that it is possible to construct a philosophical case in which the moral obligation to assist those worse off than ourselves is understood to play a necessary part. To recap, we outlined first the Hobbesian Social Contract Theory, now modified and rearticulated by Robert Nozick. This version of the theory establishes a minimal moral principle along the lines of 'Do not harm me, and I shall not harm you.' We then argued that a second kind of social contract theory to be found, for example, in the works of John Rawls establishes a further moral principle which can be expressed as 'I have an obligation to aid those who are worse off than myself.' Although adopting a different line of reasoning to Rawls, Singer (1993) nonetheless wishes to affirm the same moral principle.

However, our concern in this chapter is the issue of human rights, and the way in which we can connect the notion of human rights to the moral obligation to aid the poor, the disadvantaged and the vulnerable. Consider the following incident:

In July 1993 a roving death squad made up of off-duty and retired policemen opened fire on a group of street children who were sleeping rough near a church in Rio de Janeiro, Brazil. Seven children aged between eight and fifteen were killed. According to estimates two children a day are killed by such death squads whose job it is to clear the streets of this 'human debris'.

What can moral theory make of this? Well, a number of things may be said. Firstly, from a deontological perspective we could easily apply Kant's Respect for Persons Theory summed up in his Practical

Imperative: 'Treat all persons as ends in themselves and never as a means only.' In the Rio case the children were viewed as mere commodities, as human waste that needed to be cleared up and swept away so that a) the wealthy and well-heeled would not have to witness such squalor and so spoil their champagne lunches, and b) the likelihood of begging and stealing was avoided. The street children are seen not as ends but as means, and their eradication is the means to other people's happiness and contentment.

The deontological response is quite unequivocal. The killings are simply morally wrong. However, our second perspective, that from a utilitarian position, may not be so clear cut. We may well emerge with two widely differing interpretations depending upon the number of 'facts' we have at our disposal. Remembering that, at root, the utilitarian is committed to the greatest happiness principle the two competing interpretations may be as follows:

i) The pain, suffering and deaths of the children themselves are likely to contribute to an increase in the fear and suffering experienced by the remaining street children. This suffereing is not counterbalanced by the increased contentment felt by the rich or the increased satisfaction of 'efficient policing' felt by the death squads. Moreover, the intense moral repugnance expressed by other countries may be thought, even by the perpetrators of the deed, to be more damaging to their personal and collective happiness than the act itself.

ii) Alternatively, the strict utilitarian may argue that the children were likely to have been orphans whose passing would go virtually unnoticed. Their lives would more than likely have been full of pain and suffering in any case. Therefore, on balance, the stability, quietude and contentment among the majority of the local population justifies the involuntary euthanasia carried out by the police.

An emotivist response and an intuitionist response are both likely to be different again. So where can we look to find a suitably consistent and practical moral response to such problems as poverty, disadvantage, vulnerability and oppression? One answer might be to make an appeal to the concept of human rights, a concept which has become almost universal, although there are philosophical problems attached to it.

Consider these few facts:

a) Literacy
• In Afghanistan 69 per cent of the adult population cannot read;
• In Liberia the figure is 62 per cent;
• In Djibouti it is 54 per cent.

b) Life expectancy

Iceland	:	79 years	Guinea	:	50 years
Canada	:	78 years	Bhutan	:	53 years
Holland	:	78 years	Afghanistan	:	45 years
Norway	:	78 years	Somalia	:	49 years
Sweden	:	78 years	Liberia	:	49 years

c) Child deaths per thousand

United States	:	8	Guinea	:	210
United Kingdom	:	7	Angola	:	209
Sweden	:	5	Uganda	:	141
Singapore	:	5	Sierra Leone	:	284

(All these figures are taken from the United Nations statistics for 1998.)

These figures speak for themselves, and yet rights to life, health and shelter are some of the many rights formally enshrined in the Declaration of Human Rights established by the United Nations (UN).

United Nations and human rights

The United Nations (UN) was officially launched in 1945. The original fifty-one signatory nations include Australia, Brazil, Canada, China, Egypt, France, Greece, India, Iran, Iraq, New Zealand, South Africa, USSR, UK, USA, Yugoslavia. By 1987 the member states numbered 159, the latest additions being Zimbabwe, Belize and Brunei Daruassalam. The Preamble to the UN Charter reads:

> the people of the United Nations ... reaffirm faith in funda-mental human rights, in the dignity and worth of the human person, in the equal rights of men and women and of nations large and small.

Embedded in this Preamble is a principle akin to Kant's Practical Imperative. Irrespective of race, creed or colour all persons are deserving of respect. This is then connected with another principle, that to do with equality. The assumption is that all persons are born equal and are therefore deserving of equal consideration. The life of Queen Elizabeth II should not be counted as intrinsically more valuable than the life of a Somali girl born during the famine. Or, to put the argument the other way round, Orwell's famous *Animal Farm* dictum ' All animals are equal but some animals are more equal than others' is a flagrant abuse of the moral status of people. However, what does it really mean in practice to say that:

a) People have rights?
b) People are equal?

Before going on to explore these two questions a brief account of the kinds of rights the UN affirms will be of value in providing some background information.

So what kinds of rights are there? *The Universal Declaration of Human Rights* (1948) was later divided into *Civil and Political Rights* on the one hand, and *Economic, Social and Cultural Rights* on the other. This was engineered in 1966. Specific rights include:

- right to life, liberty and security
- right not to be held in slavery
- right not to be subjected to torture or degrading treatment
- right to equality before the law
- right to freedom of thought, conscience and religion
- right to a standard of living adequate for wellbeing of self and family, including food, clothing, housing and medical care and necessary social services
- motherhood and childhood are entitled to special care and assistance
- right to security in event of unemployment, sickness, disability, widowhood and old age
- right to work, and just and favourable conditions of work
- right to equal pay for equal work
- right to education
- right to rest and leisure, and periodic holidays with pay
- right to freedom of movement within and beyond state borders
- right to effective remedy for violation of human rights.

This is nowhere near the complete list, although it gives us an indication of the kind of rights that are considered to be universally applicable. Of course, there is a vast gap between the rhetoric of rights and the reality of their application. For example, 50 per cent of the world's population has no access to clean water and decent sanitation; and a child dies from starvation every two seconds. (Christian Aid 1993). We witness on a daily basis in undeveloped, underdeveloped and developed countries the systematic abuse of many of these rights. We might well ask then, what do such rights really mean, and do people really possess them?

Natural and human rights

Before answering the question a distinction needs to be drawn between natural rights and human rights, although the long philosophical tradition associated with 'rights talk' has tended not to distinguish between the two. From Plato and Aristotle through to Aquinas it has been argued that there is a natural law (*lex naturae*) which underpins the order of the universe. This order we can discern through the power and application of reason. Later, both Hobbes and Locke deployed this concept of natural law to establish some basic and natural rights of man. For Hobbes the natural right was simply not to be harmed by another. If assaulted one could justifiably use any means to repel the assailant. But that was the only natural right one possessed. Everything else depended upon the willingness of parties to negotiate 'civil' contracts with each other. Everything else, from land, money, goods and property was, effectively, 'up for grabs'. Locke, in the *Second Treatise on Civil Government*, continued the natural rights tradition but extended the rights in order to cover 'liberty' and 'property'. As well as the right to life, one had the right to personal freedom and the right to own property. These are natural rights sanctioned by God.

Since then, much of the discussion about rights has tended to rely on some version or other of the natural law theory and, therefore, the term human rights has been synonymous with natural rights. Philosophically, however, we may say with a measure of confidence that, from a secular point of view, there are no such things as natural rights, but there are certainly things called human rights. Natural rights may be thought of as those rights accorded to a being by Nature. It would be as if each infant were born with an indelible stamp on his or her forehead indicating the list of rights which must not, under any circumstances, be interfered with because they were implanted there by Nature herself. They exist by virtue of nature alone and are not conferred on a person by society nor through common agreement. As J. B. Mabbot (1958) says of rights before rejecting them:

Natural rights must be self-evident and they must be absolute (*The State and the Citizens*, p. 57).

Much earlier, Jeremy Bentham referred to them as a 'nonsense on stilts' and more recently, Alasdair MacIntyre has dismissed them as 'fictions'. This rejection of natural rights on account of their not being self-evident is reasonable. We cannot point to a self-evident quality called a natural right held by a person in the way that we can point to a whole range of self-evident qualities such as eyes, ears and hair.

We said earlier that we could be philosophically sure of our ground about the clear absence of such things as natural rights provided we adopted a secular position. The reason is that, as we know, most religions, and Christianity is certainly no exception, insist on a version of natural rights being attached to individuals at birth or even prior to birth. The kind of natural right religion generally insists upon is a right to life, and is usually covered by what is known as the sanctity of life doctrine. That is, a human life is self-evidently sacred because that life is granted by God, and therefore, should be interefered with by no-one excepting God.

Human rights, on the other hand, are the actual products of moral, social and political agreements made between human beings. Such agreements try to establish those conditions thought necessary for a decent existence. Natural rights may be fictions, but human rights have already been enshrined in public documents, authorised by international communities and entrusted to a worldwide organisation partly established to ensure that such rights are not violated. Now whether the UN performs this last function well or badly is not the point. The point is that human rights are not fictions. They are social realities just as much as are marriage vows, legal statutes and abstract nouns like love, hate and jealousy.

It must be restated that some philosophers, like Richard Wasserstrom (1964), would not wish to draw a distinction between natural and human rights, believing that the distinction is artificial, which, in one sense, of course, it is. But then, so are most concepts of an abstract nature. We could, for example, argue that the distinction between justice and injustice is artificial. There is no self-evident object in existence called justice (unless, of course, one is committed to a form of moral objectivism or cognitivism in the way that Plato was), but we can point to documented instances of what a community has agreed are injustices. Wasserstrom prefers to talk of human/natural rights (he uses the labels interchangeably) in terms of 'moral commodities' to which people are naturally entitled on account of them belonging to the human race.

Equality

We made the point early on that the Universal Declaration connected the concept of rights to the concept of equality. Something must therefore be said about the nature of equality. It presents us with an age-old conundrum: Are people equal, and if so, in what ways are they equal? It is clearly an absurd thing to say that all people are equal if by that we mean that they are so in every respect. Some are large, some are small, some are good with paper and pen, others with spanner and saw. The list of differences is endless. So, clearly we are not born equal in the sense that we are not all born the same. It would be an exceptionally dull world if we were. Part of the wonder and richness of being human is the fact that, to a greater or lesser extent, we are all different.

However, it does not follow that because we are all different we should therefore all be treated differently, or worse still, have different sorts of laws applied to us. To follow such an argument would be to subscribe to what is known (somewhat paradoxically) as the 'formal principle of equality'. Originally ascribed to Aristotle the principle states that we ought to

treat equals equally and unequals unequally.

For example, in ancient Greece it was considered right and proper to accord equal treatment to aristocratic Athenian males because they were all equal to each other in status. A slave or a barbarian, however, must not expect treatment of a kind similar to that accorded to the Athenian for the simple reason that neither the slave nor the barbarian was considered in any sense equal to the wealthy Greek male. In fact it would have been improper or plain wrong to treat the slave or the 'foreigner' in the same way that one should treat the Athenian. Fortunately, the formal principle has become something of an antique curiosity, at least among philosophers, although not so among the death squads that roam Brazil and elswhere.

Bernard Williams (1969) draws four distinctions in relation to equality:

1 'statements of purported fact', for example, 'that (people) are equal'
2 'statements of political principle' for example, 'that (people) should be equal'.

We have substituted (in brackets) the word 'people' for the word 'men' that was in Williams' original account.

The difference between these two is clear. For some political constitutions, written or unwritten, it is deemed a self-evident 'fact' that people *are* equal, irrespective of any differences between them. Natural rights, as we have presented them, are predicated on this kind of equality. However, for others (notably constitutions based on political scepticism), equality is not a self-evident fact, although it would be a good thing if it were. Hence, such constitutions are based on the principle that people *should be* equal.

3 Equality in terms of 'distribution of goods'
4 Equality of 'respect'.

On the latter two issues Williams says:

> One might hope for a society in which there existed both a fair, rational and appropriate distribution of these goods, and no

contempt, condescension, or lack of human communication between persons who were more or less successful recipients of the distribution (B. Williams, 1969, 'The Idea of Equality' in J. Feinberg (ed.) *Moral Concepts*, p. 171).

The 'fair, rational and appropriate' allocation of goods is a form of distributive justice. For Williams then, equality is connected with both respect for persons and distributive justice. And this link between justice and equality is made more explicit by Hospers who uses a simple analogy to make the case on its behalf.

There is no doubt that in daily life we associate the idea of justice with that of equality. If a parent is kind to one child and cruel to another, we call this treatment unjust. If a judge is severe to one prisoner and lenient to another for the same offence, this treatment too is called unjust. In both cases we attribute the injustice to 'unequal treatment' (John Hospers, 1961, *Human Conduct*, p. 345).

This may be called the common-sense view. However, the defence of equality is by no means universal. David Cooper, for instance, in a tightly argued book called *Illusions of Equality* (1980), maintains that in human communities the concept of equality and its associated practices are 'at odds' with other concepts and practices which we also hold dear. For Cooper the pursuit of excellence is more important than the pursuit of equality. Consequently, he accepts 'without bashfulness, the "inegalitarian" label' (Cooper, *Illusions of Equality*, p. 163).

The case for human rights

R. S. Downie (1971) has also explored the conflict between various principles to which communities subscribe. For Downie there are four basic political principles which are in competition:

- utility
- equality
- liberty
- fraternity.

The last three, of course, were those championed by the French Revolution. The two principles that cause the problem are equality and liberty. Social equality sits uneasily with individual freedom, as the chapter on Rawls and Nozick suggests. The pursuit of individual freedom in a community soon leads to material inequalities, and from there to social inequalities. Jordan's *The Common Good* (1989) points to the real material and social inequalities in the western industrialised world which has opted more for the principle of liberty than for the principle of equality. Following Jordan's argument we see three social classes beginning to emerge. They are all unequal, particularly in terms of the distribution of goods:

- *an elite class*: generally white, male, wealthy, well-educated, working in the high-status professions;
- *an exploited class*: generally white, female, on average income, working in low-status jobs;
- *an excluded class*: a loose configuration of groups including the homeless, unemployed, ethnic minorities, disabled and the poor.

What is interesting in Jordan's critique of these inequalities is the contradiction embedded in the libertarian philosophy which has brought them about. The divisions, the gaps between the classes, have been the result of an over-emphasis on individual self-interest and personal economic gain at the expense of commitment to the community and collective responsibility. Jordan has identified the flaw in the philosophy: if the excluded class turn against mainstream society (that is, the other two classes), particularly through crime against property, it is only because it is in their self-interest to do so. In a culture which has promoted Hobbesian self-interest above anything else it is likely to find that the excluded or underclass take to the principle with a vengeance. Mainstream society has, by design or by default, excluded them. It is therefore no longer in their own interests to subscribe to its laws and values, except for the single proposition that self comes before others.

However, the appeal to a set of rights enshrined in law can do much to eradicate the growing inequalities in societies and between societies. It can, for example, open the door to mainstream society for the excluded class. Despite the assertion that natural rights probably are fictions in the true sense of the word, human rights are social facts which have as their purpose the reduction of human suffering and the maintenance of truly ethical communities in which respect for persons is taken seriously as a rational practice and not as an outdated doctrine. Lucas sums up the case:

> By conducting our deliberations in terms of rights ... we make discussion cruder but easier for others to join in, and although it may lead to some people's interests being overridden, it also, and more importantly, manifests respect for people by investing their own actual decisions with legal significance (J. Lucas, 1980, *On Justice*, p. 34).

Some problems with the argument from equality and justice

We may summarise the argument in the following way:

i) All people are equal. They all have equal intrinsic value, and that value simply depends upon them being members of the human race. Given these propositions, human rights ought to be distributed equally among human beings. Human beings, therefore, all have the equal right to life, shelter, food and respect for their intrinsic worth.

ii) As justice is inextricably linked with equality, both from a common-sense position and a formal position, it is a matter of justice that all people: a) should have equal rights, and b) that such rights are equally respected.

One of the problems is that the second part of the argument is circular. The meaning of (x) is validated by the meaning of (y); the meaning of (y) is validated by (z), and the meaning of (z) is validated by (x), and so on. It is based on the assumption that there are necessary connections between rights, justice and equality. It is arguable whether such connections do actually exist. Asserting connections between abstract nouns is easy; arguing such connections, when we are in doubt about the nouns themselves, is notoriously difficult. Philosophers throughout the ages have found this out to their cost and embarrassment.

There are (at least) two further problems, one philosophical, one practical (assuming that we are justified in making such a distinction). Let us first assume that there are such things as human rights. They are social facts in the sense that they exist in documents, and human groups have affirmed their existence. What we now wish to ask is: Which human rights are applicable to all human beings on the basis of justice and equality? This is the philosophical problem. The answer might simply be to refer to the Universal Declaration of Human Rights to see what it says there. But a problem still remains; for example: Is the right to work, and just and favourable conditions of work, on an equal par with the right to life? Presumably not. Therefore, we are faced with the problem of having 'graded human rights'. Is it possible to rank-order the list of rights? Supposing that we were able to reach some universal agreement on their priority listing, then our second problem, the practical one, would soon present itself. And this would be to do with the kind of basic political and economic commitment governments (acting on behalf of communities) would be willing to make in order to ensure that such rights were taken seriously.

Human rights as moral rights

Alan Gewirth's *Human Rights: Essays on Justification and Application* (1982, Univ. Chicago Press) is probably the most comprehensive account of the ways in which both the philosophical and practical problems may be addressed. For Gewirth, human rights are moral rights, and may be argued on the grounds of their necessity. It is a matter of moral necessity that humans have certain rights simply because they belong to a widespread moral community, namely the human race. Moreover, such rights are to do with what may be called concrete goods, such as food and shelter, and abstract goods such as freedom of belief. Being necessary, human rights are not contingent. That is, they are not dependent upon something else, for example, upon someone being white, or being European or American. However, these necessary moral rights may be distinguished from other kinds of rights such as 'legal, prudential and intellectual' rights. Such a distinction is to be found in our previous question to do with the improbable parity accorded to the right to life and the right to work and just, favourable conditions of work. In summarising his position, Gewirth argues that

> the ultimate purpose of the rights is to secure for each person a fundamental moral status (A. Gewirth, *Human Rights*, p. 5).

Such fundamental moral status ought, by necessity, to have been accorded to those children in Rio. Human rights may be the best way of ensuring that it will be so accorded in the future.

Questions for discussion

1 Do you believe in natural and human rights? If so, for what reasons?
2 Which human rights to do you believe are of primary importance? On what grounds would you distinguish them from rights of secondary importance?

3 How else might the formal principle of equality be applied? Try to give some examples.
4 Give some examples of the ways in which the principle of liberty may conflict with the principle of equality.
5 Is the pursuit of excellence more important than the pursuit of equality?
6 Do all people have intrinsic moral value?

SEVENTEEN

Animal Rights

The moral debate about animals generally revolves around five controversial areas:

1 Animals being bred and killed for food – particularly for instance, where the farming techniques prevent many chickens or pigs ever leaving a space in which they can not turn round. Vegetarians, on the whole, believe that it is ethically unjustifiable for humans to kill animals for food and, therefore, choose a diet that excludes the eating of animal flesh. Vegans go one step further by excluding the eating and drinking of all substances derived from animals. Therefore, eggs, milk and cheese are also avoided.

2 Animals being used for medical experiments. Many people have little objection to this use of animals provided that the experimentation involves the minimum amount of pain and suffering caused to the animals. It is often argued that the medically engineered deaths of some mice and cats is a morally justifiable price for the cure of say, cancer, which is causing the painful deaths of thousands of people including young children.

3 Animals used for the testing of cosmetics, detergents and other non-medical goods. Of late, the lobby which opposes the testing of cosmetics on animals has become powerful; so much so, that many shops and manufacturers use the 'not tested on animals' label as a positive advertising and marketing ploy.

4 Breeding and killing animals for their fur. Again, this is something in the west that is beginning to wane as a result of public pressure. A woman can no longer flaunt the wearing of a mink coat or a fox-fur wrap in the way that she could in the 1940s and 50s. It would be difficult to object to an Eskimo killing a seal for clothing (and food), as the Eskimo's survival is on the line. However, the range of alternative textiles available to the average westerner makes the slaughter of minks and rabbits unnecessary.

5 Finally, there is the highly-charged question of the hunting and killing of animals for sport and the breeding and training of animals for entertainment. Of these, foxhunting and deerhunting in the UK and bullfighting in Spain tend to inflame the most passion. Some theatres now prohibit the use of live animals on stage, and some councils in the UK refuse performance permits to circuses which use animal acts.

Historical and philosophical viewpoints

Traditionally, philosophy has not been effective at defending the moral status of animals. Arguably, it was Aristotle who was responsible initially for the superior attitude that western societies have taken towards animals. For Aristotle, animals were devoid of reason. The power of reason is what clearly distinguishes humans from animals. Moreover, the purpose of humankind is to use its reason. That is the function of a person, to deploy the rational mind. If that is so, what is the function of animals? Aristotle was quite clear on this:

plants exist for the sake of animals, and brute beasts for the sake of man — domestic animals for his use and food, wild ones for food and other accessories of life, such as clothing and various tools. Since nature makes nothing purposeless or in vain, it is undeniably true that she has made all animals for the sake of man (Aristotle, *Politics*).

Prior to this, however, the Pythagoreans (after the philosopher, Pythagoras, 580-500 B.C.) tended to demonstrate a care for animals, but only on the basis that in tucking in to a piece of cooked pig one might be munching on the implanted soul of an ancestor. The Pythagoreans believed in the transmigration of souls or metempsychosis. As has already been stated, this is the doctrine in which the souls of the dead may well enter the bodies not only of other people but of animals. Pythagoras is once reputed to have tried to restrain someone from whipping a puppy dog on the following grounds:

> Stop, do not beat it; for it is the soul of a dear friend – I recognised it when I heard the voice (from Diogenes Laertius, *Lives of the Philosophers*).

The Christian tradition tended to reflect the views of Aristotle. St Augustine (350-430), the patron saint of theologians, believed it was perfectly acceptable for Christ to do away with the Gadarene swine because animals, having no sense of reason, cannot exist in the same moral sphere as humans. Therefore, in effect, we can do what we like to them. Later, the great medieval theologian and philosopher St Thomas Aquinas (1225-74) reinforced this position with admirable clarity:

> It matters not how man behaves to animals, because God has subjected all things to man's power and it is in this sense that the Apostle says that God has no care for the oxen, because God does not ask of man what he does with oxen or other animals (*Summa Theologica*).

However, things have not quite been so clear cut in the biblical tradition. For example, in the book of Genesis there are two accounts of the creation of the world (Genesis 1:1-2; 4a; and Genesis 2:4b-25). In the first of these God is portrayed as making sea creatures and land animals before he made humans and God blessed these animals. However, the human beings were to have 'power over the fish, the birds, and all animals, domestic and wild, large and small' (Genesis 1:26). This gives the impression that animals are there for the use of human beings. The second account gives a different picture with human beings being told to 'cultivate and care for' (2:15) the garden of Eden and the animals and birds were brought to the first man so that he could name them. These two contrasting attitudes, of power and guardianship, have come down through the history of the religious debate. Some Christian writers have attempted to differentiate humans from animals – and thus to argue that the latter have no rights – by claiming that animals have no soul. However, as the discussion of ensoulment makes clear, this may be problematic.

Despite freeing philosophy from the yoke of theology, Descartes (1596–1650), the French philosopher and mathematician, firmly believed that animals were not capable of experiencing pain. Therefore, he had little qualms about experimenting on them without administering any form of anaesthetic. Even the German philosopher, Immanuel Kant (1724–1804), subscribed to the same view:

> so far as animals are concerned, we have no direct duties. Animals are not self-conscious, and are there merely as a means to an end. That end is man (*Lecture on Ethics*).

This long tradition of placing animals clearly outside the realm of morality or ethical significance on the grounds that they do not possess rational minds is often referred to as the 'absolute dismissal argument'. Animals are simply excluded, or dismissed, from the moral circle which binds humanity together.

As recently as 1986, Michael Fox ('The case for animal experimentation') argued that animals are not members of the moral community as they do not use sophisticated language, plan, accept responsibility for actions and are not critically self-aware. They therefore have no moral rights.

Modern statistics

Before considering some of the responses to the absolute dismissal argument, some statistics may be relevant:

Animal experiments in Britain in 1990

Total procedures	3,207,094
Without anaesthetic	2,205,360
Number of cats	3,456
Number of dogs	8,567
Procedures on mice	1,636,332
Deliberately causing cancer	59,616
Reasons for tests:	
medical/veterinary procedures	1,523,377
cosmetics and toiletries	4,365
food additives	10,822
household products	1,486

(Home Office. Source: Observer 17.11.91)

These statistics are significant. Firstly, they raise the obvious question whether one species (dogs) should be accorded a higher moral status and thus whether they should be the subject of more concern than another (mice) and what the criteria for differentiation would be. Secondly, Peter Singer in *Practical Ethics* makes the point that it is difficult to justify the testing of more cosmetics and toiletries on animals which are known to experience pain when there are already sufficient types of such products on the market to suit just about every fashion. The medical and veterinary use may seem justified on the basis that drugs used, say, on humans must first be comprehensively tested – although it can be argued that biological modelling and protein engineering are adequate substitutes for animal testing. The case of deliberately causing cancer in animals, especially mice, raises a host of ethical concerns. There is a particular technique known as transgenic manipulation. One result of transgenic manipulation is the 'oncomouse' – a mouse which carries an implanted human cancer gene which soon develops into cancer, killing the mouse within 90-100 days. In 1985, the US patent office awarded patent number 47336866 to Harvard University for its development of the oncomouse. This patent is now available for commercial use from the Du Pont company for a mere £100.

There are at least three moral concerns here. First, there is the issue of whether or not it is justifiable and therefore right to experiment on animals at all. Second, there is the question of whether or not it is morally acceptable to create living beings which are deliberately fashioned to suffer pain and an early death. Even if these are held to be justified by the greater good that may result (that is, the possible elimination of cancer), there is the third ethical dilemma of the commercialisation of such pain and suffering with a view to ensuring profitability for a company.

Animals for food

Transgenic manipulation has also resulted in the development of supposedly 'superior' farm animals which will yield greater quantities of meat. For example, there is the 'superpig' which through the insertion of human growth genes can almost double the meat yield of an ordinary pig. There are moral considerations similar to those connected with the oncomouse. In addition to the question of whether or not the rearing of pigs is desirable in order to kill them for food, there is an ethical problem attached to the deliberate manipulation of life to bring about greater economic profitability. Again, similar to the oncomouse, if we add the third problem which is that the superpig suffers a series of debilitating side-effects, such as skull deformity, arthritis, lethargy, impotence and abnormal hormone production, then the moral justification for the creation of such an animal becomes less credible. Unless, of course, we wish to adopt the 'absolute dismissal argument' in which animals are, for whatever reasons, placed completely outside the bounds of moral consideration.

However, we may want to defend a milder version of the argument. Let us call it the 'pragmatic dismissal argument'. On this view, animals are accorded moral status but it is not equal to that accorded to a human being. Therefore, in general, we may wish to treat animals with the same respect that we treat other humans, excepting that if it were a question of saving Lassie or her owner, then the animal takes second place. The moral status of animals would only be reduced in circumstances that threatened the survival of human communities or individuals. Similarly, a pacifist might hold dear to the principle of non-violence, until she is forced to defend herself and her children against a maniac aggressor. It would be difficult to accuse her of unethical behaviour, despite the fact that she had taken a pragmatic approach to her moral principles. On the face of it the ethics of pragmatism appears attractive. We can hold sincere moral beliefs until they are truly tested in certain circumstances, and then we can ignore, modify or bypass them. This, in effect, is probably what most actually do in practice.

Speciesism

The term 'speciesism' was introduced into the formal language used to describe the moral status of animals by R. Ryder in *Victims of Science: The Use of Animals in Research*. It refers to the disproportionate moral weight given to members of one species, in this case, the human species. It is an expression of stubborn preference for beings of one's own kind and a clear prejudice against members of another kind. As such, speciesism may be said to be synonymous with the dismissal argument. Moreover, it is sometimes argued that speciesism is similar to sexism and racism – more rights accorded to one's own sex or race than to another's. Singer puts it thus:

Racists of European descent typically have not accepted that pain matters as much when it is felt by Africans, for example, as when it is felt by Europeans. Similarly, those I would call 'speciesists' give greater weight to the interests of members of their own species when there is a clash between their interests and the interests of those other species (*Practical Ethics*, 1993, p. 58).

The consideration of interests is crucial in Singer's argument. For Singer, a minor interest should not count over a major interest. So, for example, the minor interest of a pleasant taste in the palate of a human should not be counted above the major interest of an animal losing its life in order that such a pleasant taste can be enjoyed. Singer maintains that as we now find racism and sexism to be morally unacceptable, we are logically committed to finding speciesism equally unacceptable.

However, Bernard Williams in *Ethics and the Limits of Philosophy* is not convinced of the moral force of speciesism. We are human beings, and therefore, it is perfectly natural that we are likely to give greater weight to the interests of human beings over animals. The language of morality is, after all, a human invention, or so it is argued. This is not, however, the same as saying, like Aquinas, Descartes and Kant, that therefore we can do what we like with animals. Indeed, inflicting unnecessary pain on animals diminishes us, morally, as human beings. Even the limited sense of caring for animals as an object lesson in teaching children how to show compassion for another living being seems to have some justifiable moral merit – although this approach bases moral care of animals on its usefulness to human beings.

Animals for hunting and entertainment

Not much has been said about the use of animals for hunting and for entertainment, and it would be difficult to write a chapter on the moral status of animals if nothing at all was said about, for example, foxhunting. Generally those who go hunting foxes use the following three arguments. Firstly, they claim that foxes have to be killed because they are such a nuisance to farmers. Foxes maim and kill lambs, pregnant sheep, and hens. What is more, a fox will often kill more than is needed for its own food. There are two responses to this. The farmer can either protect the stock more carefully, which will take time, effort and money, or he or she can accept that foxes have to eat to survive in the same way that other creatures do and that, therefore, the loss of some stock is a price worth paying for respecting the fact of the fox's existence. Clearly, though, neither response is satisfactory. There is a third response which is to defend the right to hunt and kill just as many foxes as is necessary to avoid the loss of stock and minimise the nuisance.

The second argument used by foxhunters, is to do with the tradition associated with the practice. Foxhunting, it is claimed, is an ancient country sport with a history and a tradition based on a set of rituals. The wearing of particular clothes, the riding of horses, the chasing of the fox with a pack of hounds and the ritualistic daubing of the mauled fox's blood on the forehead of the youngest recruit to the 'hunt' is all part of that tradition which binds a community together. The counter-argument is simple. Just because something has a tradition and a history that is no good reason for continuing it. Slavery had a long tradition attached to it, but we now see it as an evil to be avoided. The practice of publicly hanging criminals had a long history but we now view it as something quite barbaric and morally reprehensible. If foxes are to be culled, then perhaps it is ethically encumbent upon us to find a more humane method of doing it. The counter-argument to this is equally powerful. It is stated that foxhunting, as opposed to gassing, poisoning or any other quick means of termination, ensures that the fittest foxes survive, and that, therefore, the fox population is likely to continue, aided by natural selection, rather than die out altogether. The third argument, that foxhunting provides sport and entertainment, is perhaps the weakest of the three. Arguably, I would enjoy spraying paint over my neighbour's car, particularly when it is permanently parked in my space. Moreover, I am sure that it would provide my children with a frisson of pleasure, but emphasising its entertainment factor would hardly give me the moral right or justification to carry out the act. But this is, of course, a trivial example. The law already prohibits the deliberate fighting between dogs and cockerels on the ground that such practices are barbaric. An activity which necessarily involves the fearful chasing, painful maiming and destruction of a non-human animal arguably disqualifies itself as a sport or an entertaining pastime.

The 'difference' argument

Peter Singer points to the heart of the speciesist's problem when he asks the question: On what grounds are non-human animals different from human animals? Is being a 'person' (and therefore deserving moral status and protection) dependent upon being conscious, rational, autonomous or on having the criteria demanded by Fox (p. 211)?

The criteria used by Fox and others to support the absolute dismissal argument may be challenged, as some categories of human beings cannot use sophisticated language, be critically self-aware etc. (for instance babies, some geriatric patients, those in a coma and those who are mentally retarded). Most people would reject the idea of experimentation on such groups and, if this is accepted, why should not the same protection be extended to the more complex animals such as dolphins, whales, dogs and cats – and where does one draw the line? If we are prepared to accept the moral responsibility for experimenting on cats, rats, dogs and chimpanzees, all of which display advanced characteristics such as those described, then why rule out experimenting on certain categories of geriatric patients or even babies? Fox, in fact, changed his mind a year after his argument first appeared and he came to maintain that the basic moral obligation not to harm human beings should be extended to animals. The key to the whole issue of animal rights may well lie in determining the criteria for personhood but this is notoriously difficult – as the history of the philosophy of mind has shown.

Discussion of animal rights may sometimes be based on an emotivist approach to ethics – a person who has seen whales being killed, the intensive rearing of pigs where the sow cannot turn round or rabbits having their eyes injected with chemicals may react strongly and condemn such practices by labelling them 'immoral'. However whether this is an adequate grounding for an ethical position may be a matter of debate.

One way forward may be to argue for a form of proportionalism – maintaining that animals should be accorded moral rights unless there is a proportionate reason which would justify these being waived. What reasons might counter-balance the rights claimed for different species of animals may be the prime area of debate in the future.

Jeremy Bentham has a quotation which has become famous in animal rights discussions and which comes close to the heart of the problem:

The day may come when the rest of the animal creation may acquire those rights which never could have been withholden from them except by the hand of tyranny ... The question is not 'Can they reason?' nor 'Can they talk?' but 'Can they suffer?' (Intro. to *The Principles of Morals*, ch. 17).

Clearly animals do experience pain and suffering, but whether this is a sufficient reason to accord them rights is a matter for further debate. Moreover, to draw animals into the moral circle in the way that Singer suggests, and to accord them the kinds of rights which have normally been reserved for humans simply on the basis that many animals display characteristics of personhood (self-consciousness, autonomy, etc.) is tantamount to setting up personhood as the sole criterion for moral consideration. For humans to grant rights to animals on the grounds that animals are like humans, or more accurately, that some non-human animals are like some human animals, is somewhat arrogant, although, of course, this is far more preferable to humans morally dismissing animals altogether.

However, Stephen Clark's solution in *The Moral Status of Animals* (1977, Clarendon Press) is an interesting one. Clark argues that we ought to respect animals not on the basis of their *similarity* to humans, but rather on the basis of their *difference*. Animals are simply different creatures sharing the same planet as ourselves and, as such, are deserving of respect. This re-casting of the Kantian Respect for Persons Theory as the Respect for Living Creatures Theory avoids the need to identify various indicators of personhood in living beings before moral consideration can be extended to them.

Questions for discussion

1 Do animals have rights? And if so, what are they?
2 Is speciesism the same kind of prejudice as racism and sexism?
3 What criteria might be used to differentiate human beings from animals? Defend your choice.
4 Do animals have souls? What difference would it make if they did?
5 What are your views concerning the development of the onco-mouse? What arguments could be used to defend transgenic manipulation?
6 Analyse the statistics provided. What conclusions may we draw from them?

EIGHTEEN

Environmental Ethics

Environmental ethics has recently gained a high profile as more and more people are recognising the fact that some scientific evidence demonstrates that we are needlessly and unthinkingly destroying parts of the natural environment. Not only this, but many animal species, if they are not already extinct, are in danger of rapidly becoming so. However, before examining the ethics of environmentalism in detail it is worth exploring a particular philosophical controversy which has a bearing on ecological problems and their possible solutions.

The 'is/ought' controversy

There is a famous controversy in philosophy known as the 'is/ought' controversy. Briefly, it concerns the distinction between epistemology (theory or theories of knowledge) and ethics (theory or theories or morality). What *is* the case is the concern of epistemology, whereas what *ought to be* the case is generally the concern of ethics. One of the principal aims in epistemology is to give an account (scientific and logical) of the way in which the world is constructed. It is concerned with describing the world as it is and people as they are. One of the main aims of ethics, however, is to give an account of the way in which perhaps the world ought to be and the ways in which people ought to conduct themselves within it.

Now one line of thinking from Hume onwards suggests that the division between epistemology and ethics, or between *is* and *ought*, is clear cut. One cannot move logically between the two without making some serious category mistakes. Hence, many philosophers have maintained that you cannot derive an 'ought' from an 'is'. That is, you cannot logically derive a moral stance simply from a description of the way things are in the world. Take the following example which, for Hume and others, makes an unwarranted move from 'is' to 'ought'.

- *Is statement*: Chemically, biologically and physically the planet is in a less stable condition than it was three hundred years ago.
- *Ought statement*: That being the case we ought to begin to address the problem and make it more environmentally stable.

For Hume and others it does, of course, make some sense to say that we ought to do something about the mess around us. But it is simply false to say that what we ought to do is a necessary logical step from what is the case. To move from description to prescription is logically invalid.

Others, including Prior, Searle and MacIntyre, however, claim that there are cases in which it is logically valid to move from description to prescription. Epistemology and ethics are necessarily connected. MacIntyre, quoting Prior, gives an example:

- *Is statement*: He is a sea-captain. (Descriptive statement)
- *Ought statement*: Therefore, he ought to do what sea-captains do. (Prescriptive statement)

(A. MacIntyre, 1981, After Virtue, 2nd edn. 1985,
Duckworth, p. 57).

Proponents of environmental ethics, particularly deep ecologists or deep environmentalists, largely work from the latter assumption that when we talk of the environment as a whole, epistemology and ethics must necessarily connect with each other. For them, environmentalism is an ethical imperative. Because we are an inevitable part of the overall ecosystem, we ought therefore to examine our impact upon it, and if such an impact is damaging then we ought to do something about it.

Three categories of environmental ethics

For the past 65 million years, according to Alan Marshall (writing in the *Journal of Applied Philosophy*, 1993, Vol. 10, No. 2), there existed a natural ecological balance between animate and inanimate, living and non-living entities on this planet. When humans arrived on the scene the hunter-gatherer culture followed by the agrarian culture did little to upset the ecological balance. However, the last three hundred years of rapid industrialisation has led to a massive imbalance between humankind and nature. The various finely-tuned ecosystems have been grossly disturbed, some irretrievably so. What has been the response? For Marshall, three broad ethical approaches have been adopted over the past twenty years or so:

1 The libertarian extension

In this approach the human race has extended its own concept of individual rights to non-human animals and, occasionally, to inanimate entities. We may suppose that it is referred to as 'libertarian' in the sense that individual entities ought to be given the right to an uninterrupted freedom of existence. In this category we may find, for example, the work of Peter Singer. Singer argues along rational grounds that the 'expanding circle' or moral worth should be redrawn so that it includes non-human animals as well as human animals. Not to do so is to be guilty of speciesism. (See chapter 17). However, for Singer, it is a problematic issue whether or not such a moral boundary should also include plants and lesser life and non-life forms. In the first edition of his *Practical Ethics* (1979) Singer arued that as plants are not 'sentient' or conscious living entities it is difficult for us to know what their interests would be in staying alive. Consequently, Singer advocated a 'hierarchy of value' similar to that originally advanced by Aristotle. Singer stated:

> The hierarchy of value leaves open the possibility that when I weed my vegetable garden, the life of each weed I destroy has some value, though a value overridden by my own needs; but is

there really any intrinsic value at all in the life of a weed? Suppose that we apply the test of imagining living a life with no conscious experiences at all. Such a life is a complete blank; I would not in the least regret the shortening of this subjectively barren form of existence. This test suggests, therefore, that the life of a being that has no conscious experience is of no intrinsic value (P. Singer, *Practical Ethics*, p. 92).

However, since the work of deep ecologists such as Arne Naess and George Sessions (1984), Singer's second edition of *Practical Ethics* (1993) contains a slightly revised view of the hierarchy of value theory. Although finally unconvinced by deep ecology ethics, on account of our clear inability even to begin to imagine what sorts of interests yeasts and grasses might have in not being disturbed, Singer is prepared to admit that this

does not mean that the case for the preservation of wilderness is not strong. All it means is that one kind of argument – the argument from intrinsic value of the plants, species or ecosystems – is, at best, problematic (Singer, *Practical Ethics*, 1993, p. 282).

This category of libertarian extension may also include the work of some ecologists who wish to argue that all ontological entities (that is, beings and objects that actually exist), are deserving of moral status or ethical worth simply on the basis of their individual existence. Andrew Brennan's (1988) *Thinking about Nature: an investigation of nature, value and ecology* (London) may be said to fall within this category. Brennan prefers, however, the title 'ecological humanism' or simply 'eco-humanism'. Arguably, Robin Attfield's (1983) *The Ethics of Environmental Concern* (Oxford) also occupies the same category, although unlike Brennan, Attfield argues his position from a theological perspective.

2 Ecological extension

This approach concentrates not on the individual ethical rights and status of each and every living and non-living entity, but rather on the overall importance of:

a) the fundamental inter-relatedness of all things in the geophysiological structure of the planet (often subdivided into the biosphere and geosphere); and

b) the essential diversity of such things within the planetary structure.

It may be said that the work of, for example, Naess and Sessions (1984, 'Basic Principles of Deep Ecology' in *Ecophilosophy*, vol. 6) straddles both approaches: the libertarian and the ecologic. For Naess and Sessions there are a number of bedrock moral principles which need to be affirmed. Among them are:

i) The well-being and flourishing of human and non-human life on earth have value in themselves (synonyms: intrinsic value, inherent value). These values are independent of the usefulness of the non-human world for human purposes

and

ii) Richness and diversity of life forms contribute to the realisation of these values and are also values in themselves (Source: Singer (1993) *Practical Ethics*, p. 281).

This category of ecologic extension is also referred to as Eco-Holism, and includes James Lovelock's now famous Gaia hypothesis (1979, *Gaia: A New Look at Life on Earth*, Oxford) in which the planet is characterised as a single, unified (or holistic) living entity with its own in-built rationale.

3 Conservation ethics

This approach focuses on the importance of ecological conservation and preservation, not because of any intrinsic value ecosystems and life forms might have, but simply because of the benefits such systems and life forms bring to humankind. We must preserve the planetary environment because it is in our interests to do so, and that the environment is there for our own exclusive use and pleasure. The environment, on this view, is given instrumental or extrinsic value. It becomes not an end in itself, but a means to other ends, the means by which humans gain pleasure and/or profit. This is the most prevalent form of moral reasoning about the environment which, in turn, tends to dictate policies on the environment. Arguably, it was the principal ethic that informed the thinking of politicians during the international Rio Summit in 1992. It is an ethic very different from that which informs the Green Politics of Capra and Spretnak. In *Green Politics: The Global Promise* (1984, Paladin) there is to be found a loose configuration of spiritual values, feminist critique and rejected modernity:

> ... any vision of Green politics must reflect three essential elements ... First, Green politics rejects the anthropocentric orientation of humanism, a philosophy which posits that humans have the ability to confront and solve the many problems we face by applying human reason and by rearranging the natural world and the interactions of men and women so that human life will prosper ... (Secondly) Green politics goes beyond not only the anthropocentric assumptions of humanism but also the broader constellation of values that constitutes modernity. Modern culture ... is based on mechanistic analysis and control of human systems as well as Nature, rootless cosmopolitanism, nationalistic chauvinism, sterile secularism, and monoculture shaped by mass media ... The third cultural force that Green politics counters is patriarchal values ... the term 'patriarchal culture' in most feminist circles connotes not only injustice toward women but also the accompanying cultural traits: love of hierarchical structure

and competition, love of dominance-or-submission modes of relating, alienation from Nature, suppression of empathy and other emotions, and haunting insecurity about all of those matters (pp. 234-6).

Humanist, bio-centric and eco-holist theories

As a consequence of the growing interest in the environment, ethical arguments and positions are classified and categorised in a potentially bewildering number of ways. Michael Smith, for example, also writing in the *Journal of Applied Philosophy* (1991, Vol. 8 No. 2), has tabled a similar three-part classification to Marshall's:

1 *Humanist Theories*: those theories, like Singer's, in which moral status remains tied to a set of criteria such as sentience or consciousness. Human and non-human animals possess undisputed value because it is possible to conceive what their interests would be in remaining unharmed.
2 *Bio-centric theories:* This is a term taken from Paul Taylor's *Respect for Nature* (1986). Although recognising moral worth in all living organisms, from human and non-human animals to trees and plants, such theories are partly predicated on the belief that the expanding ethical circle ought not to include, for instance, piles of sand. The reason being that insects, plants and animals all clearly have a 'good-of-their-own' but a pile of sand could not have such a 'good-of-its-own' for the simple reason that it is a non-living entity. To attribute ethical status to non-living entities is simply absurd. This is not to say, however, that from the perspective of conservation ethics we cannot nor should not value sand dunes and mountains. Clearly we value them because we enjoy beach picnics and mountaineering, but the sand and the rockface do not possess any inherent or intrinsic worth or value of their own.
3 *Eco-holistic theories*. This category is, as has already been indicated, identical to Marshall's ecologic extension category.

What is particularly interesting about Smith's classification is his assertion that, in essence, each of the three types of theory is basically humanist in the sense that humans are still seen as occupying a central place in the expanding circle, and that any moral concern for the environment is shaped by an already rigid human vision. Instead, Smith asks us simply to consider the 'otherness' of the wilderness or the jungle:

> Perhaps the only long-term chance for the survival of the jungle lies in our coming to see it as a being of intrinsic value on its own terms. The jungle offers us a chance to escape a world where all we see reflects 'humanity' back at us (M. Smith, 'Letting in the Jungle', *Journal of Applied Philosophy*, p. 153).

Two things may be said about this. Firstly, it is difficult to see how different Smith's view is from the deep ecology perspective (of Naess and Sessions) which he terms eco-holism. Secondly, it is difficult to see how one could ever escape from some version or other of the human mirror-reflection. We happen to see, articulate, or understand things from a human perspective simply because we are human.

Williams' four effects

The philosopher Bernard Williams follows a line of enquiry similar to that taken by Smith, Naess, Sessions and other deep ecologists, except that Williams adopts a thoroughgoing conceptual analytical style in contrast to the previous 'theory-types' approach. In a paper entitled 'Must a Concern for the Environment be Centred on Human Beings?' (in C. Taylor, ed., 1992, *Ethics and the Environment*, Oxford), Williams sketches in a four-part classification based on 'effects'. The intention seems to be to consider the practicalities of, as well as drawing the theoretical distinctions within, environmental ethics.

1 *Unallocated effects* – for example, the effects of environmental policies on all future generations. The effects are based on a straight cost/benefit equation, although the questions of whether such costs should be compensated and how they can be calculated are hardly straightforward. For example, if I like loud music the benefit to me of this activity may constitute a real loss to my neighbour who has to suffer it. Is compensation an issue here? Or, to take another example, should future generations be compensated for, say, the loss of being able to ride among the North American buffalo simply because white American cowboys in the last century enjoyed indiscriminate hunting? On a more serious level, should we begin to consider compensation for future generations in respect of increased skin cancer brought about by the depletion of the ozone layer?

2 *Experiential effects.* These refer to any actual perceptions and experiences of a person consequent upon the activity of another. How is a person's experience affected by the activity of another? Bathers suffer a clear experiential effect because of irresponsible garbage dumping at sea. Weekend picnics are ruined because of untreated sewage pumped into rivers flowing through local beauty spots. And so on. Clearly and logically, these effects will have to be judged before any unallocated effects can be considered. Experiential effects may be thought of as being purely human effects.

3 *Non-human effects.* Whatever policies are pursued or activities undertaken, they will undoubtedly have some greater or lesser effect upon animal species. Foxhunting, for example, has a non-human effect which requires some ethical response. Building a new sports complex may well improve both unallocated and experiential effects on humans but may have a disastrous non-human effect in terms of the destruction of natural habitat for, say, birds, mice and voles.

4 *Non-animal effects.* Finally, there are those effects which relate to all non-animal entities. This may encompass living organisms such as trees, flowers and plants, and inanimate things such as mountains, deserts and rocky outcrops.

Interests and experiences: The Sand Dune Problem

Williams believes that non-animal entities can have 'interests' though they cannot have 'experiences'. For Singer, the two concepts are conflated. For an entity to have an interest it must first be capable of experiencing something. However, for Williams the two cannot be conflated; the difference between them is quite crucial, although the nature of that difference is not at all clear. Sentient creatures, that is human and non-human animals, clearly have experiences in the sense that they respond to situations and circumstances in such a way that one can assume something significant is going on in their brains and neurological systems. Put simply, my dog would yelp in pain and surprise if I suddenly kicked him hard. Clearly then, they (sentient creatures) also have 'interests'. My dog actually has an interest in not being kicked. As a living entity that exists in a straightforward ontological manner my dog has some kind of an interest in his own preservation. Moreover, I can guess roughly what that interest is likely to involve. He wishes not only not to be kicked, but to be fed, watered, protected and shown some kind of basic affection. We might though want to take issue both with Williams when he says that, for example, trees and plants do not have experiences, they only have interests. It is sometimes alleged that plants emit some kind of a screaming sound when the stem is plucked from the roots. Moreover, we talk of trees and plants as growing, ageing and dying, and if those aren't fundamental experiences it is difficult to know exactly what they are.

However, we know what Williams means when he wants (perhaps rightly) to draw some distinction between plants and trees on the one hand and cats and dogs on the other. It is a more clear-cut issue when one begins talking of mountains, rocks and sand dunes as not having experiences, but none the less having interests. A sand dune does not, in any sense of the word, experience any sensation if my daughter decides to reshape it with a bucket and spade. We might argue that the natural habitat of ants, sand fleas or certain types of flora is radically disturbed, and that these inhabitants are just as much part of the sand dune as the sand itself. This though is a side issue as we are concentrating on inorganic entities such as the sand itself, or the hard, granite rockface on the side of a mountain. The rock cannot experience the fact of my hitting it with a hammer in order to extract fossils. One could argue though that the sand dune or the rock, in actually having an existence at all, has an interest in being left alone and not deliberately or accidentally broken up or interfered with. However, this is perhaps taking an argument too far. We are able to identify with the experiences, and hence the interests, of cats, dogs, horses and rabbits because they seem to exhibit many of the behaviours that we identify with humans – they are loyal, responsive to affection, and pine when a significant being is absent. We may even be able to identify with the experiences of trees. In a long dry spell, plants wilt and die if they are not properly watered and cared for. We have some vague understanding of the interest in staying alive that plants possess. However, as sand and rocks have no experiences as such, it is perhaps impossible for us to make sense of what their interests might be. A stone cannot care at all if I throw it in the water or smash it with a hammer. It is difficult therefore to make proper sense of the word 'interests' in the way that Williams uses it. By default, therefore, his argument seems to be no different to Singer's 'hierarchy of value' doctrine that we have already encountered.

There are, of course, other levels of non-animal effects that we have not yet covered. These include organic entities such as viruses and bacteria which clearly can have an interest in multiplying and staying alive. If we are to preserve life forms and species then are we not logically committed to the non-interference with these? However, such a moral absolute is, perhaps, rather absurd. The moral sanctity of all living things is a doctrine that needs at least two qualifications. The logical qualification may be derived from a utilitarian balancing of interests. The interests humans and animals have in avoiding the pain and suffering likely to be experienced as a result of contracting a lethal strain of bacteria probably far outweighs any interests the bacteria might have in staying alive. The other qualification is a simple emotional one that has been given expression in culture. I just happen to be more in sympathy with the child dying from cancer than I am with the cancer cell. I am, therefore, happier and more ethically assured of my ground with the thought that the cancer cell ought to be demolished rather than the child.

Anthropocentrism

As we have suggested before in our discussion of Smith's notion of 'otherness', any talk of environmental ethics is bound, to a greater or lesser extent, to be anthropocentric, or human–centred, for the simple reason that philosophy in general and moral reasoning in particular are straightforward human activities. Anthropocentrism (Gk. *anthropos* – man; *kentron* – centre) may be understood in two ways. Firstly, a 'strong thesis' view is predicated on the belief that not only are humans at the centre of reality but that they ought to be so. Secondly, however, there is a 'weak thesis' version that is predicated on the simple understanding that reality can only be interpreted from a human point of view, and that, therefore, humans have to be at the centre of reality as they see it. This is not, however, to say that humans cannot try to imagine what reality may be like from the perspective of a non–human or even non–living entity, but it is perhaps beyond the realm of human ingenuity to discover what the internal consciousness of cats, dogs, sand–fleas and others may be like. My dog does not moralise about how I should treat him, and the trees in my garden cannot reason about their own existence.

Therefore, our concern for the environment is bound to be human–centred, if only because it is humans who deploy the linguistic concepts by which we discuss these issues, although, if we are realists we may nevertheless try to adopt an ethical approach to the environment which is not based on human self–interest.

Gaia: life without humans?

There are clearly good reasons why the Exxon Valdez oil leak disaster, the Chernobyl nuclear fire and the East European defor-estation caused by acid rain all ought to have been avoided. And not all of the reasons have to do with the effects upon people. Firstly, the animal and non-animal effects of each of these disasters are difficult to quantify. How many individual animals suffered and how many species were affected is a matter for debate. What is undeniable is the fact that humans were responsible for the disasters. Secondly, it may be that the overall scale of destruction is such that the consequences for humans is far outweighed by the consequences for all non-human entities, be they animal, vegetable or mineral. James Lovelock's Gaia hypothesis responds to these two considerations quite succinctly. Life (with a capital L), or Nature (with a capital N) might be so far committed to its own survival that the future of the human race is of no real significance to it in the long run. It might be that the planet Earth (the Gaia 'spirit'), taken as a single and unified whole, gradually alters its own geophysiological structure so that the human race is obliterated or massively reduced in order to halt the human-engineered environmental damage which threatens the survival of the planet itself. The cosmos is not primarily committed to the human race, unless, of course, one believes in a particular religious system or a particular version of the anthropic principle – that the universe exists in order to be explained by humans. However, the cosmos may be governed by some kind of ultimate imperative, and that imperative may simply be to do with ensuring that some kind of organic and inorganic substance continues to survive and evolve. There might be a blueprint for the universe, but human beings may well not be a necessary feature of it. The moral consequences of that are difficult to assess and, in the end, it is not human beings who control nature but Life and Nature which may not be prepared to tolerate human beings. If this view is taken our environmental ethics may have a fundamentally self-centred motive – to ensure that Nature allows the human species to continue to survive.

Questions for discussion

1 Where do you think the boundary of the expanding moral circle should finally be drawn? Around humans? animals? plants? inanimate objects? the planet as a whole?

   Try to give reasons for your answer.

2 How could one argue that a sand dune can have no 'experience' but it can have an 'interest'?

3 Should we seriously be considering compensation for unallocated effects? If so, what kinds of effects?

4 Is it at all possible to imagine the 'otherness' of the jungle in the way that Smith suggests? If so, how might we go about it?

5 What practical steps ought to be taken in the a) short-term, b) medium-term, and c) long-term futures to ensure that we deal with the environment in an ethical manner? (Assuming that we would want so to do.)

6 Can you detect any error of reasoning in the two principles cited by the deep ecologists?

7 In which of Smith's or Marshall's categories would you place yourself, and for what reasons?

NINETEEN

Genetic Engineering

Clarity and dispassionate analysis are often lacking in discussions about genetic engineering as the issues are complex and require some basic scientific knowledge combined with ethical analysis. The issues will be dealt with under four headings: (1) Human genetic engineering, (2) Genetic testing of human beings, (3) Genetic engineering of animals, and (4) Genetic engineering relating to plants.

Human genetic engineering

There are three main types of genetic engineering: somatic cell, germ line and enhancement gene therapy (eugenics, the attempt to use genetic engineering to improve the gene pool as a whole, is not dealt with there).

Somatic cell genetic engineering

This involves making genetic changes to particular cells. The new and altered genes can either be injected into cells where genetic change is required, they can be 'fired' in using a type of 'gun' or, more frequently, they can be introduced by using the 'retrovirus vector' to attach the new genes. As an example, bone marrow cells are responsible for generating human blood and retroviruses have been used to insert functioning genes into defective bone marrow cells in order to ensure the production of healthy blood. Another example might be in the potential treatment of cancer. At present, if cancer cells are detected then an operation is likely to remove the cancerous cells before they spread any further. This will mean removing a considerable amount of healthy tissue as well as safeguarding against the possibility of there being a small number of cancerous cells present. If these cells are not removed, they would grow and the cancer would reoccur. Thus a woman might have a breast removed if she is detected with breast cancer and, perhaps, a radical mastectomy would be performed. This involves removing not only the breast but also the lymph glands under the arm as cancer cells can spread through the lymphatic system. Somatic cell genetic engineering holds out the prospect of attaching a 'self-destruct' gene to the cancerous cells, thereby killing all the cancerous cells but leaving the healthy cells intact. The problem is to target just the cancerous cells and not the healthy ones and as these are, genetically, almost identical this is exceptionally difficult. The risks of not getting this right are obvious as it would lead to both healthy and cancerous cells being killed.

In the case of cancers that are more difficult to access (such as prostate cancer in a man) this would also make treatment much easier. It seems hard to argue that there is any moral problem with this form of treatment. There is clearly no objection to the killing of diseased cells to save a person's life and there do not seem to be any obviously identifiable risks that would make the procedure foolhardy. Somatic cell genetic engineering may also be used to stimulate the production of hormones which the body needs and which, for some reason or other, the body has ceased to produce in the necessary quantities. As examples, this engineering could be used to stimulate the pancreas or thyroid or to stimulate the production of insulin or antibodies to resist diseases.

In Britain, the Clothier Committee produced a report on the ethics of somatic cell genetic engineering. Their decision was as follows:

We conclude that the development and introduction of safe and effective means of somatic cell gene modification directed to alleviating disease in individual patients, is a proper goal for medical science ... the prospect of this new therapy heightens the familiar ethical concerns which attend the introduction of new treatment, we conclude that it poses no new ethical problems (Clothier Committee, 1992, Report of the Committee on the Ethics of Gene Therapy, HMSO, Ref. 32, p. 17).

The British government approved this decision a year later. Assuming that the technology can be developed and that clinical trials are eventually successful, then somatic cell genetic engineering would seem to hold out the hope of positive benefits for human beings with few negative elements.

Germ–line gene therapy

Germ cells are the reproductive cells – in other words, they are found in the testes of males and the ovaries of females. All a woman's eggs are present in her body by the time she is a 15-week foetus, which is why it is possible to fertilise the eggs of an aborted foetus and to implant these into another woman's womb. These eggs are then released between puberty and the menopause. Men produce huge numbers of sperm throughout their lives. In both men and women, there has been nothing individuals can do to affect the genes passed onto the next generation. This is now changing.

Germ–line gene therapy differs from somatic cell therapy because alterations are made to the germ cells. This means that any genetic alteration will be passed onto the person's children (if he or she has any). Haemophilia or hereditary diseases which are genetically transmitted may thus be capable of being eliminated by altering the genes that carry the disease. The dangers, however, are much greater than in the case of somatic cell gene therapy because once alterations are made to germ cells then these will be carried on through future generations. A mistake in somatic cell therapy should not extend beyond the patient being treated, but an error in germ line therapy for those who are still able to have children may extend into the whole of the human gene pool with potentially devastating consequences.

The key issue in assessing the morality of genetic alterations may be the balance of risk against reward. Whatever the benefits of germ-line therapy, the worry must be that there are unquantifiable risks of genetic alterations entering the human gene pool. Because of this, it may well be morally right for all germ-line gene therapy in humans to be ruled out until our present knowledge has extended further. Bernard Hoose argues that this need not be a permanent ban. It needs to be renewed in the light of our increasing knowledge. Ian Barbour agrees with this:

> I would approve germ-line gene therapy only under three conditions. Firstly, extensive studies of human somatic-cell therapies similar to the proposed germ-line therapy must have been conducted over a period of many years to acquire data on the indirect effects of the genetic changes. Secondly, the effects of similar germ-line therapy in animals must have been followed over a period of several generations to ensure the reliability and long-term safety of the techniques used. Third, widespread public approval must have been secured, since the therapy will affect unborn generations who cannot themselves give informed consent to treatment (I. Barbour, *Ethics in an Age of Technology: The Clifford Lectures 1989–1991*, Vol. 2, p. 197).

A separate problem with this form of therapy is that there may be no clear agreement on which defects are to be eliminated. For instance, whereas some would be happy to eliminate Downs syndrome, others would be less happy to eliminate a homosexual inclination (and there is some evidence, although it is not yet conclusive, that homosexual and lesbian inclinations are passed on genetically through the female line. If this proves to be correct, then the possibility would exist for being able to eliminate this characteristic). In the chapter on natural law, it was explained that the Catholic tradition holds that all human beings share a common human nature and, therefore, those who deviate from the norm are defective. A homosexual inclination is, for instance, considered to be defective. It is significant that the language of 'defect' can easily lead to the idea of 'correction of defects' and this raises the issue of what features of human beings may be regarded as 'defective' and in need of 'correction'. There is no agreement on this and there are real dangers if it is ever suggested that certain 'defects' should be compulsorily eliminated at the foetal stage. It might, for instance, be argued by a government that this would save money in the long term as children born with certain inherited defects are very expensive to care for and elimination of these defects would enable them to live 'normal' lives. The dangers, however, of regarding some human beings as 'normal' and others as partly 'defective' should not need to be spelt out – although this view is, in fact, implicit in the Natural Law tradition.

It may be argued that instead of germ-line gene therapy being something to avoid, it may be a technique that we have a moral obligation to use positively in the interests of generations yet unborn. John Harris takes this position:

> We must not act positively to cause harm to those who come after us, but we must not fail to remove dangers which, if left in place, will cause harm to future people. Thought of in this light, there is a clear dilemma about genetic engineering. On the one hand we must not make changes to the genetic structure of persons which will adversely affect their descendants. On the other hand we must not fail to remove genetic damage which we could remove and which, if left in place, will cause harm to future people (J. Harris, 'Biotechnology – Friend or Foe?' in *Ethics and Biotechnology*, ed. A. Dyson and J. Harris, pp. 216–29).

On Harris's view, therefore, there is a positive ethical obligation to remove defects which will affect future generations. The problems remain, however, of deciding which supposed 'defects' are to be eliminated and who will make the decisions. The dangers of this argument being used to carry out a form of eugenics (i.e. genetically improving the quality of the gene pool as a whole) are considerable.

Questions also arise about the nature of personhood. If one alters the genetic make-up of an individual, may this result in the destruction of one person and the creation of another? What, in other words, does it mean to be a person? If a foetus has the genes which will lead to Downs syndrome and these are eliminated, has the same person been changed or has a new person been created? The boundary lines are by no means clear.

Enhancement genetic engineering

Commercial companies are now allowed to patent sections of the human genome. This may have profound consequences as we discover more and more information about the double helix that represents the human genome. Once the sections of the genome responsible for, for instance, blond hair, blue eyes, height, athletic ability, intelligence and long life are discovered, then this opens the prospect for couples to 'design' babies to suit their wishes. Instead of a couple 'falling in love' and deciding to marry and have children with the resulting random mix of their genes, a wife may be able to say to her husband: 'I love you, I enjoy making love to you but, let's face it, I could do better genetically'.

She may then choose to have her husband's sperm genetically altered in order to develop features that are not naturally present, for instance paying to buy sections of the genome that would enable height or intelligence to be increased, athletic ability to be improved and lifespan to be extended. Alternatively she may choose to buy sperm from a donor with better genetic characteristics.

Many will view this with horror, but this initial reaction needs examination. When one decides to have children with a partner, one is effectively selecting a set of genes which will have a crucial effect in determining many things about the resultant offspring including their intelligence, looks and likely lifespan. Of course there is a random interchange of the 23 chromosomes from sperm and egg when fertilisation takes place but the genetic material is largely fixed by the parents. Instead of this selection of genetic partner being a random process due to 'falling in love' the possibility will soon exist to be able to select the features that are considered most desirable. If, for instance, a couple have a son, and the son is badly co-ordinated and not very intelligent, one could imagine him saying to his parents at age 15: 'You mean to say you bought a new car before I was born when for the same cost you could have given me better co-ordination, a higher IQ and a longer lifespan? You really are selfish!'

Or a daughter might have Downs syndrome and might then realise that her parents could have ensured that she would have been 'normal'. It may not be easy for parents to look their 13-year-old daughter who has Downs in the eyes and tell her that she could have been able to run and play like any other child but they chose not to make this possible. These situations will raise new moral dilemmas and it will not do to say that any alteration has to be ruled out because it is 'unnatural'. This argument was applied to try to prevent blood transfusions, kidney and heart transplants and many other advances in medicine. The moral issue is why genetic engineering should be significantly different. Three points need to be made:

1 Genetic selection may risk reducing the diversity of the human genome and this could, in due course, make the whole human population less resistant to disease. Having said this, it would take a very long time before this happened and it could be held that the trend may actually be in the opposite direction – namely to increase the diversity of the gene pool still further as parents choose diverse gene options.

2 These techniques will only be available to the wealthy, and this may create a 'two tier' society' in which the wealthy come to regard it as normal to 'design' their babies or at least to be aware of the potential of the combination of genes from two prospective parents.

3 All such alterations are germ line and, therefore, given the 'risk against reward' argument should not take place at the present time.

However, these issues will not go away and cool, clear, philosophic analysis is required to tackle them. To appeal to 'the will of God' may not assist the debate. The days are long gone when most theologians thought that God was responsible for implanting a human soul at some stage in the foetal development process. If God exists, then God has given human beings minds to be able to reason and to deal with the scientific discoveries that have and will be made. In principle, there does not seem to be a significant ethical difference between rectifying a disorder by surgery after a baby is born, and rectifying the same disorder at an earlier stage by adjusting the genome. If this argument is accepted as applying to rectifying defects, then the question needs to be addressed as to why the same argument should not be applied to justify enhancing various poten-tialities. The best argument against the latter may be that our knowl-edge of the genome is still very restricted and we do not know what effect any single alteration may have. On the basis of caution, there-fore, enhancement gene therapy may well not be acceptable at present. However, there seems no reason in principle why it should not be accepted in future, unless one holds a strong view of God's direct intervention to produce each unique foetus. In this case it may be argued that even defects should not be eliminated as, presumably, these are intended by God. Few, however, would be willing to hold this position.

There is a more important challenge that can be mounted against enhancement genetic engineering by those with religious beliefs. This is based on what it means to be a person. There is a real danger that increased emphasis on genetic engineering may lead to a human being coming to be regarded as 'only' his or her genes. This is rather like the playing cards in 'Alice in Wonderland' which say, 'We are only playing cards.' The religious believer's claim is that a human being is far more than simply his or her genetic make-up. To solely concentrate on genetic make-up is a radical impoverishment of what it means to be human. A couple may think they can specify the genetic make-up of their future child so that it is attractive, intelli-gent, good at music and sport and with every other apparent attribute. However, they may fail to recognise what is really important in being human, and this is a quality that cannot be determined genetically.

Already it is possible to choose to have a baby by someone other than a woman's partner. In the US it is possible to buy sperm from Nobel prizewinners, great pianists, etc. and some women choose to take this step in the hope of having a 'better baby'. In a way, much of Darwin's theory of evolution is based on genetic selection – the female (or male) choosing a mate which will optimise the chances of successful offspring. This is a natural biological approach which many biologists claim is a central part of human mating as well as that of animals. There is, here, an effective form of genetic selection at work – albeit 'naturally'. The problems arise as our knowledge increases and in the next century questions may arise as to the moral difference between a woman (a) choosing as a husband a man who is a great composer and having his children, (b) choosing to have children using the sperm of a man who is a great composer which is implanted in her womb, or (c) choosing to have the genetics of her pre-embryo or her own eggs altered so that the resultant offspring will be great composers.

It may also be that whatever our genetics, this in itself will not make someone a great composer. Human beings may be more complex than biology at present allows; in fact, this seems to be the case. In 1976, Richard Dawkins wrote *The Selfish Gene*, and since then many human behavioural characteristics, from homosexuality to intelligence, depression and alcoholism, have been linked to specific genes. When these 'discoveries' were combined with Darwin's theory of Natural Selection, a new science was born – sociobiology. This essentially holds that all human behaviour is governed by our genes and their will to survive. In the nineteenth century, Samuel Butler said that a chicken was only an egg's way of making an egg and the same could be applied to human beings and genes. Two recent books, *Lifelines – Biology, Freedom and Determinism* (by Steven Rose, Penguin) and *Figments of Reality – The Evolution of the Curious Mind* (by Ian Stewart and Jack Cohen, Cambridge), have, however, refuted this simplistic theory. Both books, as a review in the *TES* puts it, '... reject the "it's all in the genes" scenario, finding it to be a dangerously attractive but radically insufficient account of the complexities of human and animal life ...'

Both the authors reject the idea that the Human Genome Project will enable us to understand what it is to be human. Rose argues for a world of increasing complexity in which emerging wholes are more than the sum of their parts. To reduce human beings to their genes radically undermines the traditional religious and moral understanding of human freedom and can also allow for a complacency which tolerates present injustices as being in some sense necessitated by evolution. As Lachman puts it in his review, this is a comforting idea for those with a secure spot on the evolutionary tree, but '... many less "adaptive" individuals wonder why the disproportionate distribution of wealth and social freedom should be rooted in evolutionary necessity and not historical chance and human greed'.

Rose challenges one of Dawkins's most basic premises – that there are basic entities called genes. He argues that it is far from clear what a gene is. The 'genes' of the molecular biologist genes are a complex part of an organic whole with many interdependent players – they are not separate 'things'.

For Stewart and Cohen, life, minds and human intelligence are 'emergent properties' which occur when ordinary matter reaches a sufficient degree of specialisation and complexity. As they put it: 'Minds are ... processes going on inside structures made from ordinary matter.'

You cannot explain the complexities of human personality and intelligence by simply looking at genes or neurons – there is much more going on than that. It is as if you tried to explain the beauty of a painting stored in a computer by the series of binary numbers in which it is stored. There is 'more' to a painting or to being human than any number of cells or genes. As they say: 'If you experience a sunset you see orange clouds, but the reality behind that perception is a matter of light rays, light sensitive molecules, neural pathways and electro-chemical brain activity.'

Of course, genes provide us with incredibly important information about what it is to be human and exciting possibilities in disease treatment, this is incontrovertible. However, to go beyond this and to say that all human beings are is their genes is a radical oversimplification and a mistake. The beauty of a rose, a sunset or Mozart's music as well as the depth and value of an individual human being cannot adequately be captured by genetic analysis, and to reduce these things to genetic codes is to devalue an essential part of our common humanity.

Genetic testing of human beings

As knowledge of the human genome increases, it becomes apparent that a very wide range of dispositions including, perhaps, sexuality, tendencies to criminal behaviour, resistance to different forms of pollution, vulnerability to certain diseases and cancers, length of life, etc. are genetically determined. As genetic testing becomes more widespread it will become possible to predict what a person's natural life expectancy is and many other factors. Already there are young women of 20 who are choosing to have full mastectomies because they know they are likely to develop breast cancer before they are 30. Society has not begun to grapple with the implications of this information becoming available. For instance:

- Once it is possible to predict the likely age of death this will have huge social effects. Some people will be unable to obtain life insurance except at exorbitant rates. This may prevent them being able to obtain a mortgage. They will therefore be unable to buy a house.
- If the onset of diseases can be predicted, then some people may be unable to obtain employment as these individuals will need sick leave (which is expensive for an employer) and any investment in training in the early years may not pay dividends.
- Companies may be able to choose to employ only those who have a high resistance to pollution in places where pollution levels are

high. This could save the company money as not only would they cut down on sick leave but also it is possible that the companies' emission control and other environmental standards would not need to be as high as would otherwise be the case.

- Parents may choose to invest more in the education of those children with a long life expectancy than in those children whose life expectancy is low.

- Men and women may demand a genetic profile of their potential partners before having children with them (ask yourself whether you would want to know what genes a potential partner carries given that this may determine the health and length of life of your children?). This may mean that the idea of 'love' as a basis for securing a partner may still be important, but sexual activity may be separated from procreation as couples decide to emphasise genetic compatibility when deciding on the sort of baby they wish to produce.

- Employers may insist on screening for certain characteristics. One headmaster in Australia was excited by the possibilities of genetic testing as he thought this would enable him to screen potential teachers for homosexual tendencies and thereby to reduce the amount of sexual abuse in his school. In fact, this idea is flawed. The evidence is that sexual abuse is usually performed by heterosexuals rather than homosexuals, but the thought behind the head's idea could be significant as a possible indicator of the attitude of other employers.

Referring to the last point, in 1995 The US Equal Employment Opportunities Commission ruled, under the 1990 Disabilities Act, that it was illegal to use genetic information which indicated that it was likely that an individual would contract a disease as a basis for not employing a person. However, this ruling specifically does not apply to insurance companies. It is also a step that has not been taken by other developed countries.

It is important to notice that the debate about genetic testing is about who will have access to information. Already primitive forms

245

of this information are available. If a person's parents and grandparents live to an old age, he or she will be more likely to do so. Life insurance companies recognise this and routinely ask about the state of health of parents and grandparents and also whether a person has had certain tests (such as a test for HIV). They will also ask for the name and address of a person's doctor so that they may make enquiries about diseases and other factors. Life insurance companies, very reasonably, maintain that it is essential that they have this information so that they can assess the risk. If this information is not available, then a person could have genetic tests carried out and, if they are in a high-risk group, they could take out large insurance policies. The result would be that the life insurance companies would go out of business. Some governments have responded to this by proposing legislation which would make it illegal for employers or insurance companies to demand genetic tests but allowing them to ask whether such tests have been carried out and, if they have, giving them the right to demand access to the results. This sounds a good idea, but abuse is simple as a person could have the test carried out by someone other than his or her own doctor and then not disclose that the test had been done. Unless there was a central database listing every person who had a test (and civil liberties groups might well object to this on the grounds that this smacks of George Orwell's 'Big Brother') there seems no way of controlling abuse.

The Catholic Church has condemned all genetic testing but this blanket condemnation seems arguable. One motive for the ban may well be that couples may choose to have genetic tests carried out on a foetus and then may decide to abort if the foetus carries a defect. However, even if this is considered to be wrong (and this issue could be the subject of ethical debate) then this would not be a reason to ban genetic testing. The fact that a procedure may be misused is not a good reason for banning the procedure. As an example, in some areas of China ultrasound scans are used to determine the sex of some babies and, as China still has a 'one child policy', some couples will choose to abort female foetuses. This is clearly an ethically wrong use of ultrasound scanning, but this does not mean that ultrasound, in itself, is morally wrong. Similarly with genetic testing, the issue is the use to which the tests are put and who will have access to the tests.

It seems clearly to be wrong to allow access to genetic information to be given to anyone without the consent of the individual concerned. There does seem an ethical principle that access to medical records, including one's genetic profile, should only be released provided one gives permission. But this does not take the debate very far as, if employers and insurance companies can ask for the information to be made available, then refusal to comply would mean that a person could not obtain employment or get life cover. There is no easy answer to this problem as both sides have rights on their side. The individual has the right to privacy but the employer and the insurance companies have the right to the information needed to enable them to make commercial decisions without fear of abuse. The strength of the latter argument should not be underestimated. In modern society any law which has the effect of destroying an industry is not viable and to allow individuals to have access to genetic information about themselves and to forbid access by financial institutions to this information would make it impossible for life insurance companies to operate.

Genetic engineering of animals

For many years animals have been bred selectively so as to increase milk, meat and wool yields. There seems little ethical objection to this unless the breeding results in the animals becoming so unbalanced that they are in distress. For instance, if pigs are bred so that they carry so much weight that their legs cannot support them, then this clearly seems unacceptable.

The genetic engineering of animals extends the existing ethical issues raised by selective breeding. Aristotle considered that each animal species had a distinct nature, but this is no longer accepted. Lions can be crossed with tigers and the genes of glow-worms can be put into cabbages. The boundaries between species have now been reduced and animals are being genetically bred for particular tasks. Mice are bred so that they are suited for testing of anti-cancer treatments, cows and goats are genetically engineered to increase existing yields even further and some animals, such as Tracey the sheep, have been genetically bred so as to produce substances needed by human beings. Tracey is the most valuable sheep in the world as she has been bred to produce AAT – a substance used in the treatment of emphysema, a lung disease. AAT is extremely expensive and the hope is that Tracey and her offspring may make treatment more readily available at lower cost.

In a way, Tracey is a paradigm case. She is a healthy sheep living in splendid conditions and yet she is producing a substance which may do a great deal to relieve human suffering. There seems no reason why genetic engineering of animals to produce substances which will benefit human beings should be considered ethically problematic provided that the animals do not suffer. There seems little doubt that animals can feel pain and if they are 'designed' in such a way that their lives will involve suffering then this seems as ethically unacceptable as allowing any animal to suffer. This does not, however, need to be the case. The same argument can apply where animals are genetically engineered to produce greater yields. This has been done for many years by selective breeding but, in many cases, the welfare of the animals has not been sufficiently considered. There is a need for an independent body to monitor the line between the benefit to be achieved by genetic modification and the life of the animals concerned.

It may, of course, be argued that the suffering of animals is not an absolute value and that, for instance, it is morally acceptable to inflict suffering on animals if human beings will benefit. This argument is used to justify testing of cosmetics and medicines on animals. Christianity has traditionally taught that animals existed for the benefit of human beings and, if this is accepted, then the suffering of animals is a small price to pay for benefits to human beings. However, this argument is increasingly being challenged and it is held that animals do have the right not to suffer. If this is accepted, then this will impose limits on what may be acceptable in the field of genetic engineering.

The demand for transplant organs exceeds the supply. Three times as many people are on the waiting list for kidney transplants in Britain compared with the organs available (this is partly due to young people wearing seat belts and also not drinking and driving – both these steps have reduced the number of fatalities amongst young people in car crashes, thus meaning that there are less donor organs available). Using pig-heart valves to replace the patient's own defective valves has become routine, although transplanting organs such as the kidney, liver, heart or lungs is much more ambitious and, so far, has not been successful. There are grave risks in transplanting organs from the higher primates because of the dangers of disease transmission, so genetically engineered pigs (and other animals) are beginning to be bred to provide suitable organs. Such transplants are termed 'xenotransplants'. These could save many lives as well as overcoming many rejection problems due to poor tissue match but there are real dangers with disease transmission across the species boundaries. As an example, swine fever, if it could cross the genetic barrier into humans, could have terrible consequences.

There are great advantages with xenotransplants because they can be grown quickly, supplies are plentiful and the donor animal can be genetically engineered to suit the recipient. The real worry is the easy transmission of viruses and the real risk that viruses at present confined to one species may transfer to the species in which the organs are transplanted with potentially devastating consequences. Again, therefore, there is a 'risk against reward' decision to be made. Because the risks to the human population are so great, the level of certainty that the risks are not real in a particular case would need to be exceptionally high.

Genetic engineering of plants

There are various possibilities under this heading including genetic modification of plants to increase yields, to increase resistance to disease and pests, or to make plants immune to certain artificial pesticides and herbicides.

In 1998, Monsanto, Novartis and Hoechst sold all or part of their chemical engineering divisions. This is a rapid escalation of a process that sees the future lying in life sciences, in particular in genetic engineering, which they see as being a larger revenue earner than chemicals. Some are concerned about 'genetic pollution' as more and more genetically altered plants are introduced. It has long been possible to cross, say, a donkey with a horse but now the possibilities are open to cross all the genetic boundaries. The possibilities are endless and there becomes simply a fluid mix of diverse genetic material which is able to be changed almost at will. Colours, flavours, shape and various behavioural changes of plants can all, in principle, be engineered.

GMOs (Genetically Modified Organisms) are now appearing in many foods. Calgene, the US biotech company, has produced the Flava Sava tomato which is now on widespread sale. This is a genetically engineered tomato. The 'ordinary' tomato that is generally on sale is not genetically engineered but it has been sprayed and its environment artificially manipulated to prevent it bruising. Even then it has a short shelf-life. The Flava Sava does not require the same amount of pesticides but nevertheless there is a dispute about whether it requires special labelling.

Some countries are insisting that the fact that food is genetically engineered should be noted whilst others have no such requirement. However, what is not addressed is the issue of just *what* would appear on any label. If a label simply said 'Genetically modified' then this hardly gives sufficient information on which to base a decision. In order for a meaningful decision to be made the label would have to give much greater detail and most customers would not be able to interpret this. There is the danger of a label with the words 'Genetically modified' leading to the idea of 'Frankenfoods' – in other words, instilling fear in people without providing them with the information to make an informed decision. Such labelling could simply be emotive rather than informative.

There is a difference between the genetic manipulation of tomatoes used for tomato sauce and tomatoes sold in the shops. The reason is that in the former case the genetic material is destroyed in making the sauce whereas in the latter case the genetic material is still 'alive'. There are, therefore, greater risks in the latter rather than the former case. No identifiable risks have been found in these tomatoes, the debate surrounds the non-identifiable risks.

Ciba-Geigy have produced a new variety of maize that has been genetically altered so that when corn borers (a major pest which attacks maize) infects the plants, the corn borers are killed. This will increase the yield of maize but, again, there are concerns that the maize is fertile and there may be cross-fertilisation with wild grasses which might have an adverse effect on certain wildlife.

Potato blight has a terrible effect on world potato harvests and, for instance, contributed to the great Irish potato famine. Potatoes which will 'commit suicide' if infected with blight have now been genetically engineered. This means, of course, that the blight-infested potatoes do not reproduce and thus the blight should be greatly constrained. The potatoes are held not to be fertile – they reproduce *not* by the flowers being fertile but by underground multiplication from the existing plant and therefore no genetic interchange takes place.

The most significant area of genetic manipulation of plants at present is by making them herbicide or pesticide resistant. Soya beans, maize and cotton account for 90 per cent of all genetically engineered crops presently grown in the US. Of the 78.8 million hectares of land planted with genetically engineered crops in the US 71 per cent of these are resistant to herbicide. Genetically engineered soya is not identified as such in the US and, because of GATT (see Reiss and Straughan's *Improving Nature? The Science and Nature of Genetic Engineering*, pp. 198–9) genetically engineered soya is now exported round the world. No other government can do anything about this as GATT requires them to open their markets to products approved in other countries.

By far the most widely used and most famous herbicide is Monsanto's 'Roundup'. Monsanto sells both the genetically engineered seed which is resistant to the Roundup herbicide, and Roundup itself. Roundup is then sprayed by the farmer and it kills *all* weeds, but the crop is not affected because it has been genetically engineered to be resistant. The farmers can spray as much as they want whenever they want and not endanger the crop (see books such as Jeremy Rifkin's *The Biotech Century*). But it is a mistake to think that Roundup is necessarily an environmental disaster because the claim is that less herbicides will be used and this will decrease the risks to humans because of the use of such sprays. These sprays are not environmentally friendly and some have claimed that they represent a health risk, so the idea of lowering the level of spraying is an attractive one. A spokesman for Monsanto claims that Roundup will save a litre per acre of herbicide, enough to eliminate 14 large railroad tankers of such chemicals each year. It is clear, therefore, that Roundup provides both environmental benefits and risks.

The benefits come from a lowered amount of herbicides, which has positive affects on the food chain; the risks include the elimination of weeds and the possible danger of the herbicide-resistant genes included in the crops spreading to weeds. This would raise the possibility of weeds that are resistant to herbicide if, indeed, such a transfer of the genetic resistance from the crops could take place. In Britain, English Nature is urging the Government to restrict the use of Roundup until its effects on biodiversity can be determined. On the other hand, Monsanto argues that Roundup breaks up when it reaches the soil and is much less likely than Atrazine (a more conventional herbicide) to damage the environment.

In September 1998, Monsanto announced it was investing $550 million to produce Roundup in Brazil. Shortly afterwards, the Brazilian government made Roundup-resistant soya beans the first approved genetically engineered crop. Cynics might argue that these two facts are not unrelated. Five million Brazilians face starvation and famine is always present in Brazil so it could be argued that these developments will help the poor, but this is debatable. It is unlikely to be the poor who benefit from Roundup and similar products because these depend on expensive investment in genetically modified seed, herbicides and pesticides. These products can only be afforded by relatively wealthy farmers. Soya beans, for instance, are grown in Brazil for export and therefore tend to be grown by the large landowners. Subsistence farmers will not benefit at all.

Having said this, GMOs may well be needed in order to feed the increasing population of the world as it is not clear that increased yields using more traditional means will be able to feed the 10 billion people who are likely to be on this planet in 30 years. The only way that big increases in food supply may be possible is to concentrate agriculture more in the hands of the wealthy who can invest in specialised seeds, herbicides and pesticides but this will, in turn, create even more social problems.

In India, the Government has a Government-funded organisation trying to improve yields but it refused to pay Monsanto $8 million dollars to use the Bt insecticide gene which would have been of considerable help to the poorest farmers. The Indian organisation will not, therefore, be able to produce cheap, insect-resistant crops because Monsanto and other companies have patented the necessary genes and no-one can use these genes without paying substantial sums. As the speed of genetic knowledge increases, so the patents will be more and more concentrated in the hands of western companies and those who are wealthy will be able to outcompete and thus drive out of business the poor producers.

Roundup, although it has benefits, does not have all the answers. In Missouri in the summer of 1998 half the soya plants on some farms died of Fusarium mould after three-quarters of the land was planted with Roundup-resistant seed. The reason was that the seed was not resistant to the mould.

The philosophic debate in the area of genetic engineering covers a number of different areas:

• The morality of risk against advantage. Even when the advantages of genetic engineering are taken into account in terms of increased yields or a decreased use of chemical herbicides, can it ever be worth the risk that genetic engineering may open

Pandora's box? The risk may revolve around 'genetic pollution' – the possibility of genes that have been altered in some plants crossing the species boundaries, which are now much more fluid than ever in the past, thereby passing on these immunities to weeds or even to certain insects.

• At present there is no indication that genetically modified food does any harm to the human digestive system but, once again, there are dangers that may be present here of which we are at present unaware. The BSE scare which resulted in the slaughter of hundreds of thousands of cattle in Europe was not anticipated and the risks to humans from genetically modified food still exist even though we may be ignorant of them at present.

• Should genetically engineered products be labelled and, if so, how? As set out above, it is now unclear what this would achieve or what form the labelling should take. Simply to have a label saying 'GM food' conveys insufficient information on which a customer can make an informed decision.

• How far do humans have the ability to 'play God', to create new forms of life and to cross species boundaries? On the other side, is there any essential difference between genetic engineering and selective breeding?

Before the 1995 vote in the European Parliament on whether to allow companies to patent genes, Greenpeace sent a postcard with the following statement to all members of the European Parliament:

Patenting of genes

In the beginning the Lord created heavens and earth and all therein
But scientists said let the seas be populated by fish containing human, mouse and rat genes,
And Hoechst and Monsanto said let the land produce plants and trees bearing fruit containing bacteria and virus genes.

And Ciba-Geigy said let corn be grown containing scorpion genes.

And Amoco made all kinds of fruits and vegetables and they did not rot.

By the seventh day the Lord had been undone and the companies saw that they had recreated life for their own ends.

And the Parliament of Angels blessed the seventh day and made all life patentable.

This is amusing and the language is emotive but it must be recognised that it does not represent an argument. There is no moral objection to selective breeding and there seems few reasons, in principle, why genetic engineering should be ruled out, provided that the balance of risk against reward is properly assessed. This is, however, a major proviso which may not easily be achievable because of the difficulty of quantifying the dangers. Until we have more certain information great caution is required.

There is also a need for science departments in schools to educate young people who are taking these subjects into the ethical challenges and possible responses. Failure to do this constitutes an educational failure for which the senior management of many schools must bear a heavy responsibility. Too many science departments, left to their own devices, consider that science is ethically neutral and this is not the case.

Questions for discussion

1 What is the ethical difference between somatic cell and germ-line therapy?

2 Is it morally justifiable to enhance babies by genetic engineering? Who should make the decisions as to which enhancements should be permitted?

3 Would you wish to know the genetic profile of your partner before deciding to have children with him or her?

4 Can there be any ethical justification for compulsory sterilisation of a 13-year-old girl?

5 What does it mean to make cells totipotent?

6 Evaluate the ethical justification of the use of Monsanto's 'Roundup'.

7 Is it morally acceptable to modify animals genetically to benefit humans and, if so, in what circumstances?

8 Should genetically modified food be labelled? Evaluate the strengths and weaknesses of your answer.

9 Who should have access to the results of the genetic profiles of individual human beings?

TWENTY

Media Ethics

Freedom and responsibility

One of the principal discussions within media ethics is that to do with the relationship between freedom and responsibility. The issue is a fairly easy one to describe and to exemplify, but an exceedingly difficult one to resolve. Generally speaking, there is greater freedom of expression for the press in America than in the UK. The former has a written constitution which guarantees freedom of expression, and a Freedom of Information Act which guarantees the right of the press to investigate matters which are unnecessarily shrouded in secrecy, whilst the UK has neither of these two legal safeguards (see A. Belsey, 'Ethics, Law and the Quality of the Media', in B. Almond, ed., *Introducing Applied Ethics,* Oxford, Blackwell, 1995). However, irrespective of the differences in constitutional law in the US and the UK, the basic moral dilemma for the media is still one of the relationship between freedom and responsibility.

In 1997–8 the American Press began uncovering some rather lurid details of President Clinton's private life. The Clinton family, along with a third party, Monica Lewinsky, suffered some humiliating personal attacks as detailed descriptions of private sexual acts were publicly aired on a daily basis in newspapers and on television. Now, there are dozens of moral issues embedded in what has famously been dubbed as the Monica Lewinsky Affair – or more disparagingly, Zippergate (a tasteless pun on the name given to a former president's scandal to do with break-ins and burglary, namely the Watergate Affair); there are issues to do with power relations between a middle-aged and powerful president and a young, impressionable White House intern; issues to do with sexuality and marriage, adulterous and sexually promiscuous behaviour in a religiously and theoretically monogamous culture; issues to do with lying under oath, and so on. However, the concern here is principally to do with the freedom of the Press to print what it likes irrespective of the outcome. What are the rules, if any, governing the public revelation of private practices?

There are two general responses to the question. The first claims that in every case, freedom – freedom of the Press to publish what it likes – should outweigh, or take priority over any responsibility it has to individuals or groups, some of whom might be seriously affected by such expression or publication. No censorship at all, even if we may not like some of the consequences, is far better than any curtailment of free expression. The second claims that freedom should never be held above responsibility; that, ideally, they should always be balanced through the careful scrutiny of: (a) the possible adverse consequences of publication, (b) the kinds of ethical justifications governing publication, and (c) what is sometimes called the 'ethical efficiency' of media staff themselves. So, the particular form of our question could be reframed thus: Should the freedom of the Press to invade and reveal the private sexual life of President Clinton outweigh any responsibility the Press may have towards him, the office of president, or the international reputation of American politics? The question, though, is not quite as easy as that, for there is a difficulty in deciding to whom the Press is responsible. The media may quite legitimately claim that their responsibility is not to the president and his reputation, but to the public who elected him and who now need to be told just what sort of a man they have voted into the White House.

Censorship

From Plato onwards, notions of freedom and responsibility have been systematically argued. Plato, for example, was quite clear that overall responsibility, charged to legislators or government (in this case, the philosopher–kings, philosopher guardians or rulers), always outweighs freedom of expression. Hence, Homer's descriptions of the moral lapses of the gods, kings or heroes (Zeus's pathologically adulterous behaviour, for instance, or King Priam's 'grovelling in the dung') should be carefully censored and rewritten in order that always the 'right and proper' image of divine and royal conduct is created and fostered. It is interesting to note the differences in media treatment meted out to President Clinton in the 1990s and President Kennedy in the 1960s. By all accounts, President Kennedy was a far more promiscuous individual than President Clinton, but the press believed then that it was their responsibility to keep the Kennedy image publicly untarnished. No such belief is now held, with either an incumbent or an ex-president.

Freedom argument and the right response theory

D. Gordon writing in *Controversies in Media Ethics* (Longman,1996, pp. 30–35), takes what is often called the libertarian view, namely that the liberty of any single individual always takes priority over anything else, in this case their responsibilities towards anyone else. The basis for Gordon's argument rests on the primacy of the First Amendment of the US Constitution which guarantees freedom of expression. Gordon cites a case in 1974 in which a court of law upheld the view that freedom of expression – especially editorial expression in newspapers – was of paramount importance. By all accounts a candidate running for political office was the victim of a well-executed campaign of character assassination in the editorial column of a newspaper. As the accusations brought against him were largely untrue and certainly unfair, he requested that he be given newspaper space to reply to his accusers. The court ruled that newspapers did not have to justify or redress their publication excesses by granting such space. Gordon agrees with the legal verdict. As soon as any restriction is placed on freedom of expression, then what follows becomes a tangled and never-ending debate about when and how far legal injunctions and restrictions can operate: 'In our society, mass media ethics must be based on a "first principle" that ensures zealous protection for freedom of expression while leaving us fallible mortals free to chart our own ethical (or unethical) courses' (p. 31).

Gordon does, however, acknowledge that some restrictions already exist in three grey areas: obscenity, incitement to violence, and the threat to 'national security', although the 'first principle' should, he claims, always take precedence. Instead of banning or censoring false or accusatory speech, we should be campaigning simply for 'more' speech. The proper response to 'wrong, dangerous or offensive speech should be more speech by those who disagree with the original statements' (p. 32). The first and most obvious objection to this theory is that if (under the First Amendment Ruling mentioned in the court case previously cited) there can be no obligation placed upon newspapers (or, presumably, others) to provide space for more speech by those who disagree with the original statements, then the theory itself collapses at the first base.

'Hate speech' and the balanced outcome

Leaving this objection aside for the moment, Gordon discusses what has become known as 'hate speech' indulged in by extremist groups such as neo-Nazi parties, the Ku Klux Klan or the British National Party. Such 'hate speech' ought not to be censored, but rather countered through alternative or response speech and media campaigns. The purpose is, of course, either to nullify the original hate speech, or to raise the quality of the speech campaign overall. This latter purpose echoes the well-known Hegelian idea of thesis, followed by antithesis, culminating in synthesis. This idea, known as 'dialectical thinking', rests (at least for our purposes) on the following:

- *Thesis*: All people with blue eyes are good, whereas all people without blue eyes are not good (hate speech).
- *Antithesis*: All people with brown eyes are good, whereas all people without brown eyes are not good (response speech).
- *Synthesis*: All people with either blue or brown eyes are good.

The theory is that if we give airtime or print space to the Ku Klux Klan, and follow it with equal airtime and/or print space for civil rights activists, then a balanced view can be had and, hopefully, a better outcome will emerge. And even if there isn't a better outcome, the upholding of the absolute right of freedom of expression will have been maintained, and surely that is an excellent outcome in itself. One of the best philosophical statements of this position is to be found in J. S. Mill's famous *Essay on Liberty* (1859):

> The time, it is hoped, is gone by when any defence would be necessary of the 'liberty of the press' as one of the securities against corrupt or tyrannical government ... Unless opinions favourable to democracy and to aristocracy, to property and to equality, to co-operation and to competition, to luxury and to abstinence, to sociality and to individuality, to liberty and to discipline, and all the other standing antagonisms of practical life, are expressed with equal freedom and enforced and defended with equal talent and energy, there is no chance of both elements obtaining their due; one scale is sure to go up, and the other down. Truth, in the great practical concerns of life is ... a question of the reconciling and combining of opposites ... Only through diversity of opinion is there ... a chance of fair play to all sides of truth (J. S. Mill, 1859, *Essay on Liberty*, J. Gray , ed., 1991, Oxford, Oxford Univesity Press, pp. 20,53–54).

Two objections

There are, at least, two objections to this view, apart from the particular objection outlined earlier.

1 *Rational spectator fallacy*: First, it assumes that all media spectators – viewers, readers and listeners – are purely rational and knowledgeable beings able to make sensible and balanced judgements having examined and assessed the relative merits of competing arguments, and are not unduly influenced by the hidden messages

contained either in the hate speech or the subsequent response speech. Marshall McLuhan, the famous American philosopher of the 1960s and 70s was well-known for his catchphrase 'the medium is the message'. It does not really matter what one says, it is how one says it that ultimately matters. The entire advertising and publicity industry, not to mention the public relations business, are all well aware of this dictum. If, with a frown and a hurried air, I gruffly ask my neighbour how his health is, he would rightly infer that I am not all interested in the answer, whereas if I asked in a considerate and unhurried manner, he is likely to assume that I am genuinely concerned about his well-being.

2 *Neutral media fallacy*: Second, there is the underlying assumption that the world of media – of newspaper and television news – is a neutral one and that, therefore, it would automatically allow for equal space, time and resources to be given to sensationalist and anti-sensationalist material alike. It assumes a state of affairs similar to that proposed by the contemporary German philosopher, Jürgen Habermas. Habermas proposed the *ideal speech situation*: an event in which participants could debate a controversial issue without let or hindrance. In other words, any interested party could contribute to the debate or discussion without fear or prejudice, and where differences in power, influence, class and wealth would be eradicated, or simply 'left at the door', as it were. This is, however, a utopian ideal (as its very name suggests) which does not take account of the realities of everyday inequalities in power relations. It would be like having a concentration camp commandant pitted against a prisoner of war (POW) in a debate about conditions in the camp, and expecting that the poor POW has the same rights and privileges to speech and participation as does the commandant. Clearly, he does not. Similarly, an impoverished, unemployed and badly educated female would find great difficulty in competing on the same ground as a wealthy, well-educated male stockbroker in a debate about economic policy. This is not to say that it is impossible, simply highly improbable.

A final example returns us to the Monica Lewinsky affair. The president of the United States of America, by virtue of his very position, exerts enormous power and influence over the press and media in general. Assisting him in this task is a host of 'spin doctors' whose sole job is to 'manipulate' the news in order that the president's image remains (virtually) intact. President Clinton was thus able to maintain his position in the war of words over the 'truth' of the affair, whilst the relatively powerless Monica Lewinsky soon became a victim in the ensuing struggle between Kenneth Starr, the public prosecutor, and the president's legal and political advisers. However, the scales of power quickly tipped in favour of the victim, Miss Lewinsky, when the existence of the incriminating evidence (the infamous 'dress') became public knowledge.

However, Gordon's arguments do support Mill's more general thesis that an unpopular minority view, seen in one century as an absurd social lie, may well in the next century be understood by the majority as an unassailable moral truth. As Gordon claims 'women's suffrage, civil rights and opposition to the Vietnam War' (p. 34) all began as minority movements condemned as both sinister and subversive. If the freedom to express such unpopular views was in any sense restricted, then progress in such profound matters would never have taken place. Instead, the vigorous exchange of views – sometimes heated, sometimes offensive – is always considered far better than the cautious and uniform support of received wisdom on matters of responsibility. To prevent intellectual and moral stagnation, freedom should always have priority over responsibility.

To return to our original example, at the close of the Monica Lewinsky Affair, despite the somewhat 'damaged goods' reputation of President Clinton, the public's 'right to know' argument claimed by the media may have had some justification. The debate about the relationship between private life and public life had at least been aired, and the general American public seemed to have demonstrated a level of mature compassion in that, despite Clinton's private sexual lapses, his standing as a leader and a politician was not unduly affected throughout the period of the inquiry. The public may have judged him on the Aristotelian dictum described by Anscombe (see chapter nine) that here was a politician centrally concerned with justice who, like all people with frailties and foibles, 'missed the mark' or 'made a mistake' on this occasion. An alternative explanation for the public's willingness to forgive and forget is one founded on individual and collective self-interest. The economy under President Clinton was doing exceptionally well and unemployment was the lowest for years. The assumption is that Clinton's immoral private life, therefore, could be ignored if, in economic terms, he was 'delivering the goods'. It raises an interesting question: Are private moral lapses always outweighed by significant public goods?

Freedom and responsibility

C. Reuss, also writing in *Controversies in Media Ethics*, counters Gordon's argument not with the claim that responsibility should override freedom but that both should have equal priority. She quotes Meyer (Editors, Publishers and Newspaper Ethics, Washington D.C., American Society of Newspaper Editors,1983) in arguing for something called the 'ethically efficient' media worker, someone who is always critically aware of her own prejudices and is, therefore, doubly careful about the selection, presentation and analysis of news items. Instead of, as it were, withdrawing from the ethical problem – in Gordon's words 'charting an ethical (or unethical) course' – by simply offering a so-called neutral platform to any individual or group who wishes to engage in 'hate speech' or 'counter speech', the ethically efficient media worker will analyse the judgement as to whether or not permitting such neutral space is morally justifiable at all.

Similar to Meyer's ethically efficient media worker is Lambeth's virtuous journalist (*Committed Journalism: An Ethic for the Profession*, Bloomington, Indiana University Press, 1992), also analysed at length by Klaidman and Beauchamp in *The Virtuous Journalist*,

Oxford, Oxford University Press, 1987, and summarised by Belsey in 'Ethics, Law and the Quality of the Media' (in B. Almond, ed., *Introducing Applied Ethics*, op. cit. p. 257). The virtuous journalist has to balance two sorts of moral scales:

• the balance between freedom and responsibility
• the balance between media freedom and individual freedom.

The UK royal family is a case in point. Was the persistent chasing of the late Princess Diana by the press a matter of media freedom (to stalk a story and sell a newspaper) overriding individual freedom (Diana's right to some kind of private life)? As such, was press freedom placed above press responsibility? Given that the eventual outcome was the accidental death of Princess Diana in a Parisian tunnel after the relentless pursuit by the paparazzi, our response might be an unequivocal 'Yes'. However, the issue is a good deal more complex. Princess Diana had already freely consented to become a fully-fledged public figure, and to enjoy all the benefits that went with it: marrying into almost unimagined wealth and luxury, participating in a privileged and glamorous lifestyle, and freely enagaging in high-profile media campaigns. Of course, there is what is known as the 'downside' – a broken marriage, psychological damage and faithless friends and acquaintances. But by readily promoting herself as the 'People's Princess' and the 'Queen of Hearts' she had deliberately sacrificed much individual and private freedom to the public through the media. It is, however, a matter of degree. How much individual and private freedom does, or can, a public figure expect to sacrifice?

Truth telling and the qualities of competence and commitment

Reuss's argument depends largely on the ethical standards of the responsible individual journalist who works in the media, rather than on the abstract notion of media neutrality which, according to Gordon, ensures freedom of expression. One of the obvious problems with this, however, relates to the spheres of responsibility. To whom and/or for whom is the journalist responsible? Is her primary responsibility to herself, to those about whom she is writing, or to her editors and paymasters? The short answer is, of course, that she owes a responsibility to all of them. Her real difficulty is in balancing the competing responsibilities owed to each. In a further article (in *Controversies in Media Ethics*) Reuss expands this notion of the ethically efficient journalist – one who takes responsibility doubly seriously – by reference to two further central terms: 'competence' and 'commitment'. The competent journalist is one who makes every effort to check the veracity of the story given to her, to investigate thoroughly the event to be covered by her, to examine critically the opinions fed to her and to maintain the highest standards of truth in her subsequent reporting. When deadlines for 'copy' are pressing, it is even more vital that these fundamental issues are kept to the forefront of the media worker's mind, otherwise sloppy media coverage soon descends into semi-fiction and squalid sensationalism. In discussing the notion of competence Reuss reiterates a set of five principles laid down originally by Lambeth (*Committed Journalism: An Ethic for the Profession*). These are truth telling, justice, freedom, humaneness, and stewardship. Of these, arguably, truth telling is the most important.

Truth telling is, of course, a Kantian imperative and, arguably, is the key principle for journalists. Media workers, especially those who work specifically in the news industry are charged with the responsibility of telling stories. As the chapter on MacIntyre indicates, human beings are essentially 'story-telling animals'. However, what we seek, even in fictional writing, are stories which 'aspire to truth'. Great literature – the novels of Dickens and Hardy, of James and Scott Fitzgerald, the drama of Sophocles and Shakespeare, and the poetry of Wordsworth and Eliot – all identify and illuminate in unique and memorable ways the central truths of humankind. These truths are what George Santayana (1863–1952), the great American philosopher, called symbolic truths ('A General Confession', in P.

Schlipp, ed., 1951, *The Philosophy of George Santayana*, Open Court)
– what it is like to love and to be loved, to inflict and to bear
suffering, to marvel at, and be terrified of, Nature, and to experience the strange variety and richness of human experience. Non-
fiction, the realm of the scientist, the geographer and the historian, is
concerned with, so far as is possible, stories which tell us particular
truths about certain instances in the world. Journalists, no less than
geographers and historians, should also be primarily concerned
with true, factual accounts of what has happened in the world. They
may, and generally do, add their own interpretation of the meanings
behind such accounts, but they should be careful about where to
draw the line between fact and interpretation, and be clear about
when they are doing it.

Hermeneutics and the 'fusion of horizons'

In one sense, therefore, the journalist is concerned with what is
known as hermeneutics, the science of interpretation (from the
Greek *hermeneutikos*,'interpretation'). The great German philosopher, Hans Georg Gadamer, whose works include *Truth and Method*
(trans. W. Glen-Doepel, Sheed and Ward, 1975), claimed that
whenever we give an account of something or whenever we read
something that someone else has written we are inevitably involved
in 'interpreting' whatever it is that has happened or been written.
One's own subjective understanding will always distort, however
slightly, the objective facts of the situation or the text. This, he
argues, is inevitable. We consciously or unconsciously leave certain
'minor' facts out and tend to embellish other (what we may believe
to be) 'major' facts. Hence, we end up with what Gadamer calls
a *fusion of horizons* where either the original intentions of a text's
author meet with our own particular understanding of that text, or
where the objective facts of a case meet with our own selective
understanding and account of it. In the case of interpreting a text,
for example, it is quite clear that when Plato wrote the *Republic*, he
was not talking about elephants, unicorns or aliens. We are not at

liberty to interpret the text so widely as to imagine that any of these could be inferred from anything Plato said. However, when it comes to talking about the theory of forms, (see the early chapter on Plato) we are on much trickier ground, and we are at liberty to question what it was Plato was really talking about when he posited a world of universals, of ideas, of forms. Is this really another world in which the ideas of all particular things exist in a timeless, spaceless and changeless way, or is it really a kind of complex philosophical metaphor which allows us more forcefully to recognise the grave moral and intellectual pitfalls confronting us when we take the physical world and its inhabitants at simple face value? The work of some women and feminist philosophers, from Julie Ward to Martha Nussbaum, have begun to suggest the latter is a better interpretation than the former. In the case of interpreting an event or a happening, the journalist who writes a murder report will never have all of the facts to hand, and will never be able to give a complete, objective account of it. Instead, she constructs, out of the facts at hand, an account which makes both sense to her, her editor and hopefully her readers. In this sense, she is engaged in a hermeneutical quest for the truth.

It is interesting to note that another media theorist, Kittross (in *Controversies in Media Ethics*) also holds up truth telling as fundamental, along with its associated concepts of objectivity, accuracy and fairness. A wholly objective account in which all truths and facts are given a full and proper airing is an impossibility, as the hermeneutic argument of Gadamer points out. However, some attempt at objectivity is possible if the accuracy of known facts is checked out, and a sense of fairness is achieved if the resulting story or account corresponds to the reality of the actual event which is being reported. Given these and the above remaining principles it is quite clear what kind of a premium Reuss, Lambeth, Meyer and others place on the notion of responsibility – individual and collective – within the media. Those in the media, no less than anyone else, work within environments governed uneasily by competing values – between those who, like Gordon, are willing (even if not entirely

Media Ethics

happily) to follow 'unethical courses' in the pursuit of freedom of expression, and those who, like Reuss, believe themselves to be under some kind of deontological (or duty-bound) imperative to pursue ethically responsible ends. As such, Reuss has framed a series of 'ethical' questions which she believes it is important for media personnel to ask themselves:

- Is it ever acceptable for media people deliberately to deceive a potential source of information about their professional identity or intentions?
- Is it ever acceptable to steal documents, photographs, or other material from a source or to copy them without first asking permission?
- Is it ever acceptable to stage or re-create an event without telling the audience?
- Is it ever acceptable for media people to accept gifts, tickets or other freebies?
- Is it ever acceptable for media people to seek or give special treatment for themselves, their families, or causes they favour?
- Finally, is it ever acceptable for media people to violate laws, including speeding and parking laws? Are they 'above' them?' (p. 50).

Working largely from a utilitarian perspective, but also from a modified deontological view (modified by the works of, for example, W. D. Ross, who saw that the truth-telling principle would in many circumstances be outweighed by the life-saving principle), the answer to many of these questions would be 'Yes, in certain situations and for certain reasons.' The *Washington Post* journalists Woodward and Bernstein would never have got to the bottom of the famous Watergate scandal if they had always stuck rigorously to the letter of the law and answered 'No' to all of the above questions. To use Singer's consequentialist calculation, they were always in the business of balancing relatively minor interests (say, the deliberate violation of parking laws) in favour of pursuing major interests:

the exposure of criminal activities by rich and politically powerful people. What is undoubtedly clear is that one's response to these kinds of questions depends very much on the type of ethical theory one is inclined to follow, and that in turn depends upon one's obvious willingness to think through the arguments and objections to each of the theories dealt with in the first section of this book.

The problem of chequebook journalism

Kittross further argues that 'chequebook journalism', 'the buying for cash of information that one can print or air' (in *Controversies in Media Ethics*, p. 281), devalues both the seller and the buyer, the person who wishes to sell their story and the newspaper or television station which agrees to purchase it. His argument is based on the notion that news, and by association, those figures who become newsworthy, are reduced to commodities, and are thereby made morally deficient. Increasingly it is the size of the cheque or the cash handout that then becomes the single, all-encompassing factor in who reports news. This results in fine-honed judgements concerning freedoms and responsibilities, as well as complex proce-dures involved in balancing individual and collective interests, all going by the wayside. We can buy and sell objects (cars, dishwashers and houses) without too much thought about their moral status (although we really ought to, given the pressure on the environment – see the chapter on environmental ethics) but we ought not to buy and sell narratives and stories attached to human beings without in any sense considering their moral status. This kind of devaluation is especially true, claims Kittross, in the case of crime. He cites two examples of the way in which the credibility of witnesses in trials has been seriously damaged as a consequence of their having sold their stories. In the O. J. Simpson trial one witness was dismissed by the judge for having already been interviewed in *Hard Copy* by the public media, whilst two witnesses in the Michael Jackson sexual assault trial had sold distorted and sensationalised versions of their forthcoming evidence to television shows. Needless to say their subsequent evidence was given very little credence (Kittross, in *Controversies in Media Ethics*, p. 281). Moreover, the media itself will begin to lose credibility when the public sees it as nothing more than a profit-making machine which treats all information – from serious political events to trivial social stories – merely as commodity material to be bargained for, haggled over and finally bought and sold, with the biggest chequebook holder eventually dominating the news, and newspapers being designed to appeal to the lowest common denominator to guarantee market share (the British newspaper the *Sun* with its topless girls and explicit sex stories is a good example). This domination is beginning to happen with, for example, Rupert Murdoch owning and having influence over the bulk of the international media industry, from extraterrestrial television to national newspapers. The power of the Murdoch news empire and other similar organisations not just to report news but to 'gloss' the way it is presented is enormous and makes such organisations more powerful than many governments as they can effectively control the views that people hold and even their political opinions. Rupert Murdoch has used this influence throughout the world to further his corporate ambitions and many governments stand in fear of disapproval by the Murdoch-controlled press. Incidentally, Rupert Murdoch was awarded a knighthood by Pope John Paul II in 1998.

Media competition: Power and money

One final ethical problem faced by 'virtuous journalism' is that to do with the internal competition within the media industry itself, the competition which exists between rival media groups, between competing news stations and newspapers. Here, pure profit margins and 'market share' targets (percentage of the reading public a particular newspaper secures) inevitably compromise the standards of the ethically efficient journalist, assuming that there is such a person. Is there a moral justification for, say, printing a full front-page picture of the private grief of a bereaved woman in Kosovo or

Northern Ireland, or, for example, broadcasting a potentially explosive piece of information, given 'off the record' by a voluntary public servant? Or is the need to make instant headline news in order to beat a rival local network with newsworthy items sufficient justification in itself?

Questions such as these highlight the deep problems about how to characterise the overall complex relationships between ethics, the media, power and money. Two points clearly emerge from these relationships; the first is to do with the nature and function of 'news' as it is currently being conceived; and the second is to do with the nature and function of philosophical discourse about such 'news'. In relation to the first, B. Franklin (1997, *Newszak and News Media*, Arnold) argues that the quality of the media has declined over the years, partly as a consequence of the desire by news corporations to increase shareholder dividends through wielding greater power and influence over larger markets. In order to secure their goals, quality news has been transformed into *newszak* – 'a product designed and "processed" for a particular market and delivered in "snippets" which makes only modest demands on the audience. Newszak is news converted into entertainment' (Franklin, p. 5). News items converted into entertainment (sometimes referred to as 'infotainment') become commodities, devoid of serious ethical content and stripped of moral status. All that matters, eventually, is the size of the financial dividend. The second point is both paradoxical and worrying. It would appear that as the political power, financial size and cultural influence of national and international business (including media) corporations increase, so the impact of rational ethical debate about such matters actually decreases. At least, so says MacIntyre, in a recent, pessimistic article about the current status of philosophical discourse in western democracies. The size of the chequebook outweighs the quality of the argument, in the same way that the size of the shareholder dividend outweighs the quality of the news. As MacIntyre claims:

'What we have ... in contemporary society are a set of small-scale academic publics ... whose discourse is of such a kind as to have no practical effect on the conduct of social life ... [and] a public life in which ... decisions and policies are by and large outcomes of the distributions of power and money and not of the quality of argument'.

(Alasdair MacIntyre, 'Some Enlightenment Projects Reconsidered', in R. Kearney and M. Dooley, (eds, 1999, *Questioning Ethics: Contemporary Debates in Philosophy*, Routledge, p. 257).

Questions for discussion

1 Are there any grounds for censorship of the media?
2 What qualities are deemed necessary for the 'virtuous journalist', and what obstacles might stand in the way of their development?
3 With specific reference to contemporary events, discuss the relationship between freedom and responsibility in the media.
4 How far do power and money influence the media?
5 Examine the range of ethical issues raised by either the 'Watergate scandal' or the 'Monica Lewinsky affair'.
6 Should public figures expect a right to personal privacy? If so, how much privacy should they reasonably expect to enjoy?
7 Compare the way a single story is reported by different newspapers and evaluate the reasons for their differences in treatment of the story.

TWENTY-ONE

Conclusion

Vlaclev Havel is a philosopher, poet and playwright. Under the Communist government of Czechoslovakia he was imprisoned for his views although after the fall of Communism in Eastern Europe he rose to become President of Czechoslovakia and then of the Czech Republic. He was allowed to write one letter a week whilst he was in gaol and he wrote to his wife, Olga. The letters have been published in a collection called *Letters to Olga*. In one of these letters dated January 1980 he wrote about what he considered the cornerstones of human freedom. He found these in the human sense of responsibility – a responsibility exercised not just by the individual to him- or herself, not just to the community, but to something ultimate (although Havel never identified this with God or even in religious terms). In his book *Living in Truth* (Faber & Faber, 1986) in an essay entitled 'The power of the powerless' he wrote about the same theme.

He gives an example of a Prague greengrocer to illustrate his point:

> The manager of a fruit and vegetable shop places in his window, among the onions and carrots, the slogan 'Workers of the world unite!' Why does he do it? What is he trying to communicate to the world? Is he genuinely enthusiastic about the idea of unity among the workers of the world? ... That poster was delivered to our greengrocer from the enterprise headquarters along with the onions and carrots. He put them in the window simply because it has been done that way for years, because everyone does it ...

If he were to refuse there would be trouble ... It is one of the thousands of details that guarantee him a relatively tranquil life 'in harmony with society', as they say (p. 41).

Havel's greengrocer, living under a Communist government, is afraid – and the sign in the window is the mark of his fear. It is a sign placed there to appease society, to appease those in power – to show his obedience to the system. People who pass the greengrocer's shop ignore the slogan – there are thousands of similar slogans in other shops – but the slogan nevertheless has an effect, it confirms his uniformity, his obedience. Finally, however, Havel asks us to imagine that:

> ... one day something in our greengrocer snaps and he stops putting up the slogans merely to ingratiate himself. He stops voting in elections he knows are a farce. He begins to say what he really thinks ... He discovers once more his suppressed identity and dignity. He gives his freedom a concrete significance. His revolt is an attempt *to live within the truth*.
>
> The bill is not long in coming. He will be relieved of his post as manager of the shop and transferred to the warehouse. His pay will be reduced. His hopes for a holiday in Bulgaria will evaporate. His children's access to higher education will be threatened. His superiors will harass him and his fellow workers will wonder about him. Most of those who apply these sanctions, however, will not do so from any authentic inner conviction but simply under pressure from conditions, the same conditions that once pressured the greengrocer to display the official slogans ... (p. 55).

Havel's greengrocer eventually wakens to exercise a sense of responsibility – he becomes an individual, willing to act and to take responsibility for his action. He is no longer prepared to go along with the crowd, to accept convention in return for a secure life. He stands in the name of truth and, by so doing, shows up the world around him for the sham that it is. By *living in the truth* the greengrocer, as an individual, challenges the whole system because he illuminates it and shows its true nature. In taking his stand, the greengrocer stands in the shoes of Socrates whose similar stance led him to his death.

To live in the truth may be the highest that a human being can achieve and it will always bring confrontation with the established order – whether this is the society in which we live, the religious group to which we belong or the government that claims to speak for us. Because truth cannot be confined within these groups it always seeks to break free and to bring light to a dark and murky world (cf. Peter Vardy's *What Is Truth?*, University of New South Wales Press, 1999).

Philosophy is not simply an academic subject – or at least it should not be. It is about life and how it should be lived. No branch of philosophy is more practical than that of ethics which governs every aspect of our dealings with our fellow human beings, with the animals on this planet and the world in which we live.

This book has attempted to outline major ethical theories and to show how practical ethical issues have been approached by a number of philosophers. If we would truly become human individuals, we will have to think for ourselves and to consider carefully the ethical choices that confront us and the societies in which we live.

Thinking, however, is a precursor of action and we must be willing to take the next step and to act for the good – however we define this. Such a course may well not be popular and certainly will not be easy, but it is to this path that Socrates, Plato, Aristotle and their many successors call us. It will always be easier to be one of the crowd – it will always be more comfortable to be like Havel's green-grocer. However, the greengrocer finally wakes up to the fact that there is more to life than this and recognises that exercising human responsibility and living in the truth are the keys to being an indi-vidual – perhaps there are no higher objectives which we can set for ourselves.

Further Reading

General

B. Hoose, 1998, *Christian Ethics* (Cassell) – strongly recommended.
B. Mayo, 1986, *The Philosophy of Right and Wrong* (Routledge)
J. Smart, 1984, *Ethics, Persuasion and Truth* (Routledge)
J. Finnis, 1983, *Fundamentals of Ethics* (Clarendon)
D. D. Raphael, 1981, *Moral Philosophy* (Oxford)
R. Norman, 1983, *The Moral Philosophers* (Oxford)

For a clear and detailed account of the principal moral theories see:
W. D. Hudson, 1983, (2nd edition), *Modern Moral Philosophy* (Macmillan)

For an excellent defence of applied ethics see:
B. Almond & D. Hill (eds), 1991, *Applied Philosophy: Morals and Metaphysics in Contemporary Debate* (Routledge)
B. Almond, 1987, *Moral Concerns* (Humanities Press Int.)

For a good and extremely readable general introduction to moral problems see:
J. Rachels, 1986, *The Elements of Moral Philosophy* (Random House)

Also for an excellent collection of essays on various ethical problems, including: war, punishment, prejudice and discrimination, abortion and foetal research, euthanasia, suicide; poverty and hunger see:
J. Rachels (ed.), 1979, (3rd edition) *Moral Problems* (HarperCollins)

For an elegant defence of the utilitarian/consequentialist position in relation to equality, animal rights, abortion, euthanasia, gap between rich and poor, environmental ethics see:
P. Singer, 1993, (2nd edition), *Practical Ethics* (Oxford)

For a robust criticism of the way in which rationality alone has tended to dominate ethical theorising see:
B. Williams, 1985, *Ethics and the Limits of Philosophy* (Fontana)
J. Glover, 1984, *What Sort of People Should There Be?* (Penguin)
R. M. Hare, 1981, *Moral Thinking* (Oxford)
S. Kagan, 1989, *The Limits of Morality* (Oxford)

For a very readable introduction to the major moral theories see:
G. J. Warnock, 1967, *Contemporary Moral Philosophy* (Macmillan)

For a thorough text on utilitarianism:
J. J. C. Smart & B. Williams, 1973, *Utilitarianism: For and Against* (Cambridge)

The following texts on some of the specific chapters will also be of value:

Justice and equality

For a good introduction to the two theories by Rawls and Nozick, plus extracts from the two works in question, see:
T. Honderich & M. Burnyeat (eds), 1979, *Philosophy As It Is* (Pelican)

For a readable summary of both theories and some problems raised by them, see:
A. Brown, 1986, *Modern Political Philosophy* (Penguin)

Also useful are:
R. Barrow, 1982, *Injustice, Inequality and Ethics* (Barnes & Noble)

J. Horton & S. Mendus, 1985, *Aspects of Toleration: Philosophical Studies* (Methuen)

Animal rights

P. Singer (ed.), 1985, *In Defence of Animals* (Basil Blackwell)

K. Tester, 1991, *Animals and Society: The Humanity of Animal Rights* (Routledge)

R. G. Frey, 1983, *Rights, Killing and Suffering* (Basil Blackwell)

M. Midgley, 1983, *Animals and Why They Matter* (Penguin)

Abortion

L. W. Sumner, 1981, *Abortion and Moral Theory* (Princeton University Press)

J. Glover, 1977, *Causing Death and Saving Lives* (Penguin)

J. Mahoney, 1984, *Bioethics and Belief* (Sheed and Ward)

J. Jarvis Thomson, 1986, 'A Defence of Abortion', in P. Singer (ed.), 1986, *Applied Ethics* (Oxford)

Euthanasia

D. Humphrey & A. Wickett, 1986, *The Right to Die* (Bodley Head)

J. Harris, 1985, *The Value of Life* (Routledge)

G. Oosthuizen, 1978, *Euthanasia* (Oxford University Press)

Aristotle

The three works mentioned at the end of the chapter are:

J. Ackrill, 1981, *Aristotle the Philosopher* (Oxford University Press)

G. Lloyd, 1968, *Aristotle: the Growth and Structure of His Thought* (Cambridge University Press)

A. E. Taylor, 1955, *Aristotle* (Dover Books)

One of the most accessible accounts of Aristotle's philosophy is to be found in:

J. Barnes, 1982, *Aristotle* (Oxford. Past Masters series)

Environmental ethics

In addition to the texts mentioned see:

T. Regan, 1984, *Earthbound: New Introductory Essays in Environmental Ethics* (New York)

Also, there is a good summary of the theories and issues by R. Elliott 'Environmental Ethics' in:

P. Singer (ed.), 1991, *A Companion to Ethics* (Oxford)

For a good introduction to the Is/Ought controversy see:

W. D. Hudson (ed.), 1969, *The Is-Ought Question: A Collection of Papers on the Central Problem in Moral Philosophy* (London)

M. White, 1981, *What Is and What Ought To Be Done* (Oxford)

Human rights

R. Dworkin, 1977, *Taking Rights Seriously* (Duckworth)

Finally, the *Journal of Applied Philosophy* (published twice a year) contains up-to-date articles on the entire range of ethical issues from terrorism to psychosurgery, and from insider trading to embryology.

Truth

Peter Vardy, 1999, *What Is Truth?* (University of New South Wales Press)

Index

281